Troubling Sex

Law and Society Series
W. Wesley Pue, General Editor

The Law and Society Series explores law as a socially embedded phenomenon. It is premised on the understanding that the conventional division of law from society creates false dichotomies in thinking, scholarship, educational practice, and social life. Books in the series treat law and society as mutually constitutive and seek to bridge scholarship emerging from interdisciplinary engagement of law with disciplines such as politics, social theory, history, political economy, and gender studies.

A list of titles in the series appears at the end of the book.

Troubling Sex

Towards a Legal Theory of Sexual Integrity

ELAINE CRAIG

UBCPress · Vancouver · Toronto

20 19 18 17 16 15 14 13 12   5 4 3 2 1

Printed in Canada on FSC-certified ancient-forest-free paper (100% post-consumer recycled) that is processed chlorine- and acid-free.

Library and Archives Canada Cataloguing in Publication

Craig, Elaine

Troubling sex : towards a legal theory of sexual integrity / Elaine Craig.

(Law and society series, ISSN 1496-4953)
Includes bibliographical references and index.
Also issued in electronic format.
ISBN 978-0-7748-2180-3 (bound); ISBN 978-0-7748-2181-0 (pbk.)

1. Sex and law – Canada. I. Title. II. Series: Law and society series (Vancouver, B.C.)

KE8928.C73 2012   345.71'0253   C2011-903719-X
KF9325.C73 2012

Canadä

UBC Press gratefully acknowledges the financial support for our publishing program of the Government of Canada (through the Canada Book Fund), the Canada Council for the Arts, and the British Columbia Arts Council.

This book has been published with the help of a grant from the Canadian Federation for the Humanities and Social Sciences, through the Aid to Scholarly Publications Program, using funds provided by the Social Sciences and Humanities Research Council of Canada.

Printed and bound in Canada by Friesens
Set in Myriad and Sabon by Artegraphica Design Co. Ltd.
Copy editor: Stacy Belden
Proofreader: Jenna Newman
Indexer: Mary Newberry

UBC Press
The University of British Columbia
2029 West Mall
Vancouver, BC V6T 1Z2
www.ubcpress.ca

FOR JW

Contents

Acknowledgments

I would like to thank Ronalda Murphy. Without her intellect, creativity, generosity of both time and spirit, and her confidence in me, this book would not have been written. I would also like to thank Stephen Coughlan and Richard Devlin. The wisdom, insight, and tremendous overall support that both Steve and Richard have given to me for the past many years have been overwhelming. I could not have completed this project without them.

Many other people also helped in different ways throughout this process: Jocelyn Downie, Kim Brooks, Scott Campbell, Rebecca Johnson, Dianne Pothier, Constance MacIntosh, Sheila Wildeman, Vaughan Black, Jennifer Llewellyn, Constance Backhouse, Alexandra Dobrowolski, Jillian Boyd, Robert Leckey, Vicki Schultz, Illana Luther, Andrea Baldwin, Karyn Dolmont, Josée St-Martin, and the Trudeau Foundation community.

I am also grateful to Randy Schmidt for his guidance and encouragement and to the anonymous reviewers at UBC Press who assessed the manuscript and whose valuable comments improved it significantly. I would like to thank the faculty, staff, and students at the Schulich School of Law at Dalhousie University for fostering an enriching environment in which to research and write. I would also like to acknowledge the financial support I received from the Trudeau Foundation and the Social Sciences and Humanities Research Council of Canada throughout my doctoral research (which constituted the basis for this book). In addition to financial assistance, the intellectual and administrative support that I received as a consequence of my involvement with the Trudeau Foundation has been invaluable.

Finally, I would like to thank Chris, Donna, Duncan, Eric, Collin, and Chrissy for supporting me throughout this process. And thank you to Heather for the encouragement, reassurance, and countless hours spent talking through ideas and editing numerous drafts.

Troubling Sex

Introduction

Sex has been, and remains, a societal repository for distinctions between right and wrong, and law is frequently employed as the site, sentinel, and archivist for this social warehouse of distinctions. But the relationship between law and sexuality extends far beyond simply using law to make sexual norm-based judgments between right and wrong. Sexuality, as will be argued throughout this book, is an aspect of human experience that is at once produced through society, regulated by society, and used to regulate society. As such, the intersection of law and human sexuality is both complex and profound. Jeffrey Weeks identifies five areas as being integral to the social organization of sexuality: "kinship and family systems, economic and social organization, social regulation, political interventions and the development of cultures of resistance."[1] One might just as easily identify these five areas as being integral to the social organization of law or as the five areas integral to the legal organization of sexuality. All of which is to suggest that this complex intersection of law and sexuality pervades every area of social and individual life.

Given this complexity, it is important to examine how courts tend to understand sexuality, whether it is context dependent, and whether the conceptual approach they adopt best promotes legal reasoning that can account for, and accommodate, the complexity of issues, interests, and perspectives that arise when law and sexuality intersect. Issues of sexuality are found in both public and private legal contexts: tort law, contract law, constitutional law, family law, administrative law, education law, immigration law, and criminal law. The intersection of law and sexuality has been examined through feminist perspectives, critical race theory, liberal theories, postmodernism (and, more specifically, queer theory), gay liberation theory, gender theories, cultural legal studies, law and economics, and political legal philosophy. There have been debates over essentialism versus constructivism, liberty versus equality, sex versus gender, assimilation versus subversion, assimilation versus resistance, universalism versus particularism, universalism versus relativism, harm versus morality, and private versus public.

Less examined is what, if any, connection exists *between* legal issues in terms of the intersection of law and sexuality. Often, legal discussions about "good sex," sexual liberty, and the rights and/or oppression of sexual minorities tend not to include much focus on issues such as rape, sexual violence, and the "bad of sex." Similarly, discussions about sexual harm – for example, those that reflect on the sexual oppression of women and children – do not tend to emphasize theories or legal approaches that are overly concerned with also recognizing and accommodating the good of sex – the benefit, joy, and power produced through and by sexuality.

Is there a discernible conceptual approach to sexuality developed and/or applied by the courts that is common to all areas of law and sexuality? Do courts reveal the same understanding of sexuality regardless of whether they are dealing with issues of, for instance, sexual liberty, equality, tolerance, or individual and public safety? Related to these questions, can there be one legal theory of human sexuality that accounts for the good of sex but that identifies and rejects the bad, which ensures equality without assimilation, diversity without exclusion, and liberty without suffering?

Trouble Me with Three Notes about Theories Incomplete

⋆ *I know of a fourteen-year-old who sat at the kitchen table and watched as her father took his, and her mother's, Sears credit cards and, with a black magic marker, crossed out Sears and wrote "Queers." He put the cards in an envelope, mailed them to the company's customer service department, and informed her family that they no longer shopped at Sears – all in response to the department store's recent announcement that it would begin granting spousal benefits to employees in same sex relationships. Apparently, it was one of the first nation-wide companies in Canada to make this decision. For him, it was a sign (of the apocalyptic variety) that the normative universe as he knew it was in serious jeopardy – the Queers were taking over. In contrast, for those who willingly label themselves with the intended slur smeared in black felt pen on that family's credit cards, legal activism aimed at issues such as the acquisition of pension and health benefits for gay and lesbian couples is often considered a misdirected effort because it perpetuates conformity to social norms rather than subversion of them – for them, it is misguided because it is not queer enough. It can be troubling to think about how vast the space is between the perspectives of this father and the Queers.*

⋆ *I recently attended a conference on feminist constitutionalism. During breakfast on the second day, I had the pleasure of sitting next to a professor who had given a presentation the day before that offered an insightful feminist argument advocating for certain reforms to the criminal law. At breakfast, she was discussing Justice Wilson's ground-breaking interpretive approach to section 1, based as it was on a contextual analysis of proportionality. I mentioned a piece I had read, in which the author argues that Justice Wilson's contextual approach was in a sense postmodern. This professor immediately dismissed the author's work – which seemed to me to be consistent with the particular argument she was making, but which used the term postmodern in its conceptual approach – with one statement. "Yes, well ... her feminist credentials are questionable." I was immediately concerned. Were my feminist credentials questionable and, if so, would my ideas be dismissed just as easily? I did not know whether I had the "right" feminist credentials and, if I did, whether I had packed them. What if they asked me to produce them?*

⋆ *A few years ago, I was browsing through the queer theory section at Glad Day Bookshop in Toronto. Glad Day describes itself as the first Canadian lesbian and gay bookstore – it has been "serving the queer community since 1970."[2] I overheard a conversation two aisles over between two men who looked to be in their late forties or early fifties. They were bemoaning the heteronormativity and homophobia of Western attitudes towards Afghani Imam and their supposed practice of taking adolescent boys as "lovers." They expressed their disgust at Western society's failure to learn from the lessons of the ancient Greeks and their "boylovers." I had recently finished reading Khaled Hosseini's The Kite Runner and just the previous week had watched the movie based on his novel. Images of the graphic depictions of the sexual interaction between the protagonist's young nephew and the Imam who had kidnapped him were still with me.*

There are three broad theoretical approaches that have likely done the most work in terms of theorizing concepts of sexuality in a contemporary legal context. They are liberal rights theories, postmodern and queer theories, and feminist theories, in particular, radical feminism. Each of these approaches, in their various manifestations, offers significant insight into certain aspects of the relationship between law and sexuality. Each of these approaches has, at different times, helped me to grapple with the troubling tensions that arise when law and sexuality intersect. At other times, each has left me with a sense of incompleteness, even dissatisfaction.

Equality theory provides a solid theoretical foundation to defeat laws that discriminate against gays and lesbians. It provides strong support for the assertion of rights to spousal benefits for the gay and lesbian employees of Sears, but it is less able to provide a theoretical basis for the contention that the distribution of economic privileges ought not to be based on sexual relationship status. It does not accommodate well the argument that gay and lesbian pornography ought to be treated differently under the law than heterosexual pornography. Nor will it avoid the model of exclusivity inherent in any rights-based social justice movement – a model whose identity politics demand that lines be drawn in the sands of sexual normativity between which sexual deviants are in and which are out, always at once constituting new sexual outlaws while, at the same time, permitting sexual citizenship for some.[3]

Queer theory (and postmodernism more generally) can avoid drawing such lines. Queer theory can, for example, provide the basis for transgender folks to argue for the disruption of regulatory gender norms or for women to argue that context encodes (female) bodies with meaning, not the other way around.[4] However, queer theory cannot really draw lines in the sands of sexual normativity. It cannot, properly understood, provide a basis from which to argue that homosexuals ought to be in and hebophiles out. Queer theory and postmodernism offer important theoretical arguments that can promote notions of sexual justice and women's equality. However, they alone cannot coherently defend the choice to pursue either sexual justice or women's equality.

Radical feminism offers a clear theoretical basis for the assertion that violent pornography is anti-democratic (and that a failure to prohibit it is a failure to treat all citizens equally). Radical feminist thought has contributed enormously to the development of a contextual and more sophisticated understanding of sexual violence in Canadian law. It fails, though, to treat equally sexual minorities oriented towards consensual sadomasochism. Nor does it handle well women who sexually harass men, women who rape,[5] or the importance of promoting female heterosexual desire.[6] None of these approaches provides a particularly convincing theoretical basis from which to argue in favour of a legal theory of sexuality that understands sexuality as a collective interest without, that is, an assertion of sexual morality.

Can there be one legal theory of human sexuality that cuts across the space between good sex and bad sex, public sex and private sex, dominant sexual practices and minority sexual practices, assimilation and tolerance, suffering and desire? Is there a theoretical approach that can resolve or reconcile all of these tensions? I doubt there is such a theory. But it may be that law does not need a theory that can accomplish this. The ideas and theoretical approach developed throughout this book are not an attempt to provide *the* answer, or resolve these tensions – quite the opposite, in fact. Indeed, the sense of discomfort that has motivated me to pursue this project remains with me as I finish it. Instead, my objective, upon examining how the Supreme Court of Canada currently conceptualizes sexuality, is to suggest that so long as law is developed, interpreted, and applied in a manner that acknowledges the social contingency of sexuality, and so long as it tries to stay open to new ideas and the possibility of new meaning, there will always be trouble up ahead, and this may be a "good thing."

Pursuing a Legal Theory of Sexuality

This book focuses on Supreme Court of Canada jurisprudence in an effort to determine how the Court understands sexuality and whether this understanding changes depending on the type of legal issues that are involved. It examines the ways in which the Court's understanding of sexuality influences its reasoning, the changes in the Court's conceptual approach in recent years, and the factors that have influenced these changes. In exploring these questions, I have focused primarily on areas of public law, including sexual assault law, equality for sexual minorities, sexual harassment claims, and obscenity and indecency laws. I have reviewed all of the Court's jurisprudence in these areas in the past twenty years as well as a significant amount of the lower court case law on these legal issues. There are a number of factors that make Canada, and the Supreme Court of Canada in particular, a good case study for this topic. In Canada, in the past twenty-five years, there have been at least three significant macro shifts in the relationship between law and human sexuality. The first is a shift in the law's construction, interpretation, and regulation of non-consensual sex; this includes, among other changes, replacing the criminal charge of rape with sexual assault, major changes in evidence law regarding the testimony of women and children victims of sexual assault, changes to the criminal law's definition of consent and the age of consent, recognition of vicarious liability on the part of institutions who negligently employ individuals guilty of child sexual abuse, the addition of charges under the *Criminal Code* for non-penetrative child sexual abuse (such as sexual interference and invitation to sexual touching), and some limited recognition of a right to privacy for sexual assault victims.[7] The second macro shift is a change in the relationship between law and heteronormativity, which includes recognition by the Court of a right not to be discriminated against on the basis of sexual orientation, legal recognition of gay and lesbian couples in a variety of contexts, a shift in the legal significance of sex to legal relationship status, and modifications to the legal definition of family. The third is a shift from morality-based reasoning towards harm-based reasoning in the regulation of sexually expressive activities, which includes revisions to the definition of indecency under the *Criminal Code* and changes to the criminal law's regulation of pornography.

While my focus is mainly on public law, I have included some consideration of private law issues (such as liability for breach of fiduciary duty). The main reason for narrowing my focus in this respect was to control the scope of the project. I chose to focus on issues of public law rather than private law because the macro-level shifts in the area of law and sexuality just described have produced more jurisprudence from the Court on public law issues than on private law ones. I did examine many lower court decisions, but my primary focus is on the decisions of the Supreme Court of Canada. The Supreme Court of Canada has played, and continues to play, roles in both the formation of social policy and the complex, interrelated relationship between changing law and changing culture. One of the predominant arguments the Court has used to justify such intervention in a Canadian constitutional context – the dialogue metaphor[8] – was first discussed in *Vriend v. Alberta*, in which the Court determined that the Alberta government's failure to include sexual orientation as a protected ground under their human rights legislation was discriminatory.[9] The Court has been similarly active in cases involving a variety of sexual assault law reforms.

In general, the Court's decisions across legal contexts reveal a tendency to conceptualize sexuality as innate, as a pre-social naturally occurring phenomenon, and as an essential element that is constitutive of who we are as individuals. However, there is an exception to this trend. There has been a shift in the way that the Court understands sexuality in the context of sexual violence between adults. It is a shift away from understanding it as pre-social and naturally occurring and towards understanding it as a product of society – as a function of social context. This is an exciting development with implications that have already begun to reveal themselves in cases in other legal contexts. This change in the Court's conceptual approach towards sexual violence has engendered a shift in the law's moral focus as well – a shift away from a moral focus on specific sexual acts and sexual propriety and towards a moral focus on sexual actors and sexual integrity.

In this book, I have woven together the analytical observations about the jurisprudence just described, with a theoretical argument that is both grounded in the case law and that draws upon feminist, liberal, and postmodern theories. The argument developed suggests that the Court, regardless of the legal issue involved, ought to conceptualize sexuality as socially constructed, that it ought to orient itself towards protecting sexual integrity, and that it ought to understand this sexual integrity as a common interest. I begin Chapter 1 by outlining the theoretical frameworks that have informed this study. I clarify what is meant by the term social constructivism and explain how different queer and feminist theorists have used the concept. I also introduce the argument that a constructivist legal conception of sexuality is to be preferred over an essentialist conception.

In Chapters 2 and 3, I demonstrate that across different legal contexts courts have tended towards an essentialist conception of sexuality. These chapters examine the Supreme Court of Canada's jurisprudence (as well as some lower court decisions operating on the tension ostensibly structured by the Court's judgments) in four different legal contexts – human rights complaints regarding sexual harassment, sexual minority claims under section 15 of the *Canadian Charter of Rights and Freedoms,* the use of similar fact evidence in sexual assault trials, and the criminal regulation of child pornography.[10] The cases that I discuss reveal how the Court's essentialist reasoning limits the availability of legal remedies for certain types of claimants and precludes legal recognition of the social factors that produce problematic and harmful sexual behaviour.

Chapters 4 and 5 consider the Court's shift towards a more constructivist account of sexuality in the context of adult sexual violence. In Chapter 4, I demonstrate the way in which the Court has adopted a radical feminist-influenced understanding of sexual violence. It is an approach that conceptualizes both the perpetuation of sexual violence and the harm caused by sexual violence from a more constructivist perspective. Chapter 4 examines how the concept of sexual integrity has been incorporated into sexual assault law. I consider the ways in which feminist-influenced changes to sexual assault laws have resulted in a legal conception of sexual violence that better accounts for its social contingency. The old essentialist legal understanding of sexual violence – that is, the notion that sexual violation is a function of male sexual arousal gone awry – focused either on the perspective and (hetero)-sexual motives of the accused or on the sense of sexual propriety of the community. The complainant's perspective did not figure prominently in legal analysis under this approach. Under this new, more constructivist conception of sexual violence, both the legal definition of what constitutes a sexual assault and the legal test for consent to sexual touching have undergone change. Both now focus more on power dynamics, context, and the perspectives of all sexual actors involved and less on (hetero)sexual gratification, body parts, and community propriety. Chapter 4 suggests that sexual integrity be thought of as both the freedom from unwanted, or not chosen, bodily violation and the conditions for sexual fulfillment, sexual diversity, and sexual literacy. I argue that the law ought to recognize sexual integrity as a social good, like language, that individuals require in order to be autonomous.

Chapter 5 examines the laws prohibiting obscenity and indecency. I consider how this feminist-influenced constructivist perspective towards sexual violence adopted by the Court has encouraged legal reasoning that, in the obscenity context, regulates sexual conduct and assesses sexual depictions on the basis of political morality rather than sexual morality. This shift was instigated in *R. v. Butler* with the Court's radical feminist-influenced definition of obscenity.[11] It culminated in the Court's rejection of the community standards of tolerance test in *R. v. Labaye* thirteen years later.[12] The outcome of this change is a legal definition of indecency that is based on the political morals of our society (as reflected in the Constitution) rather than an assessment of the community's sexual morals. It is a legal approach to the regulation of obscenity and indecency that is more concerned with protecting sexual actors than with protecting one particular (essentialist) moral account of sex itself. Chapter 5 concludes by demonstrating how this change in the law's moral compass has the capacity to better protect individual sexual actors by suggesting how this shift ought to be applied to the interpretation of criminal laws regulating sex work.

In Chapter 6, I examine the Court's analytical approach to the tort of sexual battery and to the criminal regulation of gay pornography. This chapter reveals that a legal approach that conceptualizes sexuality from a partially constructivist perspective, while maintaining an essentialist foundation, will continue to rely on sexual morality. It will do so in a way that fails to adequately protect interests such as the sexual autonomy of women or to accommodate the specificity of diverse sexual choices and preferences that exist.

Chapter 7, the final chapter, further expands on the suggestion that the Court ought to continue its shift towards a constructivist conception of sexuality. It ought to do so by subscribing to the notion that sexual integrity is a common good and that legal reasoning should be oriented towards promoting and protecting this common good. It concludes by exploring the concept of iconoclasm and suggesting how it might be used in this context to deploy the insights of postmodernism while accommodating the reality of law's judgment.

There are two key themes that run throughout all of these chapters. The first is that constructivist conceptions of sexuality better account for its complexity and, as a result, lead to better legal reasoning. The second is that there is an irreconcilable tension between the theoretical underpinnings of the claim that sexuality is socially constructed and acknowledgment that the legal regulation of sexuality, for it not to be arbitrary, requires criteria by which to distinguish good sex from bad sex. I have suggested one account of how a legal conception of sexuality as socially constructed might attempt to accommodate this tension. It is an account that considers the tension between the recognition that what sexuality is is constituted through the norms, social practices, relationships, and discursive regimes that describe and regulate it and law's need, despite this, to use these norms, social practices, and discourses to judge that which is constituted through them. The aim is to pursue a legal theory of sexuality that conceptualizes sexuality as socially produced – one in which sexual integrity is considered a common good and in which the law is oriented towards protecting this common good through an open-ended and infinite re-evaluation and reconstitution of the relationships and interactions that constitute, promote, and threaten it.

1 Essentialism and Constructivism in Law

> I believe that there are no innate, intrinsic differences among a human being, a baboon or a grain of sand.
>
> – OLIVER WENDELL HOLMES, JR.

Social and legal understandings of sexuality have typically been bound up in, and inextricably linked with, perceptions about what is natural and what is unnatural. But for morality and race (with which it is often married), the concept of nature is likely the most common framework through which law has approached issues of sexuality. Whether informed by natural law concepts, God's law, or the scientific pursuits of sexual enlightenment, the notion that sexuality is a force of nature has deeply influenced how law characterizes families, criminal offences, and equality claims as well as sexual actors, sexual identities, and sexual acts.

Another description of the notion that sex is natural (or "of nature") is the term sexual essentialism. Sexual essentialism refers to "the idea that sex is a natural force that exists prior to social life."[1] It is the notion that sexuality is innate, unchanging, ahistorical, and pre-cultural. Queer theories, in contrast to sexual essentialism, adopt a social constructivist conception of sexuality. A social constructivist conception of sexuality suggests that "sexuality is as much a human product as are diets, methods of transportation, systems of etiquette, forms of labour, types of entertainment, processes of production, and modes of oppression."[2] The most significant contributions to the theorization of sexuality made by queer theories are the challenges to, and disruptions of, the concept of sexuality as natural or pre-social.

One issue that has received more attention than any other in the constructivist/essentialist debate is the "cause of homosexuality." This issue is sometimes manifested as the "it's a choice" (and you should not choose it or you should not question it – depending on one's perspective) argument versus the "it's not a choice" (I was born this way or it's not my fault – again depending on one's perspective) argument. To interpret the argument that homosexuality is socially constructed as asserting that homosexuality is chosen is to fail to grasp the entirety or complexity of constructivist theories. To argue that an aspect of human behaviour or human "nature" is a product of social construction and not mother nature is not necessarily to suggest that it is mutable or unstable. Many queer theorists and pro-gay scholars argue that the causation question is not the correct question anyway.[3] Instead of concerning ourselves with the cause of "homosexuality," we ought to be concerned with the broader social and legal implications of labelling someone, or being labelled, homosexual.

Regardless, the notion of social constructivism and its implications for understanding sexuality are much broader than simply establishing "the cause of homosexuality." To understand how law regulates sexuality, it is important to identify how conceptions of sexuality inform legal reasoning and legal outcomes. In order to understand how conceptions of sexuality inform law, it is first necessary to ask whether courts understand sexuality as immutable and essential or as fluid and contextually contingent. It is necessary to ask what aspects of sexuality are considered pre-social by courts and whether this determination depends on the legal issue the court is addressing. Legal distinctions between "the natural" and "the unnatural," and legal conceptions concerning the essentialist or constructed "nature" of sexuality, carry significant weight regarding legal approaches to, and the regulation of, sexual conduct, sexual identity, and sexual safety. These distinctions can significantly impact how a court addresses, for example, the legal definition of indecency or the admission of similar fact evidence in sexual assault trials. The significance of such distinctions extends far beyond simply the issue of sexual orientation. As Jeffrey Weeks argues, "appeals to nature, to the claims of natural, are amongst the most potent we can make. They place us in a world of apparent fixity and truth. They appear to tell us what and who we are, and where we are going. They seem to tell us the truth."[4]

A constructivist perspective provides insight into the ways in which meaning, constituted in and through particular social contexts, allows some sexual norms (concepts, values, practices, subjects, orientations, traits, and desires) to become perceived as natural (hegemonic) and correspondingly regulative, by excluding other norms. For this reason, the analytical frameworks engendered by constructivist theories are useful for any examination of the legal regulation of sexuality – aspects of which have often been understood through a discourse of deviation (from "the norm") or diacritical modes of knowing (that is, female means not male, woman means not man, and gay means not straight). Constructivist arguments provide a powerful critique of laws, institutions, social practices, and beliefs premised on models of essentialism. They do so by identifying many of the "naturalized" assumptions about sexuality underpinning the Supreme Court of Canada's jurisprudence. As such, social constructivism provides an analytical lens through which to both examine the Court's conceptions of sexuality and to understand how these conceptions influence legal outcomes and legal reasoning.

Queer theories are premised on one specific articulation of this constructivist conception of sexuality. Constructivist accounts of sexuality have also been developed by feminist theories such as radical feminism and postmodern feminism. Indeed, the queer suggestion that sexuality is not an innate, naturally occurring, and essential constituent of the human individual was preceded by the feminist challenge to the assumption that gender is a naturally occurring and essential element of the self.[5] In the 1970s and early 1980s, feminist writers, such as Gayle Rubin and Catharine MacKinnon, began to develop social constructivist theories of both gender and sexuality. Rubin makes the argument that the biological distinctions between male and female (such as reproductive capacity) have been transformed, through social practice and systems, into gender.[6] She argues that the division of labour and the sexual hierarchy present in both family life and the economic and political spheres are premised on gender differences – a cultural construct – and not on sex (as in male/female) differences. In other words, it is the cultural interpretation of the biological differences between male and female (that is, gender) that has led to the systemic oppression of women. Equality-seeking feminists, she stresses, ought to be concerned with reconstituting the meaning of gender. Like Rubin, MacKinnon also argues that the categories of woman and man are not a thing of nature.[7] She suggests that the meaning of woman is produced through cultural, social, and legal institutions, norms, and practices defined and controlled by men in accord with male sexual desire – a sexual desire that is oriented towards dominance and that correspondingly perpetuates women's oppression.

Social constructivist theories have taken many forms. There are those who claim that sexual orientation and biological sex are fixed and predetermined and that, while these categories can be found across cultures and historical periods, the meanings attached to them and their attendant range of activities will differ across culture and history. For example in Culture A, homosexuals might be considered perverts and anal sex dirty, while in Culture B the same individuals would be considered spiritual leaders and anal sex uplifting. There are those who recognize that acultural sexual orientation categories may exist but that they are not necessarily defined by gender-of-object choice. They suggest that "some other form or forms of human variance are primary."[8] Eve Kosofsky Sedgwick, for example, argues that social categorization (erotic speciation) based on same sex versus opposite sex desire is a cultural construct. Other orientations – such as those that are monogamous or polyamorous or those who like sex a lot versus those who do not – might be more relevant but have not been constructed as such in this culture.

Some constructivists claim that the capacity for erotic pleasure is constitutive of the individual but that the manifestation of that capacity into a coherent sexual subject is culturally determined.[9] They argue that sexual object choice, behavioural repertoire, social meaning, and emotional meaning are all socially determined. The most radical social constructivists assert that "culture supplies the very terms for understanding bodily sex."[10] They argue that sexuality and gender are prior to sex (as in male/female). So, for them, even the category of sex is constructed. Judith Butler, for example, asserts that it is impossible to think about, or understand, sex (as in male/female) outside of a cultural framework. How we think about sex is always through a cultural lens. The concept of pre-social is itself a social concept.[11] Butler has been criticized by some for what they perceive to be a rejection of the materiality of the body. However, I think that at its most basic what she is suggesting is that there are cultural forces at work that preclude us from ever being able to disaggregate culture from concept. In other words, there is no Archimedean seating at the local drag show.

The view of sexuality as a key component of our "true selves" – our essence – is often described in Freudian terms. It is the notion of sexuality as a turbulent sexual drive under which a healthy conscience is charged with guarding against the sexual excesses of our subconscious.[12] Under this notion of sexuality, those that deviate from sexual norms are either unhealthy or lacking in self-control. Until recently, this conceptual approach to sexuality underpinned much of the Supreme Court of Canada's jurisprudence in the context of sexual assault. Relying on an understanding of sexuality that is similar to the one advanced by MacKinnon, feminist constructivists have successfully challenged this essentialist understanding of sexual violence. In the Canadian context, the impact on sexual assault law and the criminal regulation of obscenity and indecency affected by this particular feminist understanding of sexuality and gender has been profound. In many other legal contexts, the notion of sexuality as an essential element of our "true selves" remains the predominant legal understanding of sexuality.

Just as feminist scholars have theorized a constructivist conception of sexual violence as produced by a sexist society rather than a perverted or uncontrollable sexual subconscious, a central theme of queer theory is also a rejection of Freud's repressive hypothesis.[13] Queer theories typically have three main themes. They seek to re-conceptualize power, re-conceptualize knowledge and its relationship to power, and re-conceptualize identity and subject formation. These objectives are not dissimilar to the objectives of radical and postmodern feminist theories.

Queer is a relational concept. It is a positionality in relation to a norm.[14] Queer, conceptually speaking, is not an identity but, rather, a critique of identity the effect of which is to contest or disrupt normative understandings of the subject by suggesting that identity is not fixed. While the notion of queer theory resists definition, and the breadth of scholarship that typically falls under its label is significant, queer theories do tend to share at least one assertion – sexual identity, rather than the expression of an innate human libido, a natural urge, or predisposition, is produced socially through norms and discourse. Foucault, for example, contends that objects of discussion and investigation come into existence only as the ability to discuss them is born.[15] In this way, a discourse produces the subjects of which it speaks. This would include the formation of new sexual identities and sexual subjects.[16] What arises from these theories of discursive formation is the possibility that what constitutes the "essence" of a sexual identity today might be inconsequential or irrelevant at another time or in another culture. Social constructivists argue that this process – what Rubin calls erotic speciation – produces all sorts of erotic individuals who are then hierarchically aggregated "into rudimentary communities."[17] This notion of "erotic speciation" (that sexual subjectivity and sexual hierarchies are produced through discourse) is revealed in legal contexts such as the criminal law's approach to pedophilia and the justifications relied upon for granting equality protection to some sexual minorities but not to others.

Queer theory has been particularly occupied with examining and challenging the heterosexual biases implicated or manifested through binary understandings of sex, sexuality, and gender. As such, queer theorists often focus their critique on diacritically constituted knowledge and its implications for sexual identity and subject formation. For example, queer theorists have argued that heterosexuality is an incoherent identity category that relies completely on the presence of a homosexual identity category for its existence.[18] To put it simply, the existence of homosexuality is indispensable to those who define themselves as against it. According to these queer theorists, categories of gender, sex, and sexuality are socially constructed through the reiterative citation of dominant gender, sex, and sexuality norms – norms that are constituted through exclusion, through the discursive creation of binaries in which a norm's meaning stems from that which it is "not," and through the power that comes from the ability to define that "not." Sedgwick, for example, notes that "erotic identity, of all things, is never to be circumscribed simply as itself, can never not be relational, is never to be perceived or known by anyone outside of a structure of transference and counter-transference."[19] Underpinning queer theory is this suggestion that an identity, because it is constituted through its difference from all other identities, is never complete – there exists, therefore, a limitless field of differential identities.[20] Queer theorists suggest that hegemonic sex, sexuality, and gender norms are created through this process of exclusion and then deployed to both constitute and regulate subjects. Examples of the manner in which this process operates may be found in the social, political, and legal responses to bisexual identity claims and transgender expressions or identity claims. In identifying what he describes as bisexual erasure by both heterosexuals and gays and lesbians, Kenji Yoshino offers as one motivating factor for this erasure their shared investment in stabilizing group identities by eradicating the threat to these identities that he suggests is posed by bisexuality.[21]

Not unlike the perceived threat to sexual identity posed by the bisexual, the existence of transgenderism challenges the dyadic and biological, genitally determined understandings of gender and sexuality. In a world in which each of us is supposed to be either a man or a woman, identifying to which of "the two gender categories" another individual belongs affirms one's understanding of within which category one's own gender may be located.[22] Under a binary understanding of gender, and because gender is produced relationally, the very fact that one cannot easily or instantly determine whether another individual is "the same" as him or her or "the opposite" of him or her disrupts the affirmation of one's own gender categorization. This internal disruption is ultimately reflected in one's awkward, uncomfortable, and at times negative outward response to transgressive gender expressions. In this way, gender conformity is subtly, constantly socially rewarded. Correspondingly, gender transgression is subtly (and often not so subtly), constantly socially discouraged. This is an example of the way in which diacritical modes of knowing socially construct, and then proceed to regulate, the very dyads that they ostensibly describe. As will be revealed throughout the remaining chapters, legal reasoning that adopts an essentialist conception of sexuality reveals this dyadic method of knowing by relying heavily on the distinctions between natural (moral) and unnatural (immoral). While the focus of queer theories has often been on sexual orientation, this work is significant in any discussion regarding the distinctions, legal or otherwise, between natural and unnatural.

Sexual essentialism understands sexuality as unchanging, ahistorical, and asocial or pre-social. Essentialists maintain that sexuality is a property of individuals and that it is without social determinants. For an essentialist, because it is understood as pre-social, the source of sexuality must be nature. This assumption "that our sexuality is the most natural thing about us" is deeply embedded in the social consciousness, at least in the modern Western world.[23] Whether founded on Christian doctrine or on sexual science, an essentialist approach understands sexuality as spontaneous and natural.[24]

However, there are problems when law adopts this naturalistic understanding of human sexuality. If sexuality is rooted in nature, then it will always and forever be understood, measured, and evaluated through one specific dyadic *episteme:* natural versus unnatural. This is a problem because "we learn very early on from many sources that 'natural' sex is what takes place with members of the 'opposite sex.' 'Sex' between people of the 'same sex' is therefore, by definition, 'unnatural.'"[25] As a result, every sexual act, desire, or identity becomes understood through, and measured against, a particular heterosexual paradigm.

Some sexual minorities have also invoked the natural/unnatural dichotomy. They point to evidence of same sex sexual behaviour within other species to contest the assertion that homosexuality is unnatural. To date, this has not been a particularly persuasive line of argument. When the natural/unnatural dichotomy is invoked, the distinction continues to be understood in the manner that Weeks suggests. Underpinning an essentialist conception of sexuality tends to be a heterosexist conception of sexuality, which leads to an assumption that same sex desire is not simply abnormal but also unnatural.

The broader issue is that the natural/unnatural distinction is, like all binaries, structured on a model of exclusivity. Natural defines itself as against unnatural. The natural/unnatural binary is not the best way to distinguish between good sex and bad sex. A more contextual approach to regulating sexuality may be more inclusive – at the very least, its criteria for exclusion is less likely to be premised on "majoritarianism." Not only does a conceptual framework, which at its core understands sexuality through a heterosexual paradigm, entrench same sex desire and identity as unnatural, but it also entrenches the notion of sex (as in male/female) difference. Entrenching the notion of sex polarizes the distinction between men and women.[26] As feminists recognized decades ago, legal conceptions of gender and sex differences as innate, biologically driven, and "natural" have not tended to promote women's equality.

A third difficulty with a legal understanding of sexuality as pre-social or naturally occurring is that it, to some extent, obfuscates the ability to perceive the relational, contextual, and institutional factors that contribute to the regulation of sexuality. It does so by overemphasizing biology, heterosexual arousal, romance, and sexual morality (rather than political morality). Legal conceptions of sexuality that are founded on essentialism tend to focus the law's moral compass on sexual acts rather than on sexual interactions. It is not that acts are irrelevant. It is rather that the meaning and moral significance of any particular act is constituted by the context and relationships in which it occurs. The law (including the criminal law) often focuses on relationships rather than on acts. Think, for example, of the sexual exploitation provisions in the *Criminal Code.*[27] Sex with a seventeen-year-old with whom one is in a relationship of dependency or leadership is criminal, but if the relationship does not involve such a power differential it is not prohibited under this provision. Think of the legally imposed obligations to provide the necessities of life to one's child but not to one's neighbour's child. Think of the age of consent laws under the *Criminal Code*. A fourteen-year-old cannot consent to have sex with a forty-year-old – unless that forty-year-old is her husband. There is nothing to suggest that the criminal law could not accommodate a principled approach oriented predominantly, if not solely, towards relational interests.

A final difficulty with an essentialist understanding of sexuality is that it evinces an air of inevitability. It suggests a concession that changes to gendered and sexualized hierarchies are, and will always be, bounded by parameters that are beyond, or external to, the choices, practices, beliefs, and *epistemes* that presently operate in this society. Legal conceptions of sexuality that reflect this essentialism tend to reinforce the status quo. As will be demonstrated by a discussion of the criminal regulation of sex work in Chapter 5, this is not a circumstance that should appeal to most women, children, and sexual minorities. The alternative, or one alternative, is the view of sexuality put forth by constructivist theorists. It is an understanding of sexuality not simply as a biological fact or naturally occurring phenomenon that can be repressed or suppressed but, rather, a complex series of interactions and relationships – a "historically shaped series of possibilities, actions, behaviors, desires, risks, identities, norms and values that can be reconfigured and recombined but not simply unleashed."[28]

This is not to suggest that biological and mental factors, or the materiality of the body, do not contribute to the concept of sexuality. As Weeks explains, "[a]ll the constituent elements of sexuality have their source either in the body or the mind ... But the capacities of the body and the psyche are given meaning only in social relations."[29] Rather, it is to suggest that sexuality is as much a social product as is food, language, or familial structure. Sexual behaviour, sexual identity, and sexual norms will logically vary across culture, religion, climate, class, economic conditions, and time. For example, sexual practices might vary somewhat in warm climates from what they will be in cold ones, just as they may vary in cultures where large amounts of alcohol are consumed from cultures that tend to imbibe less. Changes to economic and political structures will bring changes to sexual practices and sexual identities.[30] Sexual practices may be different in societies whose norm it is for couples to live with one's extended family than in those where single-family households are the norm. Sexual practices and identities may vary depending upon the availability and knowledge of birth control, the prevalence of sexually transmitted infections, or the male-to-female ratio.

In light of all of these factors, the essentialist assertion that sexuality is something more than the product of social patterns, normative distinctions, and the development of meaning though choices, discourses, and practices seems almost less intuitive. In fact, it may not be a particularly radical claim to assert that sexuality is particularized and that it is a socially contingent product of discourse and a function of social practices. What is perhaps a more significant claim is my assertion that the law ought to conceptualize, and correspondingly treat, sexuality as a contextually contingent, social good. Nevertheless, a legal approach that adopts this perspective would better enable the law to remain open to the infinite re-articulation of sex, gender, and sexuality norms while, at any given moment, drawing distinctions and making judgments about how best to protect individual sexual integrity. Unfortunately, a review of the Supreme Court of Canada cases in different legal contexts – the section 15 equality claims of sexual minorities, the sexual harassment cases, the admission of similar fact evidence in sexual assault trials, and the criminalization of child pornography – demonstrates that the Court typically does not embrace such a perspective.

The cases discussed in the next two chapters reveal a Court that considers sexual object choice to be both unchanging and an element of one's true self. Many of the cases also reveal a tendency on the part of the Court to categorize sexual acts as either "natural" or "unnatural." They also show that, when the Court operates under this essentialist understanding of sexuality (including, but also beyond, the assumption of innate sexual object choice), the legal "space" in which to identify the social forces and contextual factors contributing to, or producing, many aspects of human sexuality is significantly constricted. An essentialist understanding of sex and sexuality conceals the sexual harassment of boys and men by heterosexual men; it precludes rights recognition for those sexual minorities that cannot, or will not, assimilate to the dominant norms of ostensible monogamy and immutable sexual object choice; it precludes a more radical re-valuing of same sex desire; and it obscures the contextual factors that produce child sexual abuse. When adopted by the law, essentialist conceptions of sexuality justify the hierarchical distribution of legal rights and privileges based on sexual object choice, render some victims (and perpetrators) of sexual violation invisible, and reify problematic social distinctions between men and women. This focus on the biological, on genitals, and on sex as a force of nature to be contained or liberated (depending on one's perspective) also drives the law's traditional concern with, and moral focus on, sexual acts rather than on sexual actors. A moral focus on sexual acts, rather than on sexual actors, is less capable of promoting and protecting sexual integrity as a common good.

2 Legal Conceptions of Sexual Nature and Natural Sex

> Whereas families should be able to raise their children without fear of sexual predators.
>
> – PREAMBLE, *TACKLING VIOLENT CRIMES ACT*

Across legal contexts, the Supreme Court of Canada's jurisprudence reveals an essentialist conception of sexuality that contributes to legal reasoning that fails to account for its social contingency. This failure to account for the social contingency of sexuality is problematic for different reasons in different legal contexts. The use of similar fact evidence in sexual assault trials is one such context. In admitting similar fact evidence in sexual assault trials, courts, including the Supreme Court of Canada, often rely on an essentialist conception of those who commit sexual offences – particularly those who sexually assault children. Courts adopt this same essentialist conception of "the pedophile" in the child pornography context. It is a conception in which those who sexually offend against children are understood to have an innate disposition oriented towards this type of sexual violence and in which the problem of child sexual abuse is itself understood as pre-social or acontextual. A conceptual approach of this type is problematic because it fails to develop a legal discourse or promote legal strategies to address the social factors that perpetuate the sexual victimization of children. A constructivist conception of child sexual abuse and those who perpetuate it would better account for these social factors.

Suggesting that the law adopt an approach to the issue of child sexual abuse that recognizes its social contingency risks endorsing a contention that is both highly controversial and politically questionable. If one is to suggest that "the pedophile" is socially constructed, then must one also not agree that "the victim" is a socially constructed concept? Foucault's well-known discussion of the nineteenth-century-France village idiot who molests one of the village girls and is then arrested for his simple, "inconsequential bucolic pleasures" and forced to spend the rest of his life speaking about them to the police, the courts, and the doctors reveals this problematic contention. Foucault writes of this incident: "What is the significant thing about this story? The pettiness of it all; the fact that this everyday occurrence in the life of village sexuality ... could become, from a certain time, the object not only of a collective intolerance but of judicial action, a medical intervention, a careful clinical examination, and an entire theoretical elaboration."[1]

Foucault's claim is that the intervention of the many and sundry officials and less simple-minded adults changed what was a harmless and "barely furtive pleasure" into a discourse that then socially constructed this behaviour as a particular understanding of sexual deviance. That is to say, the interaction between the child and the half-wit becomes understood as a sexual one – a sexually deviant one – because of the *truths* that are spoken about it. Foucault's description/theorization of their interaction makes two interrelated constructivist claims. The first suggests the discursive social construction of "the victim." The second suggests the discursive social construction of "the offender."[2]

Foucault's Precocious Child

The difficulty with Foucault's discussion of this interaction is that, as Robin West notes, in all of the attention given to the ensuing discourses swirling around the village idiot "neither the French officials, nor Foucault himself, nor the vast majority of social and legal critics he has influenced, have yet heard scarcely a word from the child who was molested in that eerie scene."[3] West asks whether it is actually pleasures that are transformed into discourse: "Is it as true of the 'alert child' as it is of the half-wit? Or is this Foucauldian 'truth' about how 'natural-pleasure-is-transformed-into-socially-constructed-sexuality' only maintainable because of the alert child's silence?"[4] This question is a good one. Whose truth are we to believe: the village officials' or Foucault's? The question reveals the way in which Foucault's work is at once both a description and manifestation of that which he proposes to describe.

Nevertheless, the observation that both *what* we understand to be sexual interactions and *how* we understand these sexual interactions are socially constructed through discourse is noteworthy. It is an important observation because it provides a theoretical framework from which to challenge dominant conceptions about sexuality. This is a framework that readily allows one to argue, for example, that neither homosexuality nor female promiscuity is inherently harmful or self-destructively perverted. It is a framework that has much to contribute to claims of sexual liberty and perhaps even of substantive sexual equality. Methodologically, it provides important insight into the account of sexual integrity developed throughout this book. As examined in the discussion regarding sexual harassment in Chapter 3, discursive theories offer insight into the ways in which sex, gender, and sexuality norms act as, and constitute themselves through, regulatory mechanisms in institutional settings. It is an analytical framework that permits one to examine, as will be done in the discussion that follows, how the law contributes to the conception (and constitution) of the village half-wit. However, it is only an account of social meaning formation. It describes a process – one aspect of how societies come to be organized, understood, and regulated. Whether or not the "subject is dead," so to speak, does not change the fact that one cannot be extracted from one's context.[5] Consequently, whether sex with children only causes harm because society has constructed it as harmful or whether it causes harm for some innate and pre-social reason that was subsequently labelled harmful is normatively irrelevant.

Before continuing, there are two counter-points to this assertion that should be addressed. First, while it may not be normatively relevant in this discussion of sexual assault law generally – where harm is presumed and where the primary inquiry is into the social construction of the offender – is it not relevant to, for example, an argument by the North American Man/Boy Love Association (NAMBLA) about lowering the age of consent? I would argue that it is not necessarily relevant, at least not in the example I have just given. NAMBLA advocates for an end to "the oppression of men and boys who have freely chosen mutually consenting relationships."[6] NAMBLA's argument is not that sex between adult men and pubescent boys is only harmful because society has socially constructed it as such. It argues, instead, that it is not harmful to boys but, rather, beneficial for them. The issue in the NAMBLA example turns on whose account/argument regarding the fact of, or potential for, harm is more persuasive. This is an argument that should be had. It is particularly an argument that should be had regarding issues of sexual conduct that exist in the potentially grey areas at the ends of social/sexual regulatory spectrums such as age, degree of consanguinity, and nature of commodification. While the law can and should question, critique, and challenge assumptions about sexual harm and the criteria by which it assesses harm, and while what is harmful now might not always be harmful and an approach to sexuality should accommodate this "truth," the point is that it does not matter for this argument whether sex with children is inherently harmful or harmful because of social context. I can presume that it is harmful without relying on essentialist reasoning.

In Canada, the law presumes that a young girl who, under coercion, bribery, or even just encouragement, manually ejaculates an adult man is sexually violated – that she suffers harm. Whether this harm is the manifestation of a socially constructed victim discourse or, rather, some innate and instinctively felt loss of dignity and bodily and personal autonomy, Foucault might agree that, in the here and now, the young girl suffers, or is at risk of suffering, harm. The process by which the harm came to "be" may very well be socially constructed. The harm, however, is real. Given that social constructivists do not necessarily assume that a social concept is more readily changed than is an inherent one, it is not theoretically inconsistent to stake this claim and still pursue a constructivist project of inquiry and theorization.

The second counter-argument would be that this claim suggests a problematic approach in terms of sexual liberty and non-majoritarian sexual interests. For example, does my argument not suggest then that whatever society labels harmful is, in the context of that society, harmful? Again, the answer is no. This counter-argument misconstrues constructivist claims. It miscalculates both the lengthy process through which conduct may come to be understood as harmful, and therefore be harmful, and the degree of entrenchment, stability, and permanency that this process creates and sustains. It is a misapprehension analogous to the one discussed in Chapter 1 regarding the assumption that, if sexual object preference – that is, sexual orientation – is socially constructed, this means that it can be easily and readily changed. A legislative, adjudicative, religious, political, or pedagogical statement or declaration that behaviour X is harmful does not socially construct harm any more than a drag show, fashion show, or wedding socially constructs gender. If harm is socially constructed, it is constructed through the infinite and reiterative citation of norms and social practices, of which legislative, adjudicative, religious, political, and pedagogical statements would be a part. Sexual liberty and non-majoritarian interests (as will be discussed in Chapter 7) can be protected, at least to some degree, by critical, open-ended engagement with the criteria by which the law assesses harm.

One might follow this point by asking, if this "immutability" is true of sexual assault victims and homosexuals, is it not equally true of those who sexually assault children? The answer is that it may very well be true of individual sexual actors who sexually assault children (or adults). But such an answer does not change the argument. It only raises the following question: if one accepts that harm *and* pedophiles are contextually produced and socially contingent and one acknowledges that there should nonetheless be efforts to change this circumstance – since the harm is real – the choice becomes whether to start talking/thinking about systemic approaches aimed at changing the social context and factors that produce one or the other (or both). My argument regarding the discursive production of "the pedophile" is that to change the discourse regarding sexual offenders would first entail recognizing that there are social and contextual factors that perpetuate this behaviour rather than innate biological deviations. Recognizing these factors – starting with a legal discourse that acknowledges them – seems a good place to start.

Foucault's Village Idiot

It is therefore the second constructivist claim found in Foucault's passage regarding the village idiot that reveals the main focus of this chapter. The second claim, again, is that just as the homosexual was "speechified" into existence, so too were other types of "perverts" – namely the pedophile. The suggestion that the child molester as a species is socially constructed is not a conceptual perspective that has revealed itself in the law's approach to those who sexually offend against children. Rather, both the Supreme Court of Canada's approach to the admission of similar fact evidence in sexual assault cases and its approach to the criminal regulation of child pornography suggest an essentialist conception of those who commit sexual offences – in particular, those who sexually abuse children. Child sexual abuse is considered a function of a discrete and perverted minority possessed with a sexual predisposition towards children.

While the Court's approach to the admission of similar fact evidence in sexual assault cases involving adult complainants also reveals elements of essentialism, the analysis differs. In adult complainant cases, the Court's essentialism tends to be revealed by its focus on sexual acts (not innate dispositions) and the distinctions it draws between natural and unnatural. While "the pedophile" has been, and continues to be, treated by law as a member of a discrete and identifiable sexual minority, "the rapist" is not. As is discussed in Chapter 4, the Court has shifted towards a more constructivist approach with respect to the perpetrators of sexual assault against adults. In fact, even when an essentialist understanding of sexual violence against adults was more typical, the essentialist assumption tended to be that the sexual assault was a function of an unnatural or uncontrollable sexual *arousal* rather than of an unnatural or uncontrollable sexual *pervert*.[7]

The same assumptions about "the pedophile" at play in many similar fact evidence cases also reveal themselves in the Court's approach to the criminal regulation of child pornography.

Similar Fact Evidence in Sexual Assault Trials

Similar fact evidence is factual evidence of the past misconduct of an accused proffered for the purpose of inviting the finder of fact to infer that the accused committed the misconduct at issue in the trial. The issue of similar fact evidence typically arises in the criminal law context when the Crown seeks to introduce prior bad acts as circumstantial evidence to establish the following inference: if the accused committed the prior bad acts suggested by the similar fact evidence, then by inference he is also likely to have committed the act with which he is currently charged. Similar fact evidence is presumptively not admissible. The principle behind this rule of inadmissibility is that individuals accused of a crime are to be convicted based on evidence showing that they committed the crime and not evidence showing that they are a bad person. Nevertheless, in what the Supreme Court of Canada has described as exceptional circumstances, similar fact evidence is admissible if it is relevant to an issue in the case and its probative value outweighs its prejudicial effect.

In *R. v. Handy*, the leading precedent on the similar fact evidence rule, Justice Binnie suggests that the presumptive inadmissibility of similar fact evidence is premised on a recognition of "the difficulty of containing the effects of such information which, once dropped like poison in the juror's ear, 'swift as quicksilver it courses through the natural gates and alleys of the body.'"[8] Justice Binnie's quote is taken from the following passage of Shakespeare's *Hamlet:*

> Upon my secure hour thy uncle stole,
> With juice of cursed hebenon in a vial,
> And in the porches of my ears did pour
> The leperous distilment; whose effect
> Holds such an enmity with blood of man
> That swift as quicksilver it courses through
> The natural gates and alleys of the body,
> And with a sudden vigour doth posset
> And curd, like eager droppings into milk,
> The thin and wholesome blood: so did it mine;
> And a most instant tetter bark'd about,
> Most lazar-like, with vile and loathsome crust,
> All my smooth body.[9]

The lines are those of King Hamlet's ghost, who is describing his own death at the hands of "that incestuous, that adulterate beast," his brother Claudius. *Hamlet,* in this passage and throughout the play as a whole, is laden with incestuous overtones, corporeal metaphors involving bodily invasion, references to the natural passages of the body, and allusions to sex as diseased and infectious. This particular quote was a poignant selection on the part of Justice Binnie given the factual circumstance in *Handy* (accusations of sexual assault) and more significantly in the law of similar fact evidence generally (the great preponderance of which involves cases concerning sexual assault and child sexual abuse). It is particularly significant when considered in conjunction with the analysis that follows regarding the Court's essentialist conception of certain forms of sexual assault (in particular, those involving children who have a familial relationship with the accused). Indeed, while earlier cases involved wives in bathtubs[10] and babies in the backyard,[11] for several decades now, both in the United Kingdom[12] and in Canada,[13] the leading precedents concerning this evidentiary issue have involved cases of sexual assault. It is an evidentiary issue that arises in criminal trials regarding any type of offence. Nevertheless, the case law that has determined its admissibility has been, at least in recent times, developed almost exclusively in the context of sexual assault cases.

Establishing the exceptional circumstances under which similar fact evidence will be admitted, and establishing the actual probative value of such evidence, has been a matter of considerable academic discussion and judicial consideration. The main point of contestation and confusion, and the point that is of significance to this discussion, concerns the issue of propensity-based reasoning. The issue of evidence adduced to show that the accused has a propensity to act in the very same manner with which he is now accused of acting has been difficult for courts to address. The issue of reasoning based on propensity is of particular relevance to a discussion concerning legal notions about innate, essential human (sexual) nature.

To understand what the Court's current approach to propensity-based reasoning reveals about its conceptions regarding the perpetrators of sexual offences, it is necessary to understand the conundrum historically presented by the similar fact rule. In an effort to ensure that people are tried for what they have done, not for who they are, courts have relied for nearly a century on the Privy Council's assertion that similar fact evidence was permissible only if its use came within one of a number of specific, predetermined categories (such as to rebut a defence). This categorical approach softened over time, and the courts eventually came to view the rule as stipulating that "evidence which tends to show bad character or a criminal disposition on the part of the accused is admissible if (1) relevant to some other issue beyond disposition or character, and (2) the probative value outweighs the prejudicial effect."[14] However, this articulation of the rule created a conundrum: "[I]f evidence of the accused's prior bad acts is ever relevant, it would seem that its relevance would derive from showing his bad character; yet the evidence is said not to be admissible on that ground."[15]

The Supreme Court of Canada is thought to have resolved this conundrum in *Handy* by acknowledging that it is propensity-based reasoning that constitutes the probative value of similar fact evidence.[16] In *Handy*, Justice Binnie established an analytical framework for assessing the admissibility of similar fact evidence. He determined that evidence of other discreditable conduct (that is, evidence of an accused's propensity) may be admitted where the prosecution establishes that in the context of a particular case the probative value of the evidence in relation to a particular issue outweighs its potential prejudice.[17] Probative value will outweigh prejudicial effect when the evidence of propensity is significantly connected to the facts alleged in the charge. While evidence of general disposition ("bad personhood") will not be admitted under Justice Binnie's framework, evidence of a specific propensity that is related to a particular matter at issue will be admissible. The assumption is that this will guard against the danger that an accused will be convicted for who he is rather than for what he has done, while at the same time acknowledging that an accused's propensity to act a certain way can, in some instances, be highly probative.

John Henry Wigmore defines propensity as a trait or group of traits or the sum of a person's traits – her or his actual moral or psychical disposition.[18] Regarding issues of sexuality, the law's treatment of, and approach to, "disposition" is illuminating. Whether courts treat similar fact evidence in sexual assault cases as suggesting a propensity to *act* a certain way versus a propensity to *be* a certain way reveals something about whether their reasoning is informed by an essentialist conception of sexuality. In the years just prior to *Handy*, the Court decided a number of similar fact cases in which the accused were charged with sexual offences and the Crown sought to lead evidence regarding prior sexual misconduct.[19] Critics have suggested that, prior to the Court's acknowledgment in *Handy* that the relevance of similar fact evidence was indeed about the accused's propensity, the law on similar fact evidence was unclear and the Court's rulings regarding it were inconsistent.[20]

Doctrinally, it is possible to characterize the reasoning in these pre-*Handy* cases as being inconsistent. I want to suggest an alternative interpretation based on certain trends that are evident in these cases and that are more pronounced in post-*Handy* lower court cases addressing similar fact evidence. The alternative interpretation is that there is actually a consistency in how the Court approached similar fact evidence cases in the early 1990s. The seeming inconsistency stems from a distinction in how the Court treats similar fact evidence in adult complainant cases and child complainant cases – a distinction that stems from a difference in how the "rapist" and the "pedophile" are conceptualized by the Court. The thread of continuity evident in this line of cases – the aspect of these decisions that suggests a consistency rather than the inconsistency generally attributed to them – pertains to the role that essentialism plays in the Court's reasoning. Under this interpretation, the inconsistencies in the three pre-*Handy* cases about to be discussed could be reconciled by the fact that two of them, *R. v. B.(C.R.)* and *R. v. B.(F.F.)*, involved child complainants whereas the other, *R. v. C.(M.H.)*, involved adults.[21]

The first of the trilogy of similar fact cases decided by the Supreme Court of Canada in the 1990s was *B.(C.R.)*. In *B.(C.R.)*, Justice McLachlin (as she then was) upheld the trial judge's decision to admit similar fact evidence regarding prior acts of sexual misconduct on the part of the accused. The accused was charged with sexual offences against his biological, or in the Court's words "natural," daughter. She was aged eleven to thirteen at the time of the assaults and alleged that she had been sexually abused by her father two or three times a week, progressing from fondling to oral sex and vaginal and anal intercourse. She testified that on occasion they had also urinated on each other. In order to support the complainant's testimony that the acts occurred, the Crown led similar fact evidence that, several years earlier, the accused had had sexual relations with the fifteen-year-old daughter of his common law wife – a girl with whom he had "enjoyed a father-daughter relationship."[22] His stepdaughter testified that within a year of living with the accused he had begun sexually abusing her.

Two interrelated points arising from Justice McLachlin's decision in *B.(C.R.)* should be noted. The first is with respect to her general comments regarding the use of propensity-based reasoning. It was actually *B.(C.R.)*, not *Handy*, in which the Court first acknowledged that in fact the probative value of similar fact evidence does turn on propensity-based reasoning. Justice McLachlin stated that "[i]t is no longer necessary to hang the evidence tendered on the peg of some issue other than disposition."[23] She determined that evidence of propensity may be admitted where its probative value in relation to an issue in question is so high that it displaces the heavy prejudice that inevitably arises when evidence of prior bad sexual acts on the part of the accused is admitted.

The second point regarding this case concerns Justice McLachlin's application of the law of similar fact evidence, as she states it in *B.(C.R.)*, to the facts of *B.(C.R.)* itself. She found that the probative value of the stepdaughter's evidence stemmed from its demonstration of the accused's propensity to engage in the sort of sexual misconduct with which he was charged. The main similarity in each case, according to Justice McLachlin, was that "the accused shortly after establishing a father-daughter relationship with the victim is alleged to have engaged her in a sexual relationship."[24] The differences between their testimony that Justice McLachlin highlighted as important are also significant. These include the fact that the age of the girls was different and that one was sexually mature, while the other was only a child, when the acts began. She noted that one was a blood relation, while the other was not, and that while many of the acts were the same there was no suggestion of urination on the stepdaughter.

In light of these differences, to what propensity was Justice McLachlin referring in admitting the evidence? Given that one victim was a child and the other a post-pubescent teenager, it was not a pedophilic propensity *per se*. Nor was it a propensity to engage in the "unnatural" act of incestuous sexual contact, nor a propensity for the "unnatural" practice of incorporating bodily wastes into one's sexual repertoire. Justice McLachlin was referring to a propensity to take sexual advantage of a father-daughter relationship. The Court's analysis was directly tied to what it determined to be the similarity in nature of the relationship between each of the two victims and the accused. Lower court decisions post-*Handy* regarding similar fact evidence suggest that similarity of relationship – how the accused relates to the complainants – appears to be the single most significant factor in the great majority of cases involving the admission of similar fact evidence in trials concerning the alleged sexual assault of a child.

Almost exactly one year after *B.(C.R.)*, the Supreme Court of Canada, with Justice McLachlin again writing for the majority, released another decision addressing the issue of similar fact evidence in sexual assault trials. In *C.(M.H.)*, the accused was charged with indecent assault against his ex-wife. She alleged that the accused forced her to have sexual intercourse with a dog. The Crown led evidence from the accused's subsequent common law wife that he had: (1) requested she submit to sexual intercourse with a dog; (2) made a remark suggesting that she should have sexual intercourse with a bull; and (3) requested that she engage in sexual conduct involving a cucumber and body oils and foams.[25]

Recall that in *B.(C.R.)*, Justice McLachlin determined that "[i]t is no longer necessary to hang the evidence tendered on the peg of some issue other than disposition."[26] In *B.(C.R.)*, she also rejected the need to show a "striking similarity" between the allegations and the similar fact evidence, noting that such "[c]atchwords have gone the same way as categories."[27] Yet, in *C.(M.H.)*, only one year later, she declared that evidence as to disposition is generally inadmissible, highly prejudicial, and of little relevance. She determined that it would only be admissible when it goes to "more than disposition, and will be considered to have real probative value."[28] Such probative value, according to Justice McLachlin in *C.(M.H.)*, will only arise where "the acts compared are *so unusual and strikingly similar* that their similarities cannot be attributed to coincidence."[29] She found that the evidence regarding requests that the accused's subsequent common law wife have sex with dogs and bulls was admissible. She did so on the basis that it could "be argued that the suggestion that one's spouse should participate in such unnatural acts is so remarkable that the separate incidents might be viewed as highly similar, giving the evidence sufficient probative force to take it out of the category of mere evidence of disposition."[30] Interestingly, she excluded the evidence regarding the oil and cucumbers because it was not unusual enough.

So in *B.(C.R.)*, Justice McLachlin determined that in certain circumstances evidence may be admitted to demonstrate propensity, and she admitted the similar fact evidence despite distinctions regarding factors such as the age of the victims, the type of sexual acts, and the presence or absence of blood ties. A year later, she stated that similar fact evidence will typically only be admitted where it goes to something more than disposition, and she employed the very "catchwords" that she had rejected in *B.(C.R.)*. The similar fact evidence was admitted in *B.(C.R.)* despite not sharing what Justice McLachlin would surely characterize as the unusual and unnatural character of the sexual acts alleged by the complainant (incestuous pedophiliac relations and acts of urinating on one another). The focus in *B.(C.R.)* was on similarity in relationship dynamics. In *C.(M.H.)*, the "peg on which to hang" the similar fact evidence offered by Justice McLachlin was the unusualness and unnaturalness of the alleged sexual misconduct. She found that upon re-trial the evidence regarding bestiality (but not the evidence regarding cucumbers and oil) would be admissible on the basis that it was "strikingly similar" to the allegations because of the unusualness of suggesting one's spouse engage in such unnatural acts.[31] She did not discuss relationship dynamics, and the accused's propensity to relate in a specific manner to his spouses was not referenced.

Categorizing sexual acts as "natural" and "unnatural" and determining admissibility based on this distinction clearly reveals essentialist assumptions about sexuality. To categorize in this way also has normative implications regarding the potential for judicial bias against those whose sexual practices deviate from whatever the sexual norms may be in a given community at a given time. While a distinction between usual and highly unusual sexual acts may often be relevant in a determination regarding the admissibility of similar fact evidence, it is not necessary to make this distinction by identifying which sexual practices are natural and which are unnatural.

Moreover, courts should be cautious when employing an analytical approach based on their own assumptions about what sexual practices are usual. While it may be obvious and therefore highly cogent in regard to sexual practices at the far end of the usual/unusual spectrum – such as perhaps bestiality – it is likely more often the case that situating sexual practice X on the usual/unusual spectrum requires a fairly subjective and non-quantifiable assumption on the part of the judge.

The third case in this pre-*Handy* trilogy on similar fact evidence released by the Supreme Court of Canada in the 1990s was *B.(F.F.)*.[32] In this case, the accused was the complainant's uncle, who lived with her family and was responsible for the care of her and her siblings for a number of years. The complainant alleged that the sexual abuse began when she was the age of ten and continued for a number of years, stopping only when one of her brothers caught the accused sexually assaulting her. Justice Iacobucci determined that evidence from the complainant's siblings of repeated and brutal, although not sexual, attacks against them by the accused was admissible to show the accused's pattern of domination. He held that the similar fact evidence demonstrated the accused's "system of violent control" and that this control explained why the complainant had not reported the abuse sooner.

It has been suggested that Justice Iacobucci's reasoning, like Justice McLachlin's reasoning in *C.(M.H.)*, is inconsistent with *B.(C.R.)*. Critics have argued that *B.(F.F.)* is also a retreat from *B.(C.R.)*.[33] On its face, this observation seems accurate. Justice Iacobucci did refer to the old categorical approach, suggesting that the evidence could be admitted to rebut the accused's defence of innocent association. Innocent association was one of the old categories. He did cite prior Supreme Court of Canada case law, stating that similar fact evidence was not to be admitted to show disposition.[34] However, a closer examination of his reasoning in *B.(F.F.)* – particularly when analyzed in relation to *B.(C.R.)* and *C.(M.H.)* – suggests a more nuanced conclusion. Unlike the reasoning in *C.(M.H.)*, Justice Iacobucci did not look for striking similarity between the acts against the different victims. Indeed, the similar fact evidence did not even relate to sexual behaviour. The evidence was admitted to show a pattern of relating – to demonstrate the accused's system of violent control. In *B.(F.F.)*, similar fact evidence of other misconduct on the part of the accused was admitted not because it shared with the allegations an unusualness, an unnaturalness, or a striking similarity. It was admitted in order to establish the accused's propensity to develop a certain type of relationship with the children in his care: a relationship of domination, power imbalance, and violence. Despite Justice Iacobucci's reference to the categorical approach and despite the fact that he linked the similar fact evidence to an explanation regarding the complainant's delayed disclosure, the inferential reasoning underpinning the decision in *B.(F.F.)* is much more akin to that in *B.(C.R.)* than to that in *C.(M.H.)*.

It may be true that the law pre-*Handy* was unclear doctrinally. That said, the Supreme Court of Canada's rulings were, in terms of certain factors, quite consistent with each other and with how these issues tend to be addressed in lower courts post-*Handy*. These factors include their degree of reliance on the accused's propensity to relate in a particular manner with the complainants (depending on whether the complainant was an adult or a child at the time of the offence) and whether, in the case of adult complainants, the sexual acts alleged to have occurred are outside the range of those acts considered "natural" or usual by the Court. *Handy*, with its acknowledgment that similar fact evidence is indeed evidence about an accused's propensity, is said to have resolved the inconsistencies in the law's approach to similar fact evidence. The fact that in lower court cases post-*Handy* the same trends emerge that were evident in the Court's pre-*Handy* decision suggests that certain overarching conceptions about sexual disposition were, and continue to be, at play.

All similar fact evidence cases involve a double inference. The probative value of similar fact evidence relies on the inference that the accused's propensity for X makes it extremely unlikely that it is merely a coincidence that both complainants are lying or mistaken in their allegations of X(ish). (The "ish" is meant to suggest that while they need not be identical, there must be a high degree of similarity between the propensity established by the similar fact evidence and the allegations at issue.) The first inference is that the similar fact evidence establishes a specific propensity. The second inference is that this propensity makes it highly unlikely that it is a mere coincidence that both or all of the complainants are making similar allegations. To avoid convicting someone for being a "bad person" rather than for doing the "bad act" with which they have been accused, it is critical that the similar fact evidence raise both inferences. This requires sufficient focus in a court's reasoning not only on how the evidence demonstrates a specific propensity but also on the likelihood of coincidence that both complainants are lying or mistaken given this propensity. This double inference takes on a particular flavour in the context of sexual assault cases. Propensity-based reasoning may differ depending on whether one understands sexuality as an innate and pre-social disposition or as a contextually dependent social variable. The distinction might be thought of as a distinction between reasoning based on the propensity to *act* a certain way and reasoning based on the propensity to *be* a certain way (which suggests that one will have acted a certain way).

Lower court decisions dealing with the similar fact evidence issue, which have been released since *Handy*, bring into better focus the different emphasis in cases involving child complainants as compared to those involving adult complainants. These cases highlight the continuity in the three trends both preceding and following the Supreme Court of Canada's decision in *Handy:* a pattern of relying on degree of similarity in *modus operandi* with an emphasis on likelihood of coincidence-type reasoning in adult complainant cases where similar fact evidence is adduced to help prove an element of the *actus reus;* a pattern in child complainant cases of emphasizing the presence of a propensity to sexually abuse children in the context of a particular type of relationship; and an emphasis on the accused's relationship dynamics in child cases that is not as evident in adult cases.

While lower court decisions reveal essentialist conceptions about sexuality in both adult and child complainant cases, the types of essentialist assumptions differ. In child complainant cases, the essentialism is evidenced by the courts' focus on an accused's "true nature." The focus tends to be more on the disposition of the accused (the first inference) and the reasoning is focused more on whether the similar fact evidence demonstrates a particular propensity. In adult complainant cases, the essentialism is revealed by the heavy emphasis placed on similarity between the specific sexual acts that are alleged. The courts tend to focus more on the likelihood of coincidence that both complainants are making similar allegations (the second inference). It is not that the reasoning in similar fact evidence cases involving child complainants is unrelated to the unlikelihood of coincidence, and it is not that the adult complainant cases lack reasoning through propensity. The distinction between the two types of cases is actually much like the distinction between cases in which the fact in issue is identity and cases in which the fact in issue is an element of the *actus reus*. As Justice Binnie notes in *Handy,* in comparing cases in which *actus reus,* rather than identification, is the issue, "the point is not that the degree of similarity in such a case must be *higher* or *lower* than in an identification case. The point is that the issue is *different* and the drivers of cogency in relation to the desired inferences will therefore not be the same."[35] Similarly, the post-*Handy* lower court cases seem to suggest that while essentialist reasoning figures into both, the drivers of cogency in adult complainant cases are not always the same as in child complainant cases.

Unlike in cases involving adult complainants, in child complainant cases the single most important factor often appears to be the nature of the relationship between the accused and the complainants. This factor seems to matter more than the similarity in the types of sexual acts engaged in, the gender of the victims, or any other element of the accused's *modus operandi*. Courts focus heavily on the accused's method or manner of relating to children, the relationship dynamic between the accused and the complainants, and the context in which the interactions are alleged to have transpired.

Factors such as the fact that "the appellant first engaged in sexually abusive conduct when the complainant was especially vulnerable" because of injury, illness, or inebriation or that "in each case the complainant came to view the appellant as a father figure" are weighted more heavily than a lack of similarity in the specific sexual acts engaged in with each complainant.[36] Similar fact evidence will be admitted under this type of reasoning to "demonstrate a specific propensity [on the part of the accused] to exploit his status as a family friend and overnight guest"[37] or as an uncle, father, or stepfather.[38]

The same observation regarding the significant weight given to relationship dynamics in child complainant cases can be observed in the Supreme Court of Canada's decision in *R. v. Shearing* (released the same year as *Handy*).[39] In *Shearing,* the accused was a cult leader accused of sexually assaulting a number of complainants – all but two of whom were members of his cult. The Court found that he had a situation-specific propensity to groom adolescent girls for sexual gratification by exploiting the cult's beliefs and that he proceeded that way with each complainant. The evidence of each of the believer complainants was also admitted with respect to the non-believing complainants because the abuse of power and *modus operandi* were similar and because, with them as well, he exploited his status as leader of the cult. The cogency of the similar fact evidence stemmed from his "gross abuse of power."[40]

In cases such as these, courts rely on, as the cogent factor for establishing the objective improbability of coincidence (and therefore demonstrating the probative value of the similar fact evidence), a specific propensity on the part of the accused to sexually exploit a specific type of relationship with children.[41] The courts in these cases draw the first inference regarding the accused's propensity and then base the second inference on an assessment of the degree of similarity in how the accused interacts with the different complainants. There is some recognition that an accused's propensity to relate in a particular manner is a critical aspect of his *modus operandi.* In child complainant cases with this type of reasoning, but where the relationship between the accused and the complainants differ, the similar fact evidence is less likely to be admitted, even where the sexual acts were quite similar.[42]

Encouragingly, in these cases, context is the single most important analytical factor. Courts identify similarity between certain important contextual factors (which are not even necessarily related to sexual conduct), such as relationship dynamics, patterns of control, and positions of power within a family, as the drivers of cogency – as was the case in the Supreme Court of Canada's decision in *B.(F.F.).* The reasoning in these cases seems sound and does not resort to essentialist conceptions that risk overemphasizing the first inference (about propensity) and underemphasizing the second inference (likelihood of coincidence). Indeed, the focus on manner of relating as a key aspect of the accused's *modus operandi* could be characterized as taking a constructivist approach (a recognition that it is the interactions, rather than the acts, that are most significant).

Less promisingly, in many lower court decisions involving child complainants, an analysis of the accused's relationship propensity is then integrated back into an essentialist approach that focuses on an offender's "true nature" or innate sexual disposition. In this way, the analysis in many child complainant cases reveals an unusual integration of both essentialist and constructivist reasoning. Where such an integration occurs, courts focus on, or refer to, factors such as the accused's fantasies and masturbatory patterns,[43] their sexual attraction, sexual interest,[44] and "proclivity towards sexual contact with children,"[45] and the accused's sexual orientation towards prepubescent bodies.[46] The most cogent factor in this type of reasoning is that the accused's behaviour displays a certain sexual arousal pattern. So, for example, in one case the court found that "the disposition [of the accused] would be described as an active interest in touching his prepubescent daughter in a sexual manner. In other words he has a sexual interest in his young daughter."[47] In this particular case, the court determined that "this overall interest is a distinct deviation from the norm of a father-daughter relationship" and went on to state that the accused's manner of relating to these girls was a manifestation of this sexual interest.[48] Only then did the court compare whether the manifestation of this sexual interest was similar in both cases. By reasoning in this manner, the analysis was driven almost entirely by the finding in regard to the accused's propensity – his "true sexual nature." In cases of this type, instead of identifying an accused's propensity to act a certain way, the court identifies an accused's propensity to be a certain way that makes him act a certain way.[49] An analytical approach that relies on underpinning assumptions that essentialize those who sexually offend against children can result in reasoning that places too much emphasis on propensity (the first inference) and not enough on coincidence (the second inference). Courts could very well arrive at the same outcome in some of these cases without overemphasizing the accused's sexual propensity. The point is that courts should not rely on reasoning that risks convicting an accused for "being" a pedophile. This approach leads to at least two problems with these lower court decisions.

The first, to which I have just alluded, is its potential to result in the type of unjust reasoning that cases from *Makin v. Attorney-General for New South Wales* to *Handy* have attempted to avoid: Mr. X is a pedophile and therefore he did what this child says he did.[50] The concern is that once the similar fact evidence establishes that the accused has a particular sexual disposition, moral prejudice or reasoning prejudice kicks in, and the accused is convicted based on who he is rather than on what he has done. Similar fact evidence should only be admitted where its ability to establish the second inference – given his propensity towards interacting/relating in this way with children it is highly unlikely that these *similar* allegations are a mere *coincidence* – is as heavily scrutinized as is its ability to establish the first inference – all of this evidence shows he has a propensity to groom, control, manipulate, and interact sexually with children with whom he has a particular type of relationship.

The second problem with this reasoning is discussed at greater length in the section to follow addressing child pornography. Briefly, and simply put, this reasoning further promotes a legal discourse that conceptualizes those who sexually assault children as a discrete minority of sexual deviants with an innate sexual orientation towards children. This reasoning is undesirable because an essentialist approach to child sexual abuse limits recognition of the social factors that produce this harmful problem. A more constructivist conception would encourage a legal discourse that acknowledges the social conditions and context in which child sexual abuse most frequently arises. A legal discourse that recognizes context in this way would help to promote legal reasoning and legal approaches oriented more towards alleviating these conditions rather than only attempting to identify and contain the "disordered other." A change in the way that courts conceptualize sexual offenders in the context of applications to admit similar fact evidence is obviously not enough to radically revamp the way that the law, legislators, courts, and policy makers approach the problem of child sexual abuse. It is, however, a start – it is perhaps even a sensible place to start.

In adult complainant cases where the Crown seeks to introduce similar fact evidence to establish an element of the *actus reus*, beyond those involving doctor-patient-type relationships, courts do not tend to look for, and rely on, a propensity to engage in a particular type of sexual behaviour tied to a specific relationship dynamic.[51] In adult cases, the focus appears to be more on the sexual acts and not on the sexual interactions.[52] Unlike in child complainant cases, in cases involving adult complainants courts seem less inclined to adopt propensity-based reasoning that relies on essentialist assumptions about an accused's "true sexual nature." Justice Binnie notes in *Handy*, which involved adult complainants, that "not only can people change their ways but they are not robotic."[53] It seems much less likely that one would read such an assertion in reference to an individual accused of having sex with multiple children. In adult complainant cases, courts are less likely to look for, make references suggesting, or rely on assumptions about, an offender's innate sexual preference or true nature. They are more likely to focus their propensity-based reasoning on the likelihood of coincidence. This is not to suggest that essentialist conceptions are absent from these adult complainant cases. More focus on the second inference typically means greater weight is given to the degree of similarity between allegations. However, for a judiciary tending to conceptualize sexuality from an essentialist perspective, this means putting an emphasis on, and making a comparison of, the specific sexual acts at issue and putting less weight on the relationship dynamics, which is the interactional aspect of the allegations. Indeed, in adult complainant cases, courts fail to do what they achieve in the child complainant cases. They fail to properly consider the cogency of similar fact evidence that demonstrates how the accused relates to women with whom the accused is sexually intimate. In other words, they focus too much on the specifics of the sexual act that has been alleged and not enough on the relationship dynamics that are involved.

The case of *R. v. G.G.* exemplifies this type of reasoning.[54] In *G.G.*, the accused's adult daughter alleged that she awoke one night to find her father's hands inside her panties. Her father had come into her house without her knowledge while she was asleep on the couch. The Crown sought to admit similar fact evidence of a prior conviction of sexual assault against the accused by the other adult daughter, G.L. G.L. had also awoken to find her father's hand inside her panties fondling her genitals. The trial judge refused to admit the similar fact evidence in part on the basis that it lacked probative value because "touching the genital area of an unconscious, vulnerable woman, who is an acquaintance or relative of the accused, cannot reasonably be described as peculiar or highly distinctive" but is instead "a generic act, which is sadly far too common or present in sexual assault cases."[55]

The relationship status between the accused and the complainants was the same, and his *modus operandi* was the same. The similar fact evidence was not admitted because from the judge's perspective the sexual misconduct – the sexual act alleged – was too common, not unusual enough. This reasoning much more closely resembles the type of reasoning used in identity cases than the reasoning in *actus reus* child complainant cases. Had this case involved allegations by these daughters as children, it is most likely that the court's examination of similarity in circumstances surrounding the allegations would have differed. The reasoning would likely have focused more on the relationships between the accused and his daughters rather than on the specific sexual act alleged and how common or unusual it might be. In adult complainant cases, power dynamics, an accused's system of control, or a particular manner of relating are not considered probative in the way that they are in child complainant cases.[56] A heavy focus on comparing specific sexual acts and ignoring relationship dynamics, combined with essentialist conceptions about sex, also means a resort to reasoning that assesses probative value based on characterizing sexual acts as natural or unnatural.

Approaching the issue of similar fact evidence with a recognition that method or manner of relating is an important part of the *modus operandi* for those who sexually assault children (and therefore ought to be given significant consideration) seems both well advised and promisingly constructivist. Where, however, this analysis is folded back into assumptions about true nature and innate sexual proclivities, its social constructivism is lost. In adult complainant cases, the problem is not that the court's inquiry is focused on discovering the accused's true nature to relate – the problem is the lack of focus on the relational elements of the accused's behaviour.

There are constructivist and essentialist elements to both of these approaches. What courts ought to do is apply an analysis that relies on the likelihood of coincidence-based reasoning (so as to eliminate the true nature/assumptions of innate sexual deviance underpinning child complainant cases) but that recognizes the significant cogency of similar fact evidence regarding an accused's propensity to relate to children, or women, or men in a particular manner. This would require an examination and comparison of relationships rather than relationship status. It would focus more on interactions and relationship dynamics than on comparisons between the specific sexual acts. In other words, for all cases, regardless of the age of the complainant, courts should maintain the more sophisticated understanding of the role of power that is currently evident in many child sexual abuse cases but lose the essentialist elements evident in both approaches. They should do this by rejecting reasoning that is based on assumptions about innate disposition and natural versus unnatural sexual acts and focus instead on the similarity in method or manner of relating as a significant element of the *modus operandi.*

The Supreme Court of Canada's Differing Approaches to Child and Adult Pornography

The assertion that courts often conceptualize "the pedophile" as a pre-social category or type of person is also supported by the Court's differing approaches to the criminal regulation of child pornography and adult pornography. Comparing the Court's reasoning in cases addressing adult pornography with its analysis in cases concerning child pornography illustrates that, while the Court identifies pedophiles as a discrete category of individuals with an innate and pre-social sexual orientation, they do not conceptualize those who sexually assault adults in the same way. Conceptualizing sexual violence as socially contingent both requires and promotes legal reasoning that acknowledges the contextual factors (such as gender hierarchy) that contribute to the perpetuation of these harms. It also better accommodates the perspectives of all sexual actors involved in an interaction (not simply the perspectives of the accused and the justice system). In contrast, understanding sexual violence as a function of the perverted arousal of a discrete minority (a conceptual approach that is evident in the Court's treatment of child pornography) produces a legal discourse that obscures the social factors that perpetuate the sexual violation of children.

As will be discussed in Chapter 5, in the early 1990s the Supreme Court of Canada began to focus on adult pornography's potentially detrimental attitudinal impact towards women – what is sometimes described as the potential for "attitudinal bias." The harm of obscenity identified by the Court turned on its potential to perpetuate inequitable perceptions about, and treatment of, women by men. The Court gave recognition to the argument that depictions of rape could normalize and perpetuate more rape.[57] The Court has not approached the criminalization of child pornography in the same way. They have refused to justify its criminalization on the basis that it risks creating attitudinal changes in society at large. While this was certainly one of the justifications that the Crown argued in *R. v. Sharpe* – the Court's leading precedent on the criminal regulation of child pornography – the Court did not justify the prohibition on possession of child pornography on the basis of systemic attitudinal bias.[58]

Sharpe involved a constitutional challenge to section 163.1(4) of the *Criminal Code*.[59] Section 163.1(4) prohibits the possession of child pornography. The defence argued that the provision, because it prohibited not just the production, sale, or distribution but also the possession of child pornography, was an unjustifiable violation of the freedom of expression protections guaranteed under the *Canadian Charter of Rights and Freedoms*.[60] But for two exceptions – what might be described as the "private diaries" and the "teenage experimentation" exceptions – the Supreme Court of Canada found that while section 163.1(4) does violate section 2(b) it was saved under section 1.[61] For the purposes of this discussion what is of most significance are Chief Justice McLachlin's reasons for finding that the general prohibition on possession of child pornography, setting aside the exceptions, bears a rational connection to the pressing and substantial objective of the law – the prevention of harm to children. The Crown argued, and the Court adopted versions of, five different harms caused by child pornography. It is the first harm alleged by the Crown – that child pornography promotes cognitive distortions – that reveals the Court's essentialist conception of those who sexually offend against children. The Crown argued that "pornography may change possessors' attitudes in ways that make them more likely to sexually abuse children."[62] They argued that people may come to see sexual relations with children as normal and have their moral inhibitions weakened and that people who would not otherwise abuse children might consequently do so. This argument tracks precisely the argument made by the Crown and accepted by the Court in *R. v. Butler* and *Little Sisters Book and Art Emporium v. Canada (Minister of Justice)* – cases dealing with the criminal regulation of adult pornography.[63]

The Supreme Court of Canada in *Sharpe* did not accept this justification. Instead, it adopted a modified version of the Crown's argument. The Court accepted that "child pornography may reduce *pedophiles'* defences and inhibitions against sexual abuse of children."[64] The nuance of their modification to the Crown's argument is significant. In *Butler* and *Little Sisters,* the Court justified the prohibition on the production and distribution of certain types of pornography based on the concern that such materials and depictions could induce individuals to change their sexual behaviour and would influence and reinforce negative perceptions about women.[65] In *Sharpe,* the Court justified the prohibition on the possession of child pornography based, in part, on the concern that such materials and depictions would incite pedophiles, making them more likely to offend.[66] Exposure to child pornography can incite – encourage or stir up – the innate sexual orientation of a pedophile (and only a pedophile). Exposure to adult pornography can induce – bring about or give rise to – the sexual violation of women by men.

This distinction raises a number of questions. Why is "the pedophile" a discrete and identifiable sexual orientation whereas "the rapist" is not? Those with a propensity for sexual interactions with children are ascribed an innate sexual orientation, while sexually violent behaviour that is directed towards adults is socially contingent and could, through exposure, be induced in an individual. This same conceptual understanding of "the pedophile" is revealed in both the majority and dissent in *R. v. Morelli.*[67] *Morelli* involved the legitimacy of a warrant obtained to search the accused's computer for possession of child pornography. The police relied upon two pieces of evidence as the basis for a reasonable belief that Morelli was in possession of child pornography. The first piece of evidence was the statement of a witness who had seen shortcut icons on Morelli's desktop suggesting he had accessed a website called "Lolita XXX." The second piece of evidence was the "expert opinion" of a police officer. In the officer's "expert opinion," there is a type of person who uses child pornography, and individuals of this type collect and hoard great numbers of pornographic images of children.

Justice Fish found the search and seizure of Morelli's computer unconstitutional. This finding was not because he took issue with the propensity-based reasoning upon which the warrant was obtained – in fact, he strongly ascribed to the same conception – but because from his perspective the police did not have enough information to reasonably believe that Morelli was indeed one of these "types of offenders."[68] Justice Fish determined that "two suspiciously-labeled links in the 'Favourites' do not suffice to characterize a person as an habitual child pornography offender of the type that seeks out and hoards illegal images."[69] In significant measure, his difficulty with this aspect of the evidence was that the bulk of the pornographic material observed at Morelli's house prior to obtaining the search warrant was "perfectly legal adult pornography,"[70] and so it was not reasonable to believe that Morelli was one of these "types of offenders."[71] His reasoning was explicitly based on the assumption that there is a type of person who views child pornographic images and that this is a different type of person than the type who views images of teenagers and adults.

It is problematic for courts to understand child sexual abuse as a function of a pre-social, acontextual sexual orientation. Essentialist conceptions of child sexual abuse conceal the larger social context – the social determinants – that produce sexual violence against children. Constructing "the pedophile" as a discrete category of people, making him the archetypical child sexual abuser, is a dangerous misapprehension of the social problem of child sexual abuse. It portrays the child abuser as atypical (and child sexual abuse as "aberrational rather than systemic and ubiquitous").[72] Under an essentialist framework, the pedophile is defined as "different in kind" from most of us, who are "normal." However, more sexual abuse against children is perpetuated by their own family members than by anyone else known or unknown to the child.[73] Less frequently are child sexual abuse victims violated by "the pedophile" – that aberrational "other" lurking around playgrounds or trolling the Internet. Children are violated in much greater numbers by their fathers, grandfathers, stepfathers, uncles, cousins, and brothers.

Understanding the issue as the "problem of the pedophile" encourages discussion, policy, and legal approaches for keeping children safe from that "other." It does nothing to keep children safe from their own families. It does nothing to recognize that child sexual abuse is often a threat that comes from within the family and not from outside of it. It does nothing to promote the need for systemic approaches (involving fundamental social changes) to prevent sexual violence against children. As a result, the focus of those criminal law approaches aimed at preventing child sexual abuse that are proactive (as opposed to reactive) are typically oriented towards keeping children safe from the sexual predator who stalks them in the playground or on the Internet. Section 161 of the *Criminal Code* provides one such example.[74] It permits a court to make an order prohibiting anyone convicted of a sexual offence against a person under sixteen from attending a park, playground, school ground, swimming pool, or community centre where children are likely to be present. It is not that laws such as section 161 are themselves problematic. It is that these legal approaches target only one specific (and small) subset of child sexual abuse. There do not seem to be parallel proactive or preventative legal initiatives aimed at preventing the larger category of sexual abuse that occurs within families and social/ educational and religious networks.[75]

The federal government's *Tackling Violent Crime Act* further exemplifies this point.[76] This act, which purports to address the issue of child sexual abuse, raises the age of capacity to consent to sexual interactions from fourteen to sixteen. Its legislative objective, as articulated in the preamble of the act, is to ensure that families are protected from sexual predators.[77] According to legislators, raising the age of consent from fourteen to sixteen will make the streets safer for our children and protect communities from sexual predators and human trafficking. Discussion about the proposed act in the House of Commons reveals the degree to which legislators seek to distance "us" from "them": "Canada has become, in some instances, a destination for those adult sexual predators, who have come from jurisdictions where their age of consent is higher. We do not want Canada to become a destination for adult sexual predators."[78]

The government's impetus for addressing the problem of sexual abuse against children in Canada was the influx of sexual predators from foreign lands and the threat that Canada will become a hotbed of child sex tourism. Enacting proactive provisions to protect children from those who lure and exploit them through the use of the Internet is desirable. Taking measures to ensure that Canada does not become the next Phuket – as ridiculous as that proposition might be – is not the problem. (Although the efficacy even of meeting the articulated objective of these measures is questionable in this instance.) The law, of course, is much more willing and able to intervene in the regulation and surveillance of public spaces. It is also more comfortable for judges and law makers to speak of, and think of, those who sexually abuse children as aliens, outsiders, and "others," than it is for them to acknowledge that it is our social structures, our educational deficits, our systemic poverty, our social dysfunction, and our families that are hurting our children. Given that the vast majority of children who are sexually abused are violated by family members and acquaintances, drawing a circle around the family, reifying the public/private distinction, and identifying the threat as from without rather than from within is dangerously imperceptive. Jurisprudence that conceptualizes "the pedophile" in this way – such as the Supreme Court of Canada's rhetoric about "clos[ing] the cyberspace door before the predator gets in to prey" in its recent (broad) interpretation of the offence of luring a child on the Internet – contributes to this problematic discourse.[79]

Legal conceptions that promote the notion that child sexual abuse is perpetuated by the anomalous and disordered "other" are likely to encourage legal approaches to prevention that focus on identifying and containing those "others" rather than approaches that offer a truthful, if uncomfortable, acknowledgment that the behaviour is prolific, that it is more often uncles, grandfathers, stepfathers, and teachers than it is sex tourists, and that, like other criminal offences, it is strongly correlated with the typical social determinants of crime. Focusing on the child pornography-consuming pedophile trolling the playgrounds rather than on the dangerous and violent landscape of the family lives of so many children is similar to the way in which courts and legislatures traditionally focused on stranger rape while ignoring the much more common rape of women by their spouses, co-workers, neighbours, and friends.[80] It does nothing to encourage an examination of the social structures that perpetuate this violence against children. An essentialist understanding of child sexual abuse, in which "the pedophile" is constructed as the archetypical offender, is unlikely to examine the possible correlation between child sexual abuse and alcoholism, poverty, drug addiction, lack of education, and other forms of child abuse. It is unlikely to recognize the generational, systemic way in which this social problem, once it has infected a family or community, is very likely to reproduce itself over and over again.

The Supreme Court of Canada in *Sharpe* did not need to rely on (and, in doing so, reinforce) an essentialist understanding of those who sexually abuse children in order to uphold the constitutionality of section 163.1(4) of the *Criminal Code*. They could have come to the same conclusion by relying on the same reasoning they endorsed in adult pornography cases. There was no analytical need, in terms of their reasoning, to modify the Crown's argument that child pornography may reduce people's defences and inhibitions against the sexual abuse of children. If the Court is willing to accept, as it did in *Butler*, that exposure to sexual violence against women could influence people's sexual behaviour in a social context where women are systematically disempowered, why could it not accept the same argument with respect to exposure to sexual images involving children – which are also a disempowered demographic?[81] The unlikelihood that elected officials will pursue legal reforms that force their voters to see child sexual abuse as a problem produced by, and typically contained within, their own families makes it all the more important for courts to adopt conceptual frameworks that promote such a legal discourse.

Conclusion

Conceptualizing those who sexually abuse children as a discrete minority possessed with an innate sexual orientation perpetuates a legal discourse that obscures the relationship between child sexual abuse and the social conditions that produce this problem. It also risks convicting people for who they are rather than for what they are alleged to have done. While the challenges to successfully prosecuting those who sexually violate children are enormous, and the law of evidence, criminal procedure, and substantive criminal law should be tailored towards overcoming these challenges, it is also critical to promote all of the fundamental principles that pursue the "just" in the criminal justice system. Essentializing the village idiot, in the context of legal responses to the problem of child sexual abuse, has done neither the law nor the precocious child any great favours.

3 Natural Categories and Non-Categorical Approaches to Law and Sexuality

> If I didn't define myself for myself, I would be crunched into other people's fantasies for me and eaten alive.
>
> – AUDRE LORDE

The pedophile is not the only inherent, biologically driven, pre-social sexual subject to emerge from the jurisprudence of Canada's high court jurists. The Supreme Court of Canada's categorical approach to equality for gays and lesbians under section 15 of the *Canadian Charter of Rights and Freedoms* also reveals the assumption that sexual preference is an innate and essential element, constitutive of who we are.[1] Some critics have suggested that the Court's essentialist understanding of sexual orientation in addressing equality claims promotes assimilation and fails to challenge those social institutions that perpetuate inequity based on opposite sex desire. Similarly, the Court's assumption that sexual harassment is a function of (hetero)sexual arousal also reveals an essentialist conception of sexuality that produces legal reasoning with comparable shortcomings. As scholars have noted, identifying (hetero)sexual arousal as the source of sexual harassment lends itself to reasoning that promotes categorical thinking, obscures the regulatory way in which sex and gender norms are used as weapons of sexual hostility, and limits the possibility for legal recognition of certain types of sexual hostility. In both section 15 equality jurisprudence and sexual harassment cases, categorical thinking relies on, and perpetuates, essentialist conceptions of sexuality.

Conceptions of Sexuality under Section 15

There now exist in Canada a number of legal instruments, some constitutionally entrenched, that provide protection against discrimination for some sexual minorities.[2] Each of these legal instruments adopts a categorical approach to the prohibition of discrimination by developing a series of legislatively enumerated, or subsequently identified or interpreted, grounds of discrimination. Each of these grounds prohibits discrimination that is based on a certain category of people. The categorical approach to human rights and equality guarantees shared by each of these legal instruments encourages claims for freedom from discrimination that are premised on essentialist conceptions of sexuality. This is because an understanding that sexual orientation, behaviour, or desire is dictated by an innate, sexual object preference, and that this preference constitutes an essential element of one's self, provides a strong justification under section 15 jurisprudence for arguing that the law ought not to discriminate on the basis of sexual preference. It supports the assertion that sexual orientation ought to be one of the protected categories.

The Supreme Court of Canada determined in *Egan v. Canada* that sexual orientation was an analogous ground under section 15. In *Egan*, Justice La Forest, writing for a plurality, characterizes sexual orientation as "a deeply personal characteristic that is either unchangeable or changeable only at unacceptable personal costs."[3] A constructivist conception of sexuality would not necessarily take issue with this characterization. For many constructivists, the problem is the combination of the assumption of immutability with the assumption that sexual object preference is a "natural" way in which to draw distinctions, identify social categories, and structure social institutions. As queer theorists have noted, assuming that sexual orientation is a naturally occurring phenomenon lends itself to distinctions between natural and unnatural – distinctions that tend to privilege heterosexuality.[4] Social constructivists and queer theorists reject the supposition that sexual object preference is a pre-social and essential element of the self, constitutive of who we are. They also challenge the assumption that it makes logical sense to make important social and legal distinctions – to form categories of people – based on this preference.

Critics of the categorical approach to equality for sexual minorities have argued that because it relies on essentialist conceptions regarding sexual identity, it means that those sexual minorities who experience their sexuality as fluid, as in transition, or as impossible to categorize will be excluded from protection under current equality guarantees.[5] They have claimed that a categorical approach means that dominant heteronormativity will not be challenged, subverted, or deconstructed – that those sexual minorities able to conform or assimilate will receive equality guarantees while those who deviate too far, those who are too "queer," will not be recognized by law.[6] They have asserted that the categorical approach to equality, in which the claims of sexual minorities are framed under the category of sexual orientation, means that other categories – prohibited grounds of discrimination – are heterosexualized.[7] Finally, they have argued that this approach to equality reinforces heteronormative discourse on social institutions such as family and marriage, rather than focusing on more transformative changes that better address the hierarchical distribution of rights and privileges in our society.[8] In this way, legal recognition of same sex relationships reinforces, rather than challenges, social institutions that are themselves inequitable (particularly for women, people of colour, and lower socio-economic families).[9]

Categorical approaches to anti-discrimination law that reify specified categories tend to obscure the "invisible background norm" operating to privilege some, while disadvantaging others.[10] While the law begins to protect certain categories of individuals who deviate from the norm, it does nothing to challenge the dominant norm against which these individuals are being measured. In fact, it does nothing to reveal that such a measurement is even taking place – the norm remains in place, permanently fixed, immutable, and "undeconstructed." Successful equality challenges expand the category of who is in, but they maintain an approach that is limited to making sure everyone who is in is treated the same rather than challenging or rejecting the necessity of a particular category.

Critics point out that categorical approaches to equality can be assimilative. They require individuals seeking equality to "fit themselves within one grouping that can be labeled disadvantaged," thus obfuscating very real differences among members of a particular category.[11] There is a second way in which categorical approaches to equality tend to be assimilative, not transformative. Not only do equality reforms premised on essentialized groups of people require excluded members of society to assimilate into an identified oppressed group, a successful equality challenge requires that the norms of that group resemble those of the majority. Susan Boyd and Claire Young offer a profound example of how this approach to equality requires and reinforces sameness in their discussion of the same sex marriage parliamentary committee hearings surrounding Bill C-23. They include a quote from a statement to the sub-committee made by a member of Parents, Families and Friends of Lesbians and Gays (PFLAG):

> When our church friend Penny was killed in a traffic accident in 1998, not only did we grieve for her but we also immediately and instinctively reached out to comfort Penny's widow ... She cried and grieved just like

> a heterosexual, because she was just as devastated, in the same way and to the same extent that a straight wife would be."[12]

Their example also demonstrates how this way of approaching equality can be at once assimilative and alienating: "She cried and grieved just like a heterosexual."

These critiques of the categorical approach to section 15 are important. Even so, as many critics would concede, certain types of sexual minority equality claims in Canada have met with a lot of success. Indeed, several of those critical of the categorical approach to social justice movements have suggested ways in which to re-consider the essentialist/constructivist binary so as to understand how essentialism can actually be invoked strategically in order to resist essentialism.[13] Foucault suggested that power was not simply a hierarchical system of domination but, rather, more a pervasive and continuous web of relations between agents, marked by continuous struggle or resistance. Power produces as much as it oppresses. The legal and social conception of sexual identity or preference as a category of folks (a "species") also produces an "it's not a choice"-type of reverse discourse, which was used successfully in the past under section 15 to radically change the legal landscape of sexual minority rights in Canada in a very short period of time. Less than ten years after recognizing sexual orientation as a prohibited ground of discrimination, almost total formal equality for gays and lesbians has been achieved in Canada – an observation that highlights one of the tensions evident in sexual orientation equality jurisprudence.[14]

The Supreme Court of Canada's reasoning in *Egan* exemplifies this tension. Both the reasoning that recognizes section 15 protection for gays and lesbians and the reasoning that denies the actual claim in *Egan* were founded on essentialist assumptions about sexual relationships. *Egan* recognized sexual orientation as a prohibited ground of discrimination under section 15 on the basis that it is unchangeable or changeable only at great personal cost. That is, sexual orientation is a stable category of identity; it constitutes a discrete type of people. Despite this finding, Justice La Forest and three others in *Egan* also determined that the heterosexual definition of "spouse" under the *Old Age Security Act* was not discriminatory.[15] This conclusion was based on their determination that heterosexuality was inextricably linked to the objective of the law. They concluded that the objective of the *Old Age Security Act* was to support and protect marriage and that because the "natural" meaning of marriage is heterosexual, the distinction was not discriminatory. Marriage, they stated, is "firmly anchored in the biological and social realities that heterosexual couples have the unique ability to procreate, [and] that most children are the product of these relationships ... In this sense, marriage is by nature heterosexual."[16] In *Egan*, essentialist reasoning gave with one hand and took away with the other.

The legal advances made by certain sexual minorities since *Egan* should not be underestimated, nor should we undervalue the future role that these advances will play in laying the foundation for further social change. It may be that until a certain degree of legal recognition is achieved, legal arguments based on disruption, transformative remedies, or a queering of the law or its subjects are likely to fail. Arguments based on the transformative potential of legally recognizing alternative familial-type relationships would have been certain to fail in a legal era in which fear of the disruption of the family was precisely the argument put forth by opponents to sexual minority rights. In fact, the Ontario Court of Appeal, in granting same sex marriage in *Halpern v. Canada (Attorney-General)*, went to some lengths to assure the Attorney General of Ontario that same sex marriage would not lead to the destruction of the family.[17] A premature argument focused too heavily on the relational interest denied by the exclusion of gays and lesbians from the institution of marriage, rather than a claim of identity-based discrimination, would have played right into the wrong hands. Those decision makers responsible for the formal equality reasoning so parsimoniously handed out in early same sex marriage decisions such as *Layland v. Ontario (Minister of Consumer and Commercial Relations)* would not have been receptive to arguments founded on a free-floating right to marry. So goes their reasoning: We are not denying gays and lesbians the right to marital *Bliss* [pun intended]. No one is saying homosexuals cannot get married – they just cannot marry each other.[18] This sort of reasoning is not fecund topsoil for achieving groundbreaking social reform through the judicial interpretations of courts.

As Brenda Cossman notes, arguments "driven by the discourse of sameness, ones which represented a 'less radical shift,' in cases such as *M. v. H.*, had greater resonance with the Court than did those in the earlier days of *Mossop* and *Egan* where at least some litigants were explicitly concerned with resisting a politics of sameness."[19] It may be, however, that while Cossman's observation is accurate, it is only now, with the wisdom of hindsight and experiential learning, that the Canadian public and its legal system, having not witnessed the collapse of life as we know it in an era of gay weddings, is ready to entertain arguments about the potential value of complicating the normative family model. Perhaps the honeymoon after "My Fabulous Gay Wedding" may lead to a court that would be more receptive today to the transformative arguments about family status made in *Mossop v. Canada (Attorney General)* twenty years ago.[20]

Regardless, it seems reasonable to assume that, at least for now, the categorical approach to equality and the obstacles that it presents for a more transformative, perhaps "queer," renovation of social structures is here to stay. There still remain ways, though, to approach section 15 that continue to pursue projects of transformative social change. One such approach that aims to create yet more inclusive social structures might be directed towards queering or disrupting the categories themselves. Sexual minority claims under section 15 have generally fallen into two categories. The first type of cases involves claims of direct discrimination. Cases such as *Vriend v. Alberta, Trinity Western University v. British Columbia College of Teachers*, and *Little Sisters Book and Art Emporium v. Canada (Minister of Justice)* are all examples of this type of case.[21] In each of these cases, the litigants argued that they had been directly discriminated against on the basis of sexual orientation. These cases are about seeking protection from unfair treatment or persecution based on sexual object preference.

The claim in the second category of cases is somewhat different. Cases such as *Halpern, M. v. H., Egan, Chamberlain v. Surrey School District No. 36, Mossop*, and *Susan Doe v. Canada (Attorney General)* all involve litigants seeking recognition of their same sex relationships (or in the case of *Chamberlain* the validity of gay- and lesbian-parented families).[22] The claim in this type of cases is about social and legal recognition of gay and lesbian relationships and families. The significance of this distinction lies in the broader, underlying purpose motivating the latter type of case – a desire for social or institutional affirmation and recognition of a relationship, or a family, that deviates from the norm. None of which is necessarily about, or even directly involves, sexual object preference. To be sure, it would be more than a little formalistic to suggest that a prohibition against same sex marriage is not also about discrimination on the basis of sexual orientation. It is about both. Nevertheless, one reason that gays and lesbians in Canada, relatively speaking, have achieved so many rights so quickly may be because of the legal battles to achieve recognition already fought and won by other non-traditional families in Canada. These battles have helped to produce a legal and social culture that is less reticent to at least consider the possibility of a family model that might include monogamous gay and lesbian couples. The subversive potential, the opportunity to queer the family, to "de-essentialize" sexual identity, starts with a recognition of the ability to transpose, and thus transcend, if not the identities then certainly the goals and motivations of various equality-seeking groups.

An analysis and critique of the decision in *Susan Doe*, which rejects a constitutional challenge to the *Processing and Distribution of Semen for Assisted Conception Regulations (Semen Regulations)*, demonstrates the promise of addressing equality for sexual minorities by attempting to disrupt the categorical approach to equality from within the categories themselves.[23] *Susan*

Doe involved a challenge to the *Semen Regulations* by "Susan Doe." Susan Doe sought assisted conception services to conceive using semen from the same gay man who had biologically fathered her and her partner's first child. Susan Doe was not in a sexual or spousal relationship with him. As a result, her donor and his semen were subject to the *Semen Regulations*. While her donor was willing to provide fresh semen for use in assisted conception, he was not willing to have his semen cryo-preserved and quarantined as required under the regulations. As a result, Susan Doe was denied access to assisted conception procedures using her chosen donor's semen.

The impetus for the *Semen Regulations* was the risk of infection from the use of semen from anonymous donors, not the use of semen from known donors. Regardless, the regulations prohibit the clinical use of all semen (anonymous or known) in assisted conception unless and until the following has occurred: the donor has tested negative for a number of communicable diseases including HIV and hepatitis B and C, the semen has been cryo-preserved (frozen) and quarantined for six months, and the donor has then re-tested negative for these diseases. The *Semen Regulations* create an exception to this protocol for women who are married to, living together in common-law relationships with, or having sex with their chosen donor.[24] They can be inseminated by their physicians without their donor first undergoing the screening and without being subjected to the wait period and the costs (both pecuniary and otherwise) imposed as a result of the *Semen Regulations*. Women who are not in a spousal or sexual relationship with their chosen donor do not have this option. In order to receive assisted conception services, these women will first have to incur the cost of having the semen cryo-preserved for six months.[25]

Susan Doe challenged the constitutional validity of the definition of "assisted conception" under the *Semen Regulations*, arguing that it violated section 15 of the *Charter* by discriminating against lesbians who by definition will not have a semen donor who is a spouse or sexual partner.[26] In rejecting her claim, the Ontario Superior Court of Justice determined that "it makes perfect sense to exclude from the scheme women seeking assisted conception with the semen of their spouses or sexual partners, because ... such women ... have already been exposed to any risk that exists, and will likely continue to be exposed."[27] Having identified this rationale as the purpose of the exclusion, the court concluded that sexual orientation was not the basis for this differential treatment. All women, gay or straight, who are not having sex with their donor are treated the same.

Undeniably, one of the legislative objectives of the *Semen Regulations* is to prevent the spread of communicable diseases. In keeping with this objective, it is logical and desirable to subject anonymous semen to the regimen of testing prescribed in the *Semen Regulations*. It would also be consistent with the legislative objective articulated by the court to subject all known donors to this regimen of testing. There does not, however, appear to be a well-reasoned and logical basis, consistent with the stated objective, to exclude from the strictures of the *Semen Regulations* some known donors but not others. The health risk certainly is not higher and may even be lower. Lesbian couples may be more likely to have their known donor tested regularly for sexually transmitted infections than would be a woman whose donor is her husband. Moreover, there is no reason to assume that women who seek assisted conception with the semen of a known donor that they are not having sex with are less likely to have already been exposed to this semen. It seems sensible to suggest that these women may be just as likely to first try things at home before seeking invasive and expensive medical assistance.

The exclusion from the *Semen Regulations* of known donors who are in a spousal or sexual relationship with the women seeking assisted conception is based on heteronormative and essentialist assumptions or understandings about family and interpersonal relationships in contemporary Canadian society. The exclusion from the regulations is premised on a monogamous, heterosexual ideal of the family that presumes that the semen of husbands ought not to be subjected to the same testing and restrictions as that of any other known donor semen. The constitutional difficulty with the definition of "assisted conception" under the *Semen Regulations* is not only that its effects impose a differential burden on some as a result of their sexual orientation but also that by relying on a heteronormative, traditional conception of the family its purpose imposes differential treatment based on family status.[28] If this is true, then even within an analytical framework that privileges purpose over effect – such as the approach adopted in *Susan Doe* – the definition of assisted conception under the *Semen Regulations* violates section 15 of the *Charter.*

Focusing on discrimination on the basis of family status would avoid the pitfalls of the formal equality approach to section 15 adopted by both levels of court in this case. In addition, it would provide a more inclusive and progressive litigation strategy for acquiring legal recognition of familial relationships that deviate from the essentialist, heteronormative paradigm assumed by the *Semen Regulations.* It may be that such an approach would encourage a more constructivist, contextual, socially contingent analysis of equality claims regarding sexuality, sexual identity, and sexual preference. As a category, family status is more conducive to maintaining open-ended and constantly re-articulated boundaries as to who is in and who is out. It is, by its structure, oriented towards litigation strategies that are intended to change its social meaning – to "queer" those relationships and those interpersonal social dynamics that constitute family. Every piece of equality litigation successfully argued under family status – a relational concept – rearticulates, and in this process of course contributes to, the social construction of family.

Susan Doe is not solely about sex or sexual orientation. It is in large measure about relationships. Yet cases such as this one are consistently presented to the public, and legally analyzed, on the sole basis of whether or not there has been discrimination on the basis of sexual orientation. The court in *Susan Doe* was right to suggest that the category of individuals disadvantaged by the *Semen Regulations* does not just include lesbian couples. It also includes heterosexual women who wish to start families with known donors with whom they are not in a sexual relationship (such as single women or families parented by three or more people). The *Semen Regulations* discriminate against anyone, regardless of their sexual orientation, who wants to start or expand a family that does not conform to the stereotypical model of a monogamous, two-parented, biologically based, heterosexual family. In addition to the possibility of success, the distinct advantage of premising a claim in this case on the basis of family status rather than sexual orientation is that it would pursue the same goal – recognition of a different way of life, a different type of family, a different choice – without capitulating to the essentializing effect of the rigid heterosexual/homosexual classification of sexual identity. While still premised on the need to establish differential treatment, a pragmatic reality under the binding analytical framework established for section 15, this approach is more in keeping with the desire to further social transformation through the disruption of loci of institutional power, such as the family.

It is true that the categorical approach to equality does nothing to challenge the fact that the law's distributive role is being dictated by, or is in reference to, certain norms. It is also true that with respect to the category of sexual orientation, this approach results in an essentialist conception of sexuality. It is not true that the success of the sexual minority equality movement has done nothing to challenge those norms upon which individuals are measured – or, to put it otherwise, upon which the distribution of rights, privileges, and legal benefits are based. Some of the power and access to cultural and social institutions achieved under this approach has successfully disrupted and replaced certain essentialist conceptions about family, sexuality, and sexual relationships. For example, the access to cultural paradigms (such as marital rites) acquired by the successes of the sexual minority rights movement lends itself well to a process of subversion (or what I would describe as iconoclasm) from within.[29]

It is likely not possible to reconcile the power produced through an essentialist conception of sexual orientation with the corresponding obstacles to more transformative approaches to equality presented by this essentialism. Such reconciliation may not be necessary though. Perhaps when we sit with this troubling tension, something productive occurs. As explained in Chapter 7 in this volume, Jacques Derrida suggests that in these moments of paradox resides the promise, albeit always only the promise, of friendship.[30] Regardless, given the legal reality – namely that the categorical approach to section 15 is unlikely to be rejected anytime soon – it is necessary to devise new equality-seeking strategies to promote more constructivist legal conceptions of sexuality, sexual relationships, and sexual preference. Claims of discrimination based on sexual orientation have had their (very successful) day in court. Yet, such success does not mean that the pursuit for equality for those whose sexual identity, sexual preferences, and relationship choices do not conform to the heteronormative paradigm is over. It does not mean that the essentialist conception of sexuality adopted and perpetuated under section 15 should be accepted. It may mean, however, that legal efforts should now be directed towards queering the categories themselves, making fewer claims based on identity and more based on status with respect to relational and interactional concepts. The downside, of course, will be that these are not claims that will benefit as significantly from those "reverse discourses" that have achieved so much for some sexual minorities. Categorical approaches to legal issues involving sexuality reveal themselves not only in the equality context but also in the area of sexual harassment law. As with equality, the connection between categorical and essentialist thinking is evident.

The Sexual Hostility of Sexual Harassment – A Non-Categorical Approach

The Supreme Court of Canada's current approach to sexual harassment was established in 1989 in *Janzen v. Platy Enterprises Ltd.*[31] In *Janzen*, the Court recognized as human rights violations those allegations of sexual harassment perpetrated against the two waitress claimants by "Tommy the Cook" and his boss (the owner of the company with which they were employed). In doing so, the Court overturned the Manitoba Court of Appeal. The lower appellate court had been of the view that to sexually harass and to discriminate based on sex are two entirely different concepts: "When a schoolboy steals kisses from a female classmate, one might well say that he is harassing her. He is troubling her; vexing her; harrying her – but he surely is not discriminating against her."[32] Justice Twaddle, in his concurring opinion, argued that sexual harassment did not constitute sex discrimination because it was not a distinction based on the category of sex but, rather, an action based on sexual attraction or "sex appeal."

On appeal to the Supreme Court of Canada, Chief Justice Dickson found that to argue that sexual harassment is not discrimination because it is based on the sexual appeal of a particular woman rather than on women as a whole is analogous to the rejected assertion that discrimination on the basis of pregnancy is not sex discrimination because it only discriminates against pregnant women and not all women who are pregnant.[33] He concluded that just as pregnancy cannot be separated from gender, "[o]nly a woman could be subject to sexual harassment by a heterosexual male" and, therefore, "sexual attractiveness cannot be separated from gender."[34] In terms of outcome, the Court's decision in *Janzen* can be considered a victory for women. The Court held, in no uncertain terms, that sexual harassment – whether it arises in the form of *quid pro quo* or a hostile work environment – was indeed a form of discrimination based on sex. Promisingly, the Court took steps towards adopting a constructivist notion of sexual harassment as a systemic product of a sexist labour market.[35] That said, Chief Justice Dickson's reasoning in *Janzen* also relies significantly on an essentialist conception of sexual harassment.

Instead of rejecting the Manitoba Court of Appeal's assumption that sexual harassment was about sexual attraction and not sex (and therefore was not sex discrimination), he found that sexual harassment was sex discrimination because sexual attractiveness cannot be separated from gender, which he assumed to be synonymous with sex (as in male/female sex). From here, he drew the analogy to pregnancy and came to the conclusion that "only a woman could be subject to sexual harassment by a heterosexual male" and that, therefore, sexual harassment constitutes sex discrimination.[36] Was this necessary in order to avoid the formalistic reasoning adopted by the Manitoba Court of Appeal? Was it consistent with Chief Justice Dickson's (feminist-informed, constructivist) recognition that sexual harassment is produced through social context (that is, through a sexist labour market)?

In fact, it was not necessary, consistent, or desirable. As feminists have long argued, it is problematic to conceptualize sexual harassment as being sourced in biology and arousal. For decades, feminists have advocated for a more contextual and systemic legal account of sexual harassment.[37] An essentialist understanding of sexual harassment fails to adequately respond to the gender inequities reflected in, and perpetuated by, its infliction on women. As Katherine Franke points out, an essentialist conception of sexual harassment also leaves less analytical space to recognize claims of sexual harassment by heterosexual men against other men (and by heterosexual women against women).[38] It encourages a categorical approach to sexual orientation in which claims of sexual harassment by men and boys that should be understood as sexual harassment are framed as claims of discrimination on the basis of sexual orientation. In addition, it leaves those sexually harassed because of transgressive gender expression less protected. An essentialist conception of sexual harassment cannot accommodate a truly complex gender analysis of the issue – something that an understanding of straight male on male sexual harassment, for example, may demand. What is more, an essentialist conception of sexual harassment is inconsistent with those aspects of Chief Justice Dickson's decision in which he recognized the role of social and contextual factors, such as power and systemic inequity, in producing sexually harassing behaviour.[39]

His overall approach does not ask or answer the question as to why sexuality is the weapon of choice in so many employment, educational, and institutional settings. It does not inquire into the other power dynamics at play – whether these are individual, institutional, political, economic, or social. It fails to fully explore why Tommy the Cook's boss, who presumably was not motivated by sexual arousal, chose to ignore his employees' complaints. Underpinning the claim that straight men will not sexually harass other men is the assumption that sexual harassment is motivated by sexual desire, sexual attraction, and sexual arousal. While such an assumption is consistent with Chief Justice Dickson's focus on sexual demands, to characterize sexual harassment in this way is precisely the understanding of sexual harassment against which feminists have argued. It also assumes that sexual desire, sexual arousal, and sexual attraction are fixed. It assumes that a heterosexual man will not sexually harass another man because sexual harassment is about sexual attraction, and it also assumes that men who identify as heterosexual are never sexually aroused by other men. Chief Justice Dickson's reasoning leaves little, if any, analytical opportunity to address cases of sexual harassment by heterosexual men against other heterosexual men. The sexual harassment by men or boys of other men or boys, which is completely irrespective of the sexual orientation of either the victims or the perpetrators, is not uncommon.[40] Indeed, one might find that the more male dominated the workplace or social context is, the more likely such harassment is to happen.[41]

The reasoning in *North Vancouver School District No. 44 v. Jubran* illustrates how an essentialist conception of sexual harassment can impede recognition of other victims in a way that a constructivist understanding of sexual harassment does not.[42] *Jubran* involved a human rights complaint against the school board by one of its former students. For Azmi Jubran, high school was a "living hell."[43] This experience was largely due to the fact that in grade eight Azmi was selected as the class "pariah" and spent the next five years being singled out and picked on by a group of fellow students. He was called a "homo," a "queer," and a "faggot." He was kicked and spit on. His tormentors drew sexually graphic pictures of him and attached the label "homo" to them. On a number of occasions, his entire class chanted "Azmi is gay" in unison.[44] Azmi claimed that he had been discriminated against on the grounds of sexual orientation.

The British Columbia Human Rights Tribunal found that Azmi was not a homosexual, nor did his tormentors perceive Azmi to be a homosexual. Regardless, the tribunal held that Azmi had been discriminated against on the ground of perceived sexual orientation and that the school board had failed, without reasonable justification, to provide a discrimination-free learning environment. The tribunal's award was quashed on judicial review to the British Columbia Supreme Court. Justice Stewart held that, given that Azmi was not a homosexual and that the students did not believe him to be a homosexual, he could not find that their harassment was discrimination based on sexual orientation. He determined that the tribunal erred by equating "discrimination through harassment by the use of hurtful words of a sexual nature with discrimination because of sex or sexual orientation."[45]

If one understands sexual orientation to be an essential part of the self, constitutive of who we are, and one determines that human rights legislation prohibiting discrimination on the basis of sexual orientation is confined to protecting those belonging to historically disadvantaged sexual minorities, then one must find that Azmi was not discriminated against based on sexual orientation. If one finds that sexual harassment is behaviour motivated by sexual arousal (as dictated by one's pre-social and innate sexual object preference), then the use of hurtful words and conduct of a sexual nature by these heterosexual students against another heterosexual student was not discrimination based on sex. Justice Stewart's reasoning is consistent with the Supreme Court of Canada's interpretation of sexual harassment in *Janzen*. It is reasoning that demonstrates how an essentialist conception of both sexual orientation and sexual harassment precludes legal recognition of this human rights violation because of an overly simplistic interpretation of the behaviour at issue. Instead of recognizing the multilayered and complex intersection of power with sex, sexuality, and gender and the relationship dynamics produced by these social practices and cultural understandings of sexuality and gender, Justice Stewart chalked these sexualized attacks up to an unexplored, and frankly uncritical, assumption of teenage cruelty. Thus, he provides his explanation for the harassment: "His high school years were a living hell. Why? Because a group of students singled him out for attack.

For reasons unknown – and probably capable of being understood only by the addled brains of certain teenagers – Jubran was a pariah."[46]

Are they reasons unknown? Are they incapable of comprehension? Azmi's classmates testified that they did not perceive him to be homosexual. They claimed that they were not targeting him because he was gay. The explanation provided by the school board and supported by the testimony of the students was that they targeted him because he was different and that the homophobic slurs were the form that their attacks took. Maura Jette, in her discussion of the *Jubran* case, argues that sexual harassment of this nature should be understood as being primarily an issue of gender norm policing.[47] From an essentialist perspective, it may be incomprehensible why a group of heterosexual students would sexually harass another heterosexual student, who they perceived to be heterosexual, by demonizing him as a "faggot." It may not be possible from this perspective to identify the behaviour as sexual. However, consider the behaviour in light of a social constructivist account of sexual harassment. A constructivist conception of sexual harassment understands it as a product of social and institutional practices – as a multiplicity of force relations manifested through webs of relationships in which sexual identity is produced and regulated through the normative practices that are typically understood to reflect it. From this perspective, the conduct of these students becomes both comprehensible as normative policing and identifiable as sexual harassment. Under this account, assuming the Supreme Court of Canada is correct that harassment that is of a sexual nature constitutes discrimination based on sex, the conduct directed towards Azmi was certainly discrimination based on sex.

The British Columbia Court of Appeal came to a different conclusion than that of Justice Stewart of the British Columbia Supreme Court. They found that "the consequences of the actions of Mr. Jubran's harassers was that he was discriminated against because of his sexual orientation, whether or not he was or his harassers believed or perceived him to be homosexual."[48] Does it really make sense to suggest that Azmi was discriminated against because of his sexual orientation or even perceived sexual orientation? Certainly, he was discriminated against. Certainly, it demeaned him in a way that interfered with his participation in school life. But Azmi was straight. His harassers knew him to be straight. His harassers were not trying to suggest that he was other than straight. To identify someone as gay, regardless of whether or not they are sexually attracted to members of the same sex, is not an act of discrimination – to suggest otherwise carries with it heterosexist, if not homophobic, normative assumptions. The issue in this case is that Azmi was persecuted and that the weapon of choice was a reliance on social attitudes of hatred and fear towards sexual minorities – Azmi was subjected to sexual hostility, not discrimination on the basis of his sexual orientation.

Sexual hostility is also sometimes the weapon of choice in circumstances where the motivation is pure animus. In *MacDonald v. Brighter Mechanical Ltd.*, the complainant alleged that he was discriminated against on the basis of sexual orientation.[49] MacDonald was not gay. There was no evidence to suggest that his alleged harassers (fellow heterosexual employees) thought that he was gay. As in *Jubran*, the complainant's claim was nonetheless framed as discrimination on the basis of sexual orientation. MacDonald alleged that, among other things, he was called a fag, asked how he liked sucking cock, and on a regular basis had sexually explicit material placed in his toolbox suggesting he try pussy for a change.[50] Having determined that no one at Brighter Mechanical perceived Mr. MacDonald to be gay, the British Columbia Human Rights Tribunal rejected his claim based on their finding that the harassment occurred because his fellow employees disliked him.

In *Janzen*, the Supreme Court of Canada found that harassment that is sexual constitutes sex discrimination because sexual norms concerning sexual attractiveness cannot be disaggregated from, and are in some loose sense dictated by, sex (as in male/female). The constructivist claim that I am making relies on the different suggestion that sex (as in male/female) cannot be disaggregated from, and is dictated by, sexual norms. Maintaining that Azmi and MacDonald were discriminated against based on their sexual orientation is not the best way to establish that the conduct they alleged occurred violates human rights legislation. Under a socially constructed understanding of sexuality, in which sexuality is not only more than nature and more than biological drives but also (or, instead, depending on the degree of constructivism) a product of social organization and a description of relationships, social interactions, and regulative sex and gender norms, sexual harassment is not understood through innate sexual object choice designations or sexual arousal. Under this account, it makes much more sense to say that these allegations, if proven, demonstrate sexual harassment (discrimination based on sex) rather than discrimination based on sexual orientation.

This is the analysis adopted by the British Columbia Human Rights Tribunal in *Mercier v. Dasilva* in response to a straight complainant who accused his straight supervisor of violating his human rights by, among other things, asking him repeatedly – in front of co-workers – to "do him a fellatio.'"[51] While they rejected his claim of discrimination based on sexual orientation, they found that he was sexually harassed. In doing so, the tribunal conceptualized sexual harassment as an act of sexual hostility – as the use of sexuality as a weapon to demean and humiliate. The tribunal's reasoning accommodated the group dynamics at play, such as the fact that the requests for fellatio did not occur coincidentally in front of other co-workers. Under this reasoning, the fact that Dasilva may have been motivated by his dislike for Mercier would not be a basis on which to dismiss the claim (unlike the reasoning in *MacDonald*). It is also reasoning that does not require the tribunal to assume that being gay, or being identified as gay, is presumptively demeaning. It is reasoning that recognizes sexual harassment as being much more complex than simply the sexualization of the workplace. It is reasoning that accommodates the fact that a straight man may sexually harass another straight man.

In *Janzen*, Chief Justice Dickson makes reference to the issue of power. He states that sexual harassment is "the concept of using a position of power to import sexual requirements into the workplace thereby negatively altering the working conditions of employees who are forced to contend with sexual demands."[52] While he recognizes the role of power, he then ties this factor to the making of sexual demands – the importation of sexual requirements. Contrast this approach with the reasoning of the tribunal in *Mercier* where an analysis of the power dynamics at play was incorporated into the tribunal's conception of the actual behaviour at issue. The benefit of adopting the more constructivist approach advocated here and by many other commentators is that claims will not turn on whether the complainant was gay or whether respondents thought that the complainant was gay.[53] This approach does not obscure the systemic way in which sex, gender, and sexuality are produced as categories of identity through social and institutional practices that are then deployed to regulate the very categories that they have produced. This can be seen in the way in which pubescent adolescents, by vigilantly policing gender norms in an effort to secure their own tentative sexual identities, produce both the identities they seek to secure and those they wish to reject. It is further revealed by the ways in which institutions, such as formal education systems, facilitate such gender policing. This alternative approach ought to (1) provide greater insight into how and why homophobia still reigns over playgrounds and many job sites and (2) better reveal that sexuality, through the policing of sex and gender norms, is so often the weapon of choice in both the social demand for sex, gender, and sexuality conformity and the mechanisms of power that inform and flow from such demand.

One might respond to this approach by asking what then would distinguish sexual harassment from other forms of harassment? What basis justifies the law's distinction between sexual harassment and plain old name-calling? The response to this critique is two-fold. First, the law often makes distinctions based on the choice of weapon. Second, the law also often makes distinctions based on the impact of the conduct or social practice at issue.

Similarly to the situation with respect to race, sexual hostility, for historical reasons as well as current social conditions, has a different impact than plain old name-calling. It has a different impact both on an individual level and on a societal one. One of the reasons why sexual hostility is so often the weapon of choice is because sexual hostility has so often been, and so often continues to be, the weapon of choice. In part, it is the very fact of this circumstance that makes sexual hostility such an effective weapon. One of the policy objectives of human rights legislation is broad or general social amelioration. One of its objectives is to reduce the efficacy of weapons such as sexual hostility.

As feminists have argued, understanding sexual harassment as a social practice – as a product of the context in which it is situated – will be more likely to produce legal reasoning aimed at discerning whether sexuality is being deployed as a weapon in a particular workplace or institutional setting. There is nothing to suggest that a more constructivist approach could not be accommodated under the current definition of sexual harassment. *Janzen* defined sexual harassment as unwelcome conduct of a sexual nature that detrimentally affects the work environment or leads to adverse job-related consequences for the victims of the harassment. While Chief Justice Dickson's essentialist reasoning should be rejected, the definition itself does not preclude the possibility of a conception of sexual harassment that recognizes it as a social, institutional, and systemic problem in which sexuality is the weapon of choice.

Conclusion

The Supreme Court of Canada's essentialist understanding of sexuality cuts across different legal contexts. While the issues that it raises differ significantly depending on the legal context, in each case, essentialist assumptions give rise to problematic reasoning – reasoning that constricts the legal "space" in which to identify the social forces and systemic factors contributing to, or producing, many aspects of human sexuality. If sexual integrity requires relational goods, is born of context, and remains contextually contingent, then legal reasoning that fails to account for its social specificity is not likely to be very good at protecting and promoting it.

Socially Constructed Conceptions of Sexual Violence

4

> The power of a thing or an act is in the meaning and the understanding.
>
> – NICHOLAS BLACK ELK

There is one area of jurisprudence in which the Supreme Court of Canada's reasoning does indicate a shift towards a more constructivist approach to issues of sexuality. In the last twenty years, the Court has adopted a more constructivist conception of sexual violence between adults. This (newly adopted social constructivist) understanding of sexual violence, which has been influenced significantly by certain feminist interventions, is reflected in the Court's approach to the regulation of obscenity and indecency. It is also revealed by how the Court defines consent to sexual touching and how the Court characterizes the harm of sexual assault. Encouragingly, this change has also promoted a shift in the law's moral focus. It is a shift from protecting sexual propriety to promoting sexual integrity – a shift from moral concern over sexual acts to moral concern over sexual interactions.

Until recently, the law conceptualized sexual violence against women the same as, or similar to, the way it often continues to conceptualize the sexual violation of children. Legal reasoning in cases involving sexual violence between adults revealed the view that rape has been perpetrated by men cursed with a natural sexual drive gone awry or with an uncontrollable or abnormal lust. Courts talked of defendants gratifying their animal lusts or satisfying their perverted impulses.[1] Under this old essentialist conception of sexuality, there was less space for the law to recognize and give import to the role that hate, anger, misogyny, power, and dehumanizing disrespect have played in sexual violence. Sexual violence was about lust and perverted urges – the greater the severity and frequency of the offensive conduct, the more perverted the offender. Arguably, this sentiment may still be revealed in contemporary sentencing cases, which often focus on whether there was penetration and also feature a discourse of psychopathology, penile plethysmographs, and personality disorder assessments. However, in a typical sexual assault trial involving an adult complainant, the perception that sexual violence is a function of a natural but uncontrolled sexual urge no longer plays the analytical role that it once did.

The issue of why the law has shifted towards a socially constructed conception of sexual violence among adults, but not as perpetuated against children, is a topic unto itself. Perhaps the difference has occurred in part because the ideas advanced by feminists regarding power and equality, if ascribed to, demand a different conceptual approach to the rape of women by men but do not necessarily engender a re-conceptualization of "pedophilia." It may be that feminist theories that are influential in the context of adult sexual violence cannot be universalized to explain or theorize other types of sexual harm. It may also be that the natural/unnatural distinction is more pronounced in the context of intergenerational sex, thus making essentialist thinking more entrenched in that context.

Regardless, feminist legal theorists, in the context of addressing sexual violence against women, have begun to explicitly advocate for the Supreme Court of Canada and law makers to conceptualize it as socially contingent. Through their success in doing so, these feminist scholars and activists have demonstrated how sexual violence is socially constructed. It is not only that the Court has begun to recognize instances of sexual violence that it previously had not, but it is also that conceptualizing sexual violence as socially contingent, rather than the product of a dysfunctional sex drive, has changed what does and does not constitute sexually violative behaviour under Canadian criminal law. The very meaning of sexual violence, as conceptualized by the law of sexual assault, has changed. Queer and postmodern feminist theories suggest that the concepts of sex, gender, and sexuality do not connote or describe an innate, pre-social essence but, rather, constitute themselves in and through their categorization via the social ascription of normative meaning. In the 1980s and 1990s, the Canadian feminist intervention on the issue of sexual violence between men and women both made, and in its successes exemplified, a similar claim.

A Construction of Sexual Violence

In the late 1980s and early 1990s, Supreme Court of Canada jurisprudence began to reflect the understanding that sex is about power and that sexual violence is an equality issue. Within the span of just a few years, the Court incorporated a power/dominance analysis into its reasoning in the context of obscenity law,[2] tort law,[3] and sexual assault law.[4] While today it might seem axiomatic to suggest that coercive or forced sex between men and women is, and ought to be, understood as an equality issue, this was not always the case. There are many implications to an equality-type approach to conceptualizing sexual violence under the law. To understand sexual violence under the rubric of equality is to adopt an analysis that will focus on relationships, on power, and on the subjective perspective of all sexual actors involved in the interaction. It is to adopt an approach that will understand sexual violence as socially contingent.

This change in the way that the Supreme Court of Canada conceptualizes sexual violence was guided in large measure by legal activism on the part of feminist scholars and feminist organizations such as the Women's Legal Education and Action Fund (LEAF). A feminist-influenced conceptual shift towards constructivist understandings of sexual violence was also evident in the law reform measures that the Parliament of Canada adopted during this period. Beginning in the late 1970s and early 1980s, feminists began to respond to issues such as rape, pornography, commercial sex, incest, public sex, and sexual harassment. These issues became the sites for legal and political activism as well as the impetus for, and subsequent target of, feminist theories that identified male sexuality as a primary source of female subordination and thus a major social problem.[5]

Feminism has many voices.[6] To talk of feminism as if it was one monolithic theory risks offering a reductionist account of what are actually a multitude of different theoretical approaches to issues of sex, gender, and sexuality. The legal activism of Canadian feminists has been influenced by the work of numerous feminist theorists working from a variety of theoretical perspectives. While the conceptual approaches of these various feminist scholars has differed, they have possessed two similarities: a social constructivist conception of sexual violence and an equality-driven perspective towards critiquing the legal system's response to the problem of sexual violence.[7] Many of them have also shared a willingness to engage with law reform in Canada – both through the courts and the legislature – while simultaneously harbouring deep apprehension about what they have identified as an androcentric legal system's limited ability to actuate real change in women's lived realities.[8] Borrowing from Audre Lorde, Sheila McIntyre, in describing the hesitation of many feminists to participate in the law reform project leading up to the substantive amendments to the sexual assault provisions in 1992, captured the sentiment underpinning this uneasiness: "Whether the master's tools can ever dismantle the master's house remains a perennial question for those struggling for social change."[9] Despite this hesitation, however, many Canadian feminists did engage with legal activism, and, as I have just suggested, in some instances this engagement had a significant impact.

One feminist approach to sexual violence that was influential in Canada in the 1980s and 1990s advanced the suggestion that rape be understood as violence rather than sex – in particular, that it be understood as systemic violence perpetrated against women by men.[10] The feminist assertion that rape is an act of violence impacted both judicial conceptions and law reform initiatives and became the conceptual framework underpinning the significant legislative reforms to sexual assault law adopted in the mid-1980s. There was considerable consensus on this aspect of the reform. During the debates on Bill C-127, the Honourable Flora MacDonald made the following statement: "This legislation makes a clear statement ... It says that sexual assault is primarily an act of violence, not of passion; an assault with sex as the weapon."[11] Rape had been included in the *Criminal Code*'s section on sexual offences and public morals.[12] The new sexual assault offences were included in the "offences against the person" section of the *Criminal Code*.

Justice Wilson's concurring opinion in *R v. Bernard* reflects this assertion that rape be understood as violence:

> Sexual assault is a crime of violence. There is no requirement of an intent or purpose beyond the intentional application of force. It is first and foremost an assault. It is sexual in nature only because, objectively viewed, it is related to sex either on account of the area of the body to which the violence is applied or on account of words accompanying the violence. Indeed, the whole purpose, as I understand it, of the replacement of the offence of rape by the offence of sexual assault was to emphasize the aspect of violence and put paid to the benign concept that rape was simply the act of a man who was "carried away" by his emotions.[13]

Under Justice Wilson's reasoning, sexual violence is violence – full stop. Her reasoning demonstrates how the "rape is violence" conception of sexual violence is a constructivist approach intended to counter the "natural urge gone awry" conception of sexual violence. If rape is violence, then, like other forms of violence it is a function of relationships, context, and interpersonal power dynamics, not biological sex drive. In this way, such an approach adopts a constructivist conception of sexual violence. It is also, however, a conception that de-emphasizes the sexual and gendered element of sexual violence.

Other feminist thought at the time opposed this gender-neutral characterization of sexual violence, arguing that it was misleading, that it depoliticized the issue, and that it obscured the reality of the crime.[14] Kathleen Lahey, for example, argued that the gender neutrality of the new sexual assault offences masked the specific harm of rape to women. She maintained that the offence of sexual assault was defined by patriarchal norms and that in defining sexual violence the criminal law must better accommodate the particularity and specificity of women's experience and perspectives by maintaining gendered crimes.

While the "sexual violence is violence" stream of thought certainly carried the day in Parliament, in the courts a more gendered, constructivist account of sexual violence was quite influential. Drawing on the theoretical insights offered by Catharine MacKinnon, Canadian feminist legal scholars such as Christine Boyle, Patricia Hughes, Maryann Ayim, and Kathleen Mahoney argued that legal approaches to issues such as the legal definition of consent to sexual touching, or the censorship of pornography, ought to be based on the understanding that the inequality between men and women is itself sexualized. Kathleen Mahoney invoked MacKinnon's theory in order to advance the argument that some pornography is itself an act of sex discrimination.[15] Similarly, in querying the definition of "sexual" in sexual assault, Christine Boyle posed the question: "[I]f dominance and submission are eroticized and if dominance is linked in some way to the cultural construction of maleness while submission is linked to femaleness, does the distinction between assault and sexual assault disappear where a man assaults a woman?"[16] Boyle suggested that courts ought to consider whether "the abuse of power in and of itself can be sexual."[17]

MacKinnon's claim was that once one takes into consideration the frequency with which women are sexually violated by men, it must be concluded that sexual violation is a sexual practice – in fact, a very common sexual practice – and that it therefore forms the meaning and content of femininity (and masculinity).[18] The way women are restricted and violated is often what sex is for men and women, and, as such, dominance will be experienced by men as sexual pleasure and submission will be experienced by women as sexual pleasure. In this way, the inequality that exists between men and women is sexualized. In less theoretical wording – of the sort that made its way into the Supreme Court of Canada's reasoning – sex is about power.[19] More specifically, it is about the power imbalances that exist (or can exist) in sexual relationships between men and women. This suggestion was often relied on by feminist interveners in Canadian sex equality, sexual assault, and obscenity cases during this period,[20] and it has often been cited by the Supreme Court of Canada.[21] If feminism has many voices, then it was certainly "feminism the chorus" and not any specific feminist soloist that engendered a feminist-inspired shift in how the Court conceptualizes sexual violence between adults. That said, the constructivist suggestion that sexual dominance is itself constitutive of gender and (hetero)sexuality and that therefore sexuality, and sexual violence in particular, is a socially produced, contextually dependent issue of power is particularly noteworthy. The impact of this approach can be readily and concretely identified through an examination of the factums of feminist interveners in sexual assault and sexual expression cases. Its impact is also revealed through the Court's articulated reliance on feminist legal scholars such as Kathleen Mahoney, Christine Boyle, Catherine MacKinnon, Elizabeth Sheehy, and Constance Backhouse.

There are two legal contexts in particular in which feminist, constructivist conceptions of sexual violence have been clearly adopted by the Supreme Court of Canada. These include the substantive meaning of sexual assault (that is, the harm to be protected against, the definition of sexual assault, and the doctrine of consent) and the criminal regulation of adult pornography. The remainder of this chapter will focus on sexual assault law, demonstrating how this constructivist conception of sexual violence promotes a shift in the law's focus away from sexual propriety and sexual acts and towards sexual integrity and sexual interactions. The chapter to follow will examine the feminist-influenced evolution of the criminal law's definition of obscenity and indecency.

Defining Sexual Assault: From Sexual Propriety to Sexual Integrity

There are two major definitional issues concerning sexual assault law that indicate that the Supreme Court of Canada has adopted the understanding that sexual violence is about power and inequality. They include how the Court designates an assault as a *sexual* assault and how the Court has come to interpret the definition of consent. The constructivist perspectives adopted in both of these reforms share the same analytical shift. Both the definition of sexual assault and the definition of consent arrived at by the Court in recent years have incorporated a new factor into the analysis of the offence. This factor is the subjective experience of the complainant.

In defining sexual assault, the subjective experience of the complainant is incorporated into the newly adopted concept of "sexual integrity."[22] In defining consent, it is manifested through an explicit determination that consent is both a part of the *actus reus* and the *mens rea* – a determination that understands consent as both attitudinal and communicative depending on whose perspective is being considered. In determining the *actus reus* for sexual assault, the question as to whether there was consent for the sexual interaction turns entirely on the state of mind of the complainant at the time the sexual interaction occurred. Consent under the *mens rea* now refers to the accused's perception of the complainant's positive expression of consent rather than to communication of non-consent or to a lack of any expression of consent.[23] These changes reflect an approach that is concerned more with power, relationships, equality, and sexual actors than with sexual arousal and sexual acts. They indicate a more constructivist understanding of the issue of sexual violence.

Consider first this shift in the meaning that the criminal law assigns to the harm of sexual violence. It is a conceptual shift from defining sexual violence based on deprivations of sexual propriety, to identifying and defining sexual violence based on violations of sexual integrity. In defining the harm of sexual violence under the *Criminal Code*, the Supreme Court of Canada incorporated into its analysis an objective assessment of the subjective experience of the victim. This definitional shift rejects, to some extent, the former essentialist understanding of sexual violence based on genitals, sexual arousal, or community standards of sexual propriety. This shift from focusing on sexual propriety to sexual integrity enables greater emphasis on violations of trust, humiliation, objectification, exploitation, shame, and loss of self-esteem rather than simply, or only, on deprivations of honour, chastity, or bodily integrity (as was more the case when the law's concern had a greater focus on sexual propriety).

Prior to the 1982 amendments to the *Criminal Code*, which revamped the criminal law's statutory approach to sexual violence, the main provisions prohibiting non-consensual sexual touching were rape and indecent assault. The offence of rape stipulated that "a male person commits rape when he has sexual intercourse with a female person who is not his wife" without her consent.[24] Under the rape provision, the offence could only be perpetrated by a male against a female – it required penile-vaginal penetration. The definition of rape turned on penises, biology, and correspondingly (hetero) sexual gratification rather than on power, relationships, and context. The complainant's perspective was not incorporated into the definition of rape.

The offence of indecent assault against a female, or indecent assault against a male, was defined by the Supreme Court of Canada as an assault that is committed in circumstances of indecency.[25] Determining whether an act or circumstance was indecent depended on an objective view of the facts and circumstances in relation to the actual assault. The offence did not require that the accused act with a specific sexual intent (although some courts did wrongly interpret it that way). Judicial interpretations of the offence were nevertheless problematic. Whether a circumstance was indecent was gauged not by violation of the sexual integrity of the complainant but, rather, by the adjudicator's or jury's perception of the moral standards of the community. The analysis focused on immorality or impropriety rather than on power and the perspective of the other sexual actor/s involved in the interaction. Indecent assault was often not defined but, rather, was assumed to be "self-explanatory" and left up to the common sense of the jury.[26] This "community standards of propriety"-type analysis resulted in an essentialist approach to potentially offensive sexual behaviour, short of intercourse or attempted intercourse (which was covered under the offence of rape). Factors such as community morality,[27] the sexual gratification or sexual motives of the accused,[28] and heterosexist assumptions[29] determined whether a particular sexual interaction constituted "circumstances of indecency." As with rape, the complainant's perception of the interaction was not factored into the definition of the offence.

The feminist-influenced 1982 amendments to the *Criminal Code* replaced the offences of rape and indecent assault with sexual assault, established three tiers to the offence, and added a definition of consent (which was again amended in 1992).[30] The replacement of the offences of rape and indecent assault with the sexual assault provisions opened the door for the Supreme Court of Canada to adopt a new conception of sexual violence that focuses more on power, relationships, and context than on sexual motives, genitals, and sexual gratification. In interpreting these amendments, the Court was clear that the new provisions did not simply re-word the offence of rape (or indecent assault). Instead, it found that the reforms were intended to create a new offence. The Court established the meaning of this new offence – sexual assault – in *R. v. Chase* in 1987.[31] In this case, the Court overturned a New Brunswick Court of Appeal finding that the act of grabbing a girl's breast and demanding that she engage in sexual intercourse with the accused did not constitute a sexual assault on the basis that sexual assault was limited to intentional and forced contact with the sexual organs or genitalia of another person without that person's consent.[32] Justice McIntyre, writing for the Supreme Court of Canada, found that

> [s]exual assault is an assault within any one of the definitions of that concept in s. 244(1) of the Criminal Code which is committed in circumstances of a sexual nature, such that the sexual integrity of the victim is violated. The test to be applied in determining whether the impugned conduct has the requisite sexual nature is an objective one ... If the motive of the accused is sexual gratification, to the extent that this may appear from the evidence, it may be a factor in determining whether the conduct

> is sexual. It must be emphasized, however, that the existence of such a motive is simply one of many factors to be considered, the importance of which will vary depending on the circumstances.[33]

Under *Chase*, an assault is a sexual assault when it violates the sexual integrity of the complainant.

Prior to *Chase*, the phrase "sexual integrity" had never before been used in a reported decision of the Supreme Court of Canada. Of the approximately 551 reported decisions in which Canadian courts in general have used the term "sexual integrity," only ten of them were prior to the Court's decision in *Chase*. Until 1980, the term had never been used in a reported decision in Canada. Today, the notion of sexual integrity is the governing concept in the legal definition of sexual assault in Canada. Not only was the adoption of this term to determine the wrong of sexual assault novel, the manner in which the Court employed it signalled a shift that has had significant impact. It is a shift towards a substantive meaning of criminally prohibited sexual violence that, at the definitional stage, flipped the analytical perspective from that of the accused or the community to that of the complainant. It is not that under the new approach the subjective experience of the complainant is determinative as to whether an assault is a *sexual* assault. Whether the complainant experienced a violation of sexual integrity is not determinative.[34] Rather, what *Chase* established is that in objectively determining whether the assault occurred in "sexual circumstances" the most salient factor will be whether the complainant's sexual integrity was violated. Determining whether the complainant's sexual integrity was violated will of necessity require consideration of the complainant's perspective and experience. This makes it different than the analysis for the former offence of indecent assault. Indecent assault based its objective determination on the sexual propriety, morality, and standards of the community, not on the integrity of the complainant.

It is not the use, per se, of the term "sexual integrity" that effected this significant impact but, rather, the meaning that the Supreme Court of Canada attached to the term sexual integrity. The term sexual integrity could have been used simply to imply protection for some notion of chastity or propriety, thus perpetuating the law's interpretation of indecent assault and maintaining an unfortunate tradition in sexual assault law's approach to women's sexuality. In fact, in the ten cases prior to *Chase* that utilized the term, several used it to connote antiquated and paternalistic notions of chastity or propriety in which the interest in prohibiting sexual violation was still understood as a proprietary interest held, in an individual sense, by a woman's husband (or father)[35] or in a societal sense by "the community."[36] In this sense, the pre-*Chase* use of the concept of sexual integrity was similar to the way that indecent assault had been understood in Canadian jurisprudence. In *R. c. Archontakis,* for example, the trial judge stated: "My prime concern has to be the protection of society. Our streets must be made safe, especially for those who are least able to protect themselves. Our wives and our daughters must be able to walk about on the streets without having their physical and sexual integrity trampled upon by such as you."[37] One question that arises is what becomes of those individuals whose subjectivity does not reach the acclaimed status of "wife" or "daughter"?

The term sexual integrity could also have been understood by the Supreme Court of Canada as being synonymous with bodily integrity. Indeed, the New Brunswick Court of Appeal in *Chase* defined sexual assault in an essentialist manner of this sort. Justice Angers determined that the grabbing of a fifteen-year-old girl's breasts was not a "sexual" assault because breasts are a secondary sexual characteristic – like a man's beard or a bird's plumage. He concluded that "it seems to me that the word 'sexual' as used in the section ought to be given its natural meaning as limited to the sexual organs or genitalia."[38] (It is odd that he selects a man's beard rather than a man's nipples as his analogue.) His reasoning explicitly invokes the notion of a natural meaning for sexual organs and genitalia (as well as, implicitly, secondary sexual characteristics and erogenous zones) while simultaneously providing an example of how law can construct the meaning of sexual organs, genitalia, secondary sexual characteristics, and erogenous zones.

While the New Brunswick Court of Appeal's reasoning was not followed in other attempts to determine the meaning of sexual assault prior to the Supreme Court of Canada's decision in *Chase,* the reasoning in these other cases was also focused on the body, reproduction, and (hetero)sexual gratification.[39] A definition that turns on these factors is problematic. It would have inadvertently created a specific intent offence for sexual acts of violation short of intercourse by requiring the Crown to show a sexual intent on the part of the accused. Moreover, its corporeal bias is premised on heterosexist, phallocentric, and essentialist reasoning, which focuses entirely on the perspective of the accused. Certainly, the notion of bodily autonomy should be included within the concept of sexual integrity, but the concept should mean something more. It should advert to the importance of the integrity of one's sexuality itself. A legal focus on sexuality more broadly, rather than bodily integrity specifically, is consistent with the constructivist suggestion that the law ought to focus its moral concern on sexual actors rather than on sexual acts.

Bodily integrity constitutes one aspect of sexual integrity, but sexual integrity should mean much more than simply "freedom from" bodily violation. It should also include, along with "freedom from," the "conditions for" sexual fulfillment, sexual diversity, the safety necessary for sexual exploration, and sexual benefit. To suggest that sexual integrity extends beyond the notion of bodily invasion invokes the notion of protecting sexuality itself (not to be confused with protecting sex itself). To suggest that sexual integrity is about one's sexuality and not simply "freedom from" bodily invasion is to suggest that the promotion of sexual integrity also requires promoting certain "conditions for" – for example, the conditions necessary to create the capacity for developing a sense of sexual self, sexual self-esteem, the opportunity for sexual exploration, and beneficial sexual interactions. Some of these conditions will necessarily entail the presence or involvement of other people, as some of them will include sexual interactions or sexual relationships with others. This will require that other members of one's community also experience a lived sexuality in which the conditions for sexual integrity are available. It suggests the need for a community of sexual actors with the capacity and opportunity to develop and maintain sexual integrity, so that each of its members might have access to the relational aspects of sexual integrity. In this way, sexual integrity is in part relational. The fact that it is in part relational suggests that it could be understood as a social good.

In fact, sexual integrity ought to be thought of as one of those social goods, like language perhaps, that individuals need in order to be autonomous. As Jennifer Nedelsky writes, "[s]ome of our most essential characteristics, such as our capacity for language and the conceptual framework through which we see the world, are not made by us, but given to us (or developed in us) through our interactions with others ... [T]here are no human beings in the absence of relations with others. We take our being in part from those relations."[40] Certain relations are necessary in order to "be" a "being" – to be autonomous. Like language, it would seem sensible to suggest that one's sexuality, and thus sexual integrity in the broader sense of the term, would be heavily contingent on, and deeply dialogic with, one's sexual interactions with the rest of society. It would also seem sensible to suggest that sexual relations (and sexuality) constitute one type of those relations from which "we take our being." (Obviously this is meant figuratively, but it would be equally true in a literal sense.)

To be autonomous, then, we need certain relational opportunities – relationships in this sense are a social good. One of those relational social goods pertains to sexuality. If sexual relations constitute one of the social goods needed for autonomy, then sexuality ought to be protected as such. Correspondingly, it seems necessary to propose a conception of sexual integrity that extends beyond "freedom from" bodily invasion to also include protection for sexual integrity itself. This proposition requires an understanding of sexual integrity that includes the conditions for the production of a community of sexual actors whose lived sexualities include the possibility of a sense of sexual self, with an ability to sexually relate to others, a faculty for sexual exploration, and a capacity for sexual benefit (whether that be economic, emotional, psychological, or physical).

If this is the case, it becomes incumbent upon the law to interpret – so that it might protect – sexual integrity as including not just "freedom from" bodily invasion but also "conditions for" an integrated, coherent (which is not to say fixed) and functional sexuality. In the context of identifying and defining the harm of sexual violence, such an interpretation of sexual integrity lends itself to a consideration of factors such as sexual shame, humiliation, violations of trust, and sexual self-esteem. Nicola Lacey argues that developing an approach to sexual violence that incorporates affectivity is critical.[41] She suggests that the criminal law, to expand beyond the concept of freedom from bodily invasion, needs to re-conceptualize its assumption of body-mind dualism and shift its focus from autonomy, as traditionally understood, to integrity. (She is referring to bodily integrity rather than to the notion of sexual integrity employed in this chapter.) She contends that rape law perpetuates a mind-body dualism and, in the process, fails to adequately respond to both the corporeal and affective elements of sexual violence. Feminists, such as Lacey, have challenged the way in which the mind-body dualism reflected in the criminal law problematically privileges the mental (typically identified as masculine) over the physical and affective (typically identified as feminine). Instead, Lacey argues, the law needs a different idea of the body. The current conception, she suggests, is an image of the body as territory, or property, divorced from reason and emotion. Under the current conception, bodies are boundaries that separate autonomous individuals. Instead, bodies ought to be understood as aspects of lived subjectivity through which people relate to one another. In this way, the criminal law might begin to protect those relational values that it currently marginalizes. Her objective is to destabilize the artificial distinction between mind and body so that the law might recognize that rape violates the victim's capacity to integrate psychic and bodily experiences – a capacity needed to achieve autonomy.

Her argument, and those of the relational feminists she draws on, supports the suggestion made in this chapter that sexual integrity be thought of as a social good. My argument, which shares Lacey's position, makes the assertion that integrity ought to include elements of body, mind, and heart and that there is a relational aspect to each of these elements. Lacey advocates for a conceptual shift from autonomy to bodily integrity – with the concept of bodily integrity including not only the corporeal but also affect and reason. My suggestion is for a shift from focusing on the body and on propriety to focusing on sexual integrity. It does not suggest conceptualizing elements of the psyche as incorporated into the notion of bodily integrity. The concept of sexual integrity developed here includes the body, affect, and reason. It recognizes that these elements of the self are fundamentally relational, and it does so without relying solely on a distinction between bodily and sexual integrity. To be clear, neither Lacey's argument nor mine should be misconstrued as a suggestion that the mental, emotional, and social elements of integrity diminished by sexual violence are a function of bodily invasion – almost like a symptom. She critiques mind-body dualism for its impoverished account of the body. I am critiquing the mind-body dualism reflected in traditional criminal law approaches to sexual violence for its impoverished account of the psyche. With respect to both, the objective is to incorporate into criminal law "the language of embodied existence," to borrow from Lacey.[42]

Adopting a constructivist understanding of sexual violence inevitably requires a consideration of issues of power, relationships, specificity, and the subjective experience of any of the sexual actors involved. To understand the harm of sexual violence (as well as the sexual goods that the criminal law is assumedly meant to protect), the law cannot focus only on unwanted penises, penetrations, and (hetero)sexual desires. It must also take into account the preservation of sexual self-esteem, sexual awareness, a sense of sexual self, and the ability to achieve sexual pleasure or benefit. It must develop language and concepts that accommodate the "conditions for" sexual integrity (and "freedom from" violation is only one of those conditions). An understanding of sexual integrity that extends beyond bodily integrity is a start.

In the criminal law context, which is only one of the legal arenas in which law and sexual integrity intersect, the interference with sexual integrity at issue will often involve a bodily component. This does not demand that the criminal law's conception of sexual integrity need be reduced to bodily integrity. It is important that the criminal law conception of sexual integrity be understood holistically. A failure to apply the notion of sexual integrity adopted in *Chase* in a holistic sense leads to reasoning such as that of the Ontario Court of Justice in *R. v. Spence*.[43] In *Spence*, the complainant was physically abducted off the street by her former pimp and two other men. She was placed in the back of their car, threatened with gang rape if she continued to refuse to remit to them the proceeds of her sex work, and forced to completely disrobe. The accused were acquitted of sexual assault on the basis that while the complainant's personal integrity had been violated, and her commercial integrity had been violated, the Crown had not proven beyond a reasonable doubt that her sexual integrity was violated. One wonders how personal integrity can be disaggregated from sexual integrity? Would the judge have considered the sexual integrity of a woman who was not already a sex worker to be violated were she physically abducted, forced to disrobe, and threatened with gang rape and other violence if she refused to prostitute herself for the benefit of her abductors?

Promisingly, it would appear that for the most part, as sexual assault jurisprudence has developed since *Chase* was decided, the concept of sexual integrity has not been reduced to merely bodily integrity. Instead, the adoption of a definition for sexual assault that involves an objective assessment of the impact on the complainant's sexual integrity has shifted the law's focus, so that what counts now is not simply the sexual motives, arousal, or body parts of the accused, or the community's standard of sexual propriety, but also the perception, experience, and impact on the complainant. It is not that bodily integrity is no longer the premier interest at stake. Rather, it is that physical integrity is not the only interest recognized by the definition of sexual assault given by the Supreme Court of Canada. It is now a definition that is corporeal and affective, relational and interactional. It is a definition that looks at the interaction, the relationships, the perspectives (both affective and corporeal) of all of the sexual actors, and the surrounding circumstances involved – a definition, in other words, that operates from a contextual, constructivist conception of sexual violence.

The doctrinal import of this shift is not to be underestimated. The first reported post-*Chase* case applying the Supreme Court of Canada's definition exemplifies this point. In *R. v. Crowe*, a former United Church minister was charged with sexually assaulting a prepubescent boy.[44] The defendant admitted to having hugged and kissed the boy on the lips but denied, and claimed he found repugnant, the allegation that he had fondled the boy's genitals or asked the boy to touch his penis. Judge Carter determined that the genital touching had not been proven beyond a reasonable doubt but convicted him of sexual assault regardless. He did so on the basis that the kiss on the lips and the hugging had been proven beyond a reasonable doubt. (It had been admitted to by the accused.) Basing his decision on the definition established in *Chase*, and noting that while the accused denied any motive of sexual gratification it did not preclude a conviction, he found that

> a reasonable observer, seeing a 71 year old man alone with an 11 year old boy who is sitting on his lap, pinch, hug and kiss the boy and then kiss him on the lips, may well put the pinching down to horseplay, the hugging and the kissing on the cheeks down to affection, but the kissing on

> the lips he would not consider normal, but violating the sexual integrity of the boy.

A definition of sexual assault that turned on sexual motives or genital contact would not, on the findings of fact made by the trial judge in this case, have resulted in a conviction.

The Supreme Court of Canada's decision in *R. v. Litchfield* provides a pronounced example of the shift from defining sexual violence based on sexual propriety and biology to defining it based on sexual integrity. The decision also demonstrates how this shift promotes a constructivist conception of sexual violence that is better able to account for the harm of sexual violation.[45] In *Litchfield*, the accused was a doctor charged with fourteen counts of sexual assault against seven of his female patients. Prior to trial, a chambers judge granted an order severing and dividing the counts such that there were to be three separate trials: one to deal with alleged assaults involving the complainants' breasts, one for those complaints involving genitals, and one for complaints of touching to other areas of the complainants' bodies. The Crown proceeded first on the counts involving vaginal exams. The trial judge refused to admit evidence of the counts involving other body parts, and the accused was acquitted.

On appeal to the Supreme Court of Canada, Justice Iacobucci found that severing the counts in this case had resulted in an injustice. The injustice stemmed from the impact that severing and dividing the counts would have on the test to be applied in determining whether an accused's conduct had the requisite nature to constitute a sexual assault. Justice Iacobucci found that

> the arbitrary distinction based on the body parts of the complainants amplified the difficulties in assessing the alleged sexual assaults in the context of all of the circumstances surrounding the conduct ... [T]he order *denied the reality of how the complainants experienced the conduct* which they alleged constituted sexual assaults, and sent an inappropriate message that a complainant's physical attributes were more important than her experience as a whole person.[46]

The difficulties in assessing the alleged sexual assaults in this case stemmed, in part, from the fact that the complainants had consented to some touching for medical purposes, including touching of their breasts and genitals. In this case, the fact that the touching occurred, and the fact that it involved touching of breasts and vaginal penetration, revealed nothing to indicate whether or not the conduct was sexually assaultive.

Justice Iacobucci notes that in light of the objective test established in *Chase,* in which all of the circumstances surrounding the conduct in question are relevant to the question of whether it violated the complainant's sexual integrity, it is essential that "courts not create unnecessary barriers to considering all the circumstances surrounding conduct which is alleged to constitute a sexual assault."[47] Of significance are the factors on which Justice Iacobucci focused. Under a sexual propriety approach, the analysis would likely have turned on the perspective of the accused, due to the fact that, given that the touching occurred in a doctor's office under the cloak of doctor-patient relations, an assessment of whether or not the community would deem it improper would likely turn on the accused's motives. It would have been necessary to establish a sexual motive. It is not that sexual motive is irrelevant under Justice Iacobucci's reasoning. It is relevant, and given the facts in this case it may be more significant than in other cases. The point is that under the *Chase* approach the sexual motive of the accused is not determinative, nor is the perspective of the accused all that is relevant in determining whether the conduct was sexual.

Justice Iacobucci's reasoning identifies the injustice that occurs if certain evidence is inadmissible – in particular, evidence regarding the nature of the relationship between the accused and the complainants, the potential power imbalances at play, and the experiences of the complainants as whole persons. He emphasizes the importance of recognizing the imbalance of power that can occur between a doctor and a patient where an alleged sexual assault is concerned. He goes on to note that not only does focusing on body parts rather than on "the larger context within which that complainant felt that the respondent's actions were inappropriate" deny coherent sexualities to the complainants, but it also sends an inappropriate message about women in general. Justice Iacobucci also determines that, in considering the evidence going to show a lack of consent, the trial judge ought to have considered "the testimony of the complainants as to their feelings of specific distress and discomfort, as well as their testimony that they had never had similar experiences with other doctors."[48] Nicola Lacey notes that one of the most typical and significant inadequacies of the criminal law's treatment of sexual offences is the virtual absence of consideration of affectivity from criminal law's doctrinal scheme.[49] Justice Iacobucci's reasoning in *Litchfield* very much incorporates affectivity into its analysis.

The Supreme Court of Canada's evolving approach towards the legal test for determining when consent to sexual touching has been vitiated by fraud provides another example of this trend towards greater concern with sexual interactions than with sexual acts. Under the common law, fraud only vitiates consent to sexual touching where the fraud goes to the nature or quality of the act consented to by the complainant. The reasoning in these older cases was essentialist. It focused on the act and nothing but the act. Under this reasoning, failing to disclose a sexually transmitted disease was not considered a fraud as to the nature or quality of the sexual act engaged in.[50] The context in which the act occurred, the relationships between the sexual actors, and the impact of the sexual interaction on the complainant were not considered. So, for example, in *Bolduc v. The Queen,* a doctor's conviction for indecent assault, arising from a medical examination conducted on a patient in front of the doctor's friend, was overturned on appeal.[51] The complainant consented to the vaginal exam based on the erroneous belief that the friend was an intern and was observing for medical/educational purposes. The Supreme Court of Canada reversed the conviction on the basis that "Bolduc did exactly what the complainant understood he would do ... to examine the vaginal tract and to cauterize the affected parts. Inserting the speculum was necessary for these purposes. There was no fraud on his part as to what he was supposed to do and in what he actually did."[52] The context in which these procedures occurred, that is, in front of a friend and not a fellow doctor, mattered not to the Court.

In recent years, the Supreme Court of Canada has revised its approach to fraudulently obtained consent in a way that now places analytical weight not only on the sexual act but also on the sexual actors and the sexual interaction. The issue was first considered in *R. v. Cuerrier.*[53] In *Cuerrier,* the accused was charged with aggravated assault. He had knowingly and repeatedly had unprotected sexual intercourse with two women without disclosing to them that he was HIV positive. Both women testified that they would not have consented to unprotected sex with Cuerrier had they known of his HIV status. The lower court acquitted Cuerrier.[54] Much like the Court's reasoning in *Bolduc,* the lower courts focused on the sexual acts, not the sexual actors. The complainants consented to a particular sexual act – unprotected sexual intercourse with the respondent – and this was the act that occurred. Justice Cory, writing for the majority of the Court in *Cuerrier,* disagreed. He determined that "it was no longer necessary when examining whether consent in assault or sexual assault cases was vitiated by fraud to consider whether the fraud related to the nature and quality of the act."[55] In addition to fraud pertaining to the nature and quality of the act or the identity of the partner, the non-disclosure of important facts combined with deprivation or risk of deprivation involving serious harm or significant risk of serious harm also vitiates consent. Rather than focusing solely on the specific sexual act, Justice Cory adopted an interpretation that takes into consideration the entire sexual interaction as well as the complainant's perspective not just regarding the specific physical act – penile/vaginal intercourse – but also regarding the context of the interaction as a whole.[56]

Where the law maintains an essentialist focus on sexual acts as opposed to sexual actors, the reasoning in *Bolduc* makes sense, as does the lower court reasoning in *Cuerrier.* A legal conception of sexuality focused on sexual actors (and thus sexual integrity) forces a different analysis. It requires the Supreme Court of Canada to ask much more than: did she say he could insert a speculum into her vagina and if so is that what he did? It requires the Court to inquire into the experience and perception of, as well as the potential impact on, all sexual actors involved. The reasoning in *Cuerrier* suggests a concern with how people treat each other sexually. The moral focus is on sexual relationships rather than on sexual acts, which is more likely to engender an emphasis on sexual integrity. It should be noted that *Cuerrier* was decided in 1996. Since then, developments in knowledge regarding the rates of transmission and regarding the treatment protocol for HIV have significantly changed the medical landscape with respect to this virus. In light of these changes, the legal response in *Cuerrier* may no longer be appropriate. The Court is soon to consider this issue in *R. v. Mabior.*[57]

By focusing on sexual interactions, the law is better able to consider the interests of the sexual actors themselves. A focus on the sexual act itself inevitably relies on essentialist conceptions about sex that are more concerned with propriety than integrity. It is not that anatomy is irrelevant. It is that its relevance is understood through a constructivist lens in which power, inequality, and the nature of the interaction are determinative, not the body parts involved. The decision of the British Columbia Court of Appeal in *R. v. Nicolaou* provides a good example of the way in which the corporeal continues to be incorporated into a social constructivist understanding of the definition of sexual violence.[58] *Nicolaou* involved numerous charges against the defendant including assault, living on the avails of prostitution, and sexual assault. The complainant alleged that Nicolaou, who lived next door to her and supplied her with drugs, had beaten her and forced her to prostitute herself in order to pay him money for drugs that he said she owed to him. The accused also ordered another woman to search the complainant's vagina against her wishes. The sexual assault charge stemmed from this non-consensual search.

Relying on *Chase,* the trial judge found the accused guilty of sexual assault on the basis that a motive of sexual gratification was not necessary and that assault for the purpose of power and control can, where it violates the complainant's sexual integrity, support a conviction. Quoting with approval the trial judge's analysis of the gendered power dynamics at play – "the evidence here clearly shows that [the appellant] was demonstrating his power and control over not only the complainant but other women present"[59] – the British Columbia Court of Appeal upheld the conviction. The Court also rejected the appellant's argument that because there was no sexual aspect to the assault the trial judge had erroneously focused on the anatomy involved. Instead, it found that "a motive of sexual gratification is not essential; the anatomy involved is relevant; [and] the exercise of power and control over the victim and his or her humiliation or subservience can engage his or her sexual integrity."[60] The involvement of sexual organs combined with the exercise of power and control equalled, in this case, a violation of the complainant's sexual integrity.

In this analysis, power becomes the salient factor. An examination of power necessitates an examination of the corporeal and the affective. Humiliation, subservience, and a contextual analysis of the gendered inequities at play (as evidenced by the reference to the domination of other women present) all become not only relevant, but also substantive, elements of what sexual assault means.

R. v. Larue, the Supreme Court of Canada's most recent interpretation of the meaning of sexual assault, reveals the significant impact on case outcomes that an understanding of the harm of sexual violence based on sexual integrity can produce.[61] The Court's basis for overturning both the trial court and the British Columbia Court of Appeal in this case also demonstrates that the shift towards a constructivist conception of sexual violence signalled by the definition of sexual assault adopted in *Chase* has been rearticulated in other cases.

The uncontested evidence at trial in *Larue* established that the accused climbed on top of an unconscious woman who was naked from the waist down and, while holding a knife to her throat, tried to force her legs apart. The complainant was unable to recall how her pants and underpants became removed. Larue slashed her throat before she was able to push him off and get help. The issue was whether this conduct constituted aggravated assault or sexual assault. A determination of such turned on whether the assault occurred in circumstances that were sexual. The trial judge found that there was a reasonable doubt as to whether the assault was sexual. His reasonable doubt was based on: (1) some evidence that there had been sexual activity between the complainant and another attendee at the party; (2) the possibility that the complainant's pants and panties had been removed by this other party; and (3) evidence that there may have been some romantic activity between the complainant and the accused before he attacked her with a knife while she was in a blacked out state (and that this prior romantic contact may have been consensual).[62]

The Crown appealed this decision arguing that the trial judge erred in law by drawing an artificial line between the potentially consensual sexual events that may have occurred prior to the attack and the attack itself. (How any sexual interactions between the accused and the complainant could have been consensual seems unclear, given the complainant's level of intoxication.) The majority of the British Columbia Court of Appeal rejected the Crown's appeal, finding that if any error occurred – which they were not convinced was the case – it was an error of fact, not law. They determined that, based on the evidence, it was open to the trial judge to conclude that there was a reasonable doubt as to whether the attack was sexual. In doing so, the Court misinterpreted *Chase.* Recall that the trial judge had accepted the uncontested fact that the complainant woke to find the defendant lying on top of her trying to pry her naked legs open. As the Supreme Court of Canada noted, under a proper application of *Chase,* it was not open to the trial judge, based on this evidence, to find that this assault was not sexual in nature.

Larue demonstrates well the significance of conceptualizing sexual assault the way the Supreme Court of Canada chose to do in *Chase.* Under an essentialist conception of sexual integrity, the actions of the accused would be interpreted through an understanding of sexual assault as about arousal and the inappropriate exercise of sexual desire. Uncontested evidence that the complainant awoke to find the accused on top of her prying her naked legs open would not necessarily be sufficient to establish that the assault ought to be characterized as a sexual assault. Under such a conceptual framework, the evidence in this case (such as that the complainant's pants may have been removed consensually by someone else) would be enough to possibly raise a reasonable doubt as to the accused's sexual motives and the sexual nature of the attack.

Now consider this case in light of the definition of sexual assault developed in *Chase.* This approach examines the context in which the acts occurred, the impact on the sexual integrity of the complainant, and interprets the accused's actions based on these factors rather than strictly on the presence or absence of arousal or sexual intentions. Under this approach, climbing on top of a partially disrobed and unconscious woman, holding a knife to her throat, and attempting to pry her naked legs open constitutes sexual assault. It does not matter who took her pants off. The definition of sexual assault in *Chase* does more than simply objectivize the *actus reus* for this offence. It alters the conception of what sexual violation is – what it means in this society. It shifts it away from an understanding of sexual violence as, or as caused by, the eruption of, or inability to control, a sexual drive. It shifts it away from an understanding that relies on the conception of sexuality as a romanticized, heterosexualized, and naturally occurring drive, away from the notion of a sexual subconscious in need of civilizing control both by the properly developed conscience of the adult mind,[63] and, for those not properly developed, away from that great surrogate, the properly developed conscience of the law. Instead, this substantive change to the legal concept of the harm caused by sexual violence reveals an understanding of sexual violation that is about interactions rather than acts – a context-dependent behaviour in which the most salient factor is power, not natural urge.

This is not to suggest that the law now fully conceptualizes sexual violence as socially constructed. Nor is it to suggest that references to, and reliance on, notions about sexual drives (uncontrollable or otherwise) are no longer to be found in cases about sexual violence. As demonstrated in Chapter 3 in this volume, in assessing admissibility of similar fact evidence in adult complainant cases, there is an element of essentialism revealed not in terms of sexual disposition but, rather, with respect to the undue focus on the "natural or unnatural" character of specific sexual acts. Whether penetration occurred may still be a factor in determining the severity of the sentence. Sentencing decisions in sexual assault cases, particularly those addressing dangerous offender and long-term offender designations, often contain references to arousal patterns. Perhaps some of this is unavoidable.

I do mean to suggest though, that in this one important respect the law has adopted a conceptual approach to defining sexual violence – to identifying the harm that sexual violence perpetuates – that is more constructivist and that this conceptual change continues to have significant impact. At this definitional stage, the law has come to reflect an understanding that whether an act between adults is sexually violative is contingent on *all* of the social factors surrounding and contributing to the act as well as an assessment of how it is experienced by *all* of the sexual actors involved.

The development of the Supreme Court of Canada's doctrine on the interpretation of non-consent as an element of the offence of sexual assault has further advanced this shift towards a less essentialist conception of sexual violence. There have been significant changes to the way in which the Court understands what the criminal law considers as consent to sexual touching. These changes, like with the changes to the definition of sexual assault, better incorporate the complainant's perspective of the sexual interaction, thus requiring the analysis to focus on the entirety of the sexual interaction rather than simply on the experience/perspective of only one of the sexual actors (the accused). The Court's decision in *R. v. Ewanchuk* affirmed two significant conceptual changes to the doctrine of consent in sexual assault law.[64] The first was the elimination of any notion of implied consent. This decision firmly entrenched consent as an element of the *actus reus,* which is based on the complainant's perspective at the time of the sexual interaction.[65] As the law now stands, in any sexual interaction either there is consent to the sexual touching or there is not consent to the sexual touching, and this determination will (for trial purposes) be based on direct and/or indirect evidence of the complainant's state of mind at the time. The second change was the characterization of knowledge of consent on the part of the accused in the affirmative rather than in the negative – the stipulation that consent means indicating yes rather than failing to indicate no.[66] Prior to the Court's decision in *Ewanchuk*, the consent element of the *mens rea* for sexual assault required that the accused believed that (or had been reckless or wilfully blind to the fact that) the complainant was not consenting. A guilty mind was a mind that knew, or was reckless as to, whether the complainant had withheld consent.[67]

The conception of consent adopted in *Ewanchuk* establishes that the accused, to be morally innocent, must have believed (or been reckless or wilfully blind to the fact that) the complainant communicated consent. *Ewanchuk* established that for the purposes of *mens rea* consent is established based on the accused's perception of the complainant's words or actions and not on the accused's speculation as to the complainant's desire for sexual contact. This means that the accused's belief that a complainant did not say no will not exculpate the accused nor will his belief that she said no but meant yes. It also means that a complainant's passivity is not a defence.[68] It is only a mistaken belief that the complainant communicated consent that will raise a reasonable doubt as to *mens rea* – not a mistaken belief that the complainant was consenting. In addition, as established by section 273.2(b) of the *Criminal Code*, the defence will not be available where the accused did not take reasonable steps, in the circumstances known to the accused at the time, to ascertain consent.

All of which means that what is now relevant in establishing *mens rea* is an assessment of the actual interaction between the sexual actors involved and not an assessment of the accused's potentially distorted perspective regarding the complainant's sexual interest. It limits the accused's (and the courts') ability to rely on essentialist understandings of what women are "like," what "certain" women are "like," or what women, or "certain" women, "want" in order to raise a reasonable doubt as to *mens rea*. These changes were directly informed by feminist legal scholarship. The conception of consent adopted by the Supreme Court of Canada in *Ewanchuk* was first articulated in Justice L'Heureux-Dubé's dissent in *R. v. Park* and (then) Justice McLachlin's dissent in *R. v. Esau*. It is a conception that was advanced by Lucinda Vandervort in the late 1980s.[69] Both Justice L'Heureux-Dubé and Justice McLachlin relied on Vandervort's work in these decisions.

The result of these modifications to the legal doctrine is a conception of consent in which all parties to the interaction must be sexual *actors* and in which the perspectives of all sexual actors involved in the interaction must be taken into account, at the definitional stage, in order to determine whether a sexual assault has occurred. Consider the case of *R. v. J.R.*, in which the complainant had no recollection of the events and could not say whether she had consented. She was able to testify that because she had, only a few days earlier, had an abortion and the doctor had told her that she should not have sexual intercourse for a certain period of time, and because she had no sexual interest in either of the two accused who had sex with her while she was passed out on the bathroom floor of a Toronto hotel, she would not have consented. Justice Ducharme found beyond a reasonable doubt that the complainant did not consent. His finding was based on her testimony regarding the abortion, the doctor's instructions, and her lack of sexual interest in either of the accused.[70]

The criminal law faces difficult challenges in identifying sexually violative and morally blameworthy sexual interactions between otherwise consenting adults. These challenges stem from the many social factors that constitute how sexuality is expressed, how sexual interactions are gendered, what norms of sexual conduct are created, and how these norms are experienced by different sexual actors. Sex involves socially contingent power dynamics, and in a society in which gendered power hierarchies are the norm in familial, social, financial, psychological, physical, and emotional contexts it is not difficult to imagine that many women would acquiesce to sexual touching that they do not desire.

Desire is used here in a broad sense. It does not refer only to sexual desire. People consent to sex for all sorts of reasons beyond physical, sexual, or emotional desires. People consent to sex for money, out of boredom or curiosity, or even out of pity. People consent to sex because they are too tired to argue with their partner and they know that next time around it might be them initiating. People consent to sex to gain social capital or to affirm their identity. While some of these circumstances might not be particularly "sexy," they do not necessarily compromise sexual integrity. In all of them, an interest is present, and so mutuality and thus sexual integrity is maintained. The need for mutuality to preserve sexual integrity does not suggest that power imbalances necessarily vitiate consent. People with less (or different kinds of) power can consent to people with more power and mutuality is still maintained. Mutuality is compromised where consent flows only as a result of power, whether perceived or real, whether exercised or not.

Distinguishing genuine consent from disingenuous consent is easier when there is violence, threat of violence, or some other form of overt coercion involved. It is more difficult when none of these are present. Nevertheless, if what the law deems important is whether the consent was genuine, then it matters not whether disingenuous consent arises because of a knife to the throat or a context of systemic inequality and gendered sexual violence in which many women have acculturated to what others might consider a conservative sense of when it feels "safe" to say no. A definition of consent that is in part based on an acknowledgment of this context reveals a conception of sexual violence that accounts for its social contingency. Post-*Ewanchuk*, the concept of consent under the *actus reus* and *mens rea* has changed. In identifying the *actus reus*, the concept of consent is used in an attitudinal sense. It is used to describe a state of mind – an unobservable feeling, sentiment, or perspective about the sexual interaction. In interpreting the *mens rea* for sexual assault, post-*Ewanchuk*, the concept of consent is used in an expressive or communicative sense. The distinction in how the term consent is understood in these two contexts reveals an attempt on the part of the Supreme Court of Canada to recognize the contextual, socially contingent, gendered factors that constitute any sexual interaction. Employing an attitudinal concept of consent to define the *actus reus* of the offence acknowledges that (often gendered) power dynamics short of overt (and therefore objectively ascertainable) coercion are just as relevant to a determination of the authenticity of consent. By rejecting the possibility of implied consent, this change also definitively draws the complainant's perspective into the legal definition of consent to sexual touching.

Employing consent as a communicative or expressive construct at the *actus reus* stage of analysis creates an approach to sexual assault that recognizes these imbalances. A communicative understanding of consent at the *actus reus* stage acknowledges that consent to sex does not mean the same thing to everyone or even the same thing to anyone in different contexts. It shifts the salient interpretation to an examination of acts or words rather than desires or natures. It ensures that all parties to the interaction are recognized by the law as sexual actors. The doctrine developed by Justice L'Heureux-Dubé in *Park* and adopted by the majority in *Ewanchuk* gives some recognition to the gender-based inequities present in sexual violence and perhaps sexual interactions generally. Contextualization is incorporated into the analytical framework of the doctrine itself. It is a recognition of this social context that gives rise to the need for a purely subjective standard of consent under the *actus reus* and a communicative notion of consent under the *mens rea*. The Court, in defining consent, in the context of individual cases – as it must do in criminal law – did so based on a consideration of the social/contextual factors that help to constitute what consent means in a "system" where sexual autonomy is not distributed equally. The substantive definition of consent to sexual touching in Canada, post-*Ewanchuk*, gives some recognition to the systemic inequalities that contribute to the production of sexual violence.

Equally important, of course, is the principle that a just criminal legal system does not convict the morally innocent. To be consistent with this principle, the criminal law, if it is to adopt a definition of consent such as the one in *Ewanchuk*, must also maintain a *mens rea* element and a mistaken belief in consent defence sufficient to ensure that the morally innocent are not convicted. An examination of the post-*Ewanchuk* case law reveals that this has been achieved. Courts have successfully applied this more contextualized approach to consent without jeopardizing the requirement for moral culpability on the part of the accused.[71] The shift towards a more constructivist conception of consent and mistaken belief in consent cannot be expected to (and has not) eradicated from the case law all remnants of essentialist reasoning. It certainly has, however, done something to challenge and replace some of the essentialist beliefs driving what the Supreme Court of Canada has described as the myths and stereotypes underpinning legal (and social) conceptions regarding sexual violence.

Conclusion

One of MacKinnon's claims was that "rape is a sex crime that is not a crime when it looks like sex."[72] This argument was based on the assertion that "what the law does not recognize is that the injury of rape is in the meaning of the experience to the victim, yet the crime is defined in the meaning of the act to the attacker."[73] The interpretation of the definition of sexual assault under *Chase* suggests that, in Canada, the Supreme Court of Canada has taken steps towards recognizing that the injury of rape is in the meaning of the experience to the victim. This is not a development that has occurred in many other jurisdictions.[74]

In addition, the doctrine of consent adopted in *Ewanchuk* establishes that where the attacker's perception is considered (as it must be under the *mens rea* analysis) it is not the meaning of the act to the attacker, but, rather, the meaning of the complainant's words or actions to the attacker, that is relevant. Together, these two doctrinal developments in the law of sexual assault, by incorporating a conception of sexual violence that takes its meaning from the social factors, circumstances, and overall context in which it is situated, do introduce a shift in the law's moral focus away from sexual propriety and towards sexual integrity.

A Moral Shift 5

> Of woman as a real human being, with sexual needs and sexual responsibilities, morality has often known nothing.
>
> – HAVELOCK ELLIS

As is the case with aspects of sexual assault law, the Supreme Court of Canada's evolving approach to obscenity and indecency also demonstrates a move away from a conception of sexual violence as a pre-social product that is more of mother nature than of culture, knowledge, relationships, and social institutions. This new constructivist approach (again an approach advanced by feminist legal thought) has precipitated a shift on the part of the Court towards a definition of obscenity that focuses less on sexual morality and more on political morality. Historically, law and "sexual morality" have consorted with one another unabashedly. Their bond, pervasive throughout all areas of law that touch upon human relationships, has been particularly evident in legal contexts such as the regulation of obscenity and indecency, the regulation of non-marital and non-procreative sexual activity, and the prohibition of the commodification of sex. What does it mean, however, to suggest that law and sexual morality have danced together throughout the years?

For one thing, it means that the law is likely to embrace, and be invested in maintaining, a particular account of sexuality. The particular account embraced by the law is an essentialist account. Indeed, when law and sexual morality consort with one another, naturalistic, essentialist understandings of sexuality are almost always there, lurking under the covers. The case law between 1958 and 1968 interpreting the offence of gross indecency (which was removed from the *Criminal Code* in 1987) provides a good example of this "threesome" between law, essentialism, and sexual morality.

Prior to 1958, the offence of gross indecency only prohibited acts of oral and anal sodomy if the act was engaged in between two men. Between 1958 and 1968, the scope of the provision was expanded such that acts of sodomy between any two people were prohibited. (In 1968, the legislature changed the offence so that it did not apply to husbands and wives or other pairs of consenting adults.) In this period between 1958 and 1968, courts struggled with what to do about husbands and wives and girlfriends and boyfriends caught in acts of oral sex. (It seems that such incidences had not been a challenge for courts under the previous definition, as it was assumed that such an unnatural thing as oral sex between two men was grossly indecent.) Courts turned to naturalistic and moralistic assumptions about sex in order to avoid this conundrum. To determine whether heterosexual acts of (oral) sodomy were grossly indecent, courts focused on factors such as monogamy, medical opinion as to the prevalence of oral sex in society, whether the oral sex at issue had been a precursor to penile-vaginal intercourse, and whether the couple caught in the act were in love.[1]

Under the traditional relationship between law, morality, and essentialism, those who are overly sexualized, under-sexualized, restricted, violated, or ignored within a given sexual morality will be less likely to see their sexual integrity promoted, or their sexual realities reflected back to them, in the laws that govern their sexual conduct. When law and morality intersect in this way, laws tend to be geared towards protecting sex itself (or, more specifically, a particular essentialist understanding of sexual acts) rather than the individuals, relationships, social practices, rights, and duties implicated in, and through which is produced, this aspect of "being" human. The difficulty with much of the jurisprudence in which the moral focus is on sex itself – whether it is in the context of sexual assault, equality, obscenity and indecency, or sex work – is that it inhibits the law's ability to accommodate in its analysis the nuance, fluidity, and complexity of human sexual interaction and sexual identity. Much less does it recognize how these interactions produce sexual identities, norms, and practices and the institutions that regulate them, which includes a failure to recognize the perspectives of all of the sexual actors engaged, the diversity of sexual actors in a society, the manner in which a society produces sexual diversity, and the manner in which this diversity, in turn, impacts a society. It is less apt to accommodate individual sexual narratives, likely because sexual stories are so often complicated and socially nuanced. Moralistic legal approaches focused on sex itself do not incorporate this social nuance because they do not conceptualize sexuality as socially constructed. Instead, sex is conceptualized as a naturally occurring and asocial or pre-social "thing" either to be feared or revered. It is either dangerous and to be controlled, or it is sacred and to be cherished or released. Yet, regardless, it is something beyond, outside of, or separate from the individuals and social contexts in which it is experienced.

One might argue, but does the law – especially the criminal law – not have to focus on *acts*? It is not that acts are irrelevant. It is that there is no inherent morality or immorality to any particular sexual act. The moral significance of a sexual act – and, in fact, the overall meaning attributed to it – is constituted by the context, interaction, and relationship in which it occurs. The relationship between law, sexuality, and morality is complicated. Morality will always play a role in the legal regulation of sex. To make legal distinctions about sex is to make judgments between good sex and bad sex. Making judgments about sex, unless they are arbitrary, is an exercise of morality. Yet there are as many sexual moralities in a society as there are people, and while the law cannot attempt to reflect all of them it can attempt to reflect a recognition of the fact of all of them. Recognition of this plurality could itself constitute the founding principles of a morality. A morality of this sort, unlike the one that has traditionally underpinned the legal regulation of sex in Canada, would not be driven to perpetuate one particular account of sexuality – a drive that has often led the law to protect sex itself rather than those subject to the law's sexual prohibitions and privileges. There is nothing to suggest that the legal regulation of sex must be motivated by a morality underpinned by essentialist thinking and based on the preservation of sex itself.

But, then, what sort of morality ought the law to adopt? How can the law make distinctions between good sex and bad sex without a static and universal account of what sex is? One possibility is to develop an approach that is grounded in political morality. Such an approach might be achieved by orienting the law such that it focuses entirely on the actors, relationships, and cultures that produce, and are produced by, sexuality rather than on sex itself. In fact, it may be that such an approach is already developing in the relationship between law, sexuality, and morality in Canada. The evolution of obscenity law in Canada illustrates how the Supreme Court of Canada's more constructivist understanding of sexual violence has led to a change in the law's focus from a moral concern with sex itself to a moral concern with sexual actors and relationships. This shift began with the incorporation of feminist thought about the social contingency of sexual violence in the 1990s in *R. v. Butler*[2] and culminated in the Court's 2005 decision in *R. v. Labaye.*[3] In the interim between the decisions in *Butler* and *Labaye,* the Court released another significant decision on obscenity – *Little Sisters Book and Art Emporium v. Canada (Minister of Justice)* – which will be explored at length in Chapter 6 in this volume.[4] One of the primary critiques of the Court's opinion in *Little Sisters* was that it both reflected, and perpetuated, a continued, albeit perhaps indirect, reliance on sexual morality. In *Labaye*, the criminal law definition of indecency was interpreted such that the law's post-*Butler* indirect reliance on sexual morality was replaced with a reliance on political morality. As discussed in the final section of this chapter (using the example of the criminal regulation of sex work), an emphasis on political morality rather than on sexual morality has the potential to better protect the interests of sexual actors rather than a particular (essentialist) account of sexual acts.

The Social Construction of Pornography in Canada

Feminists addressing the issue of pornography in Canada in the 1980s and 1990s took different approaches. Many adopted a nuanced approach to the issue of censorship,[5] and many were wary of becoming mired in the polemic sex wars debate that enveloped the feminist movement south of the border at this time.[6] While feminists developed different approaches to the issue of pornography, the definition of obscenity adopted by the Supreme Court of Canada in the 1990s was particularly informed by one feminist-inspired constructivist account of pornography. This account involved the assertion that pornography was itself a practice of subordination that constitutes sex (and correspondingly gender) hierarchies.

This conception of pornography regards it as "a practice of male power over women."[7] The most well-known advocate of this approach was Catharine MacKinnon.[8] MacKinnon argued that pornography is not speech but, rather, an act of sexual violence against women. Canadian feminists successfully relied on MacKinnon's ideas about pornography in order to encourage courts and law makers to understand pornography in its social context.[9] In both her academic work and legal activism, Kathleen Mahoney (lead counsel for the intervener Women's Legal Education and Action Fund (LEAF) in the *Butler* case) developed constitutional arguments in favour of censorship based on MacKinnon's theory.[10] In their submission to the Supreme Court of Canada in *Butler*, LEAF argued that some pornography is not protected under section 2(b) of the *Canadian Charter of Rights and Freedoms* because it constitutes a violent form of expression.[11] While the scope of protected expression under section 2(b) of the *Charter* is extremely broad, one of the limits that has been placed on its breadth is with respect to violence. Violence is not a protected form of expression under section 2(b). Had the Court adopted LEAF's assertion that pornography is itself a form of violence, they could have found that obscene depictions were not protected under section 2(b) rather than having to justify censorship of obscenity under section 1 of the *Charter*.[12] While the Court did not go this far in *Butler*, nevertheless, its decision did initiate a shift towards a constructivist conception of pornography in which the law's moral focus moved towards sexual integrity and away from sexual propriety.

In *Butler*, the Supreme Court of Canada confirmed that material will be obscene where it constitutes the "undue exploitation of sex."[13] According to the *Butler* test, determining whether material "unduly" exploits sex depends upon the degree of harm posed by the material as dictated by the community's standard of tolerance. The notion of harm has in one sense or another always been a part of the law criminalizing obscene depictions. However, in *Butler*, the notion of harm assumed a new meaning and a new role in the definition of obscenity. *Butler* established that the notion of harm was to be incorporated directly into the community standard of tolerance test: "The courts must determine as best they can what the community would tolerate others being exposed to on the basis of the degree of harm that may flow from such exposure."[14] In other words, an assessment of what the community would tolerate others doing or seeing was to be determined based on how much harm an act, or sexually explicit depiction, posed.

It was not simply that degree of harm (as tolerated by the community) was to be the ultimate arbiter in defining obscenity. *Butler* also represented a shift in the Supreme Court of Canada's understanding of the type of harm that obscenity laws were, or ought to be, concerned with. The Court in *Butler* found that the harms caused by pornography, and the harms that obscenity laws ought to be concerned with, related not to moral harm (moral corruption) but, rather, to real harm to women. It is not that *Butler* was the first time that the Court recognized that moral approbation regarding "dirt for dirt's sake" was not the proper impetus for the law.[15] It is that there was something new in the way that *Butler* conceptualized this harm to society. First, the Court recognized the potential harm as a systemic harm caused primarily to women. Second, for the first time, it began to conceptualize it as the physical and sexual harm caused to women as a result of the behavioural and attitudinal changes induced in those individuals who viewed certain types of pornography. In earlier cases, the notion of harm focused on a general sense of the need to protect from injury the moral propriety of society as a whole.

In *Butler*, the Supreme Court of Canada adopted a harm-based justification for the censorship of some pornography based on the presumption that "exposure to images bears a casual relationship to changes in attitudes and beliefs."[16] It found that it was not unreasonable for Parliament to conclude that certain types of pornography will harm society by altering the sexual attitudes and, ultimately, the sexual behaviour of those who view it. Justice Sopinka quoted with approval from the Meese Commission report on pornography:

> [T]he available evidence strongly supports the hypothesis that substantial exposure to sexually violent materials as described here bears a causal relationship to antisocial acts of sexual violence ... The evidence says simply that the images that people are exposed to bears a causal relationship to their behavior.[17]

The harm-based justification for the criminal law definition of obscenity adopted by the Court in *Butler* reflects a conception of sexuality as socially constructed. The reasoning in *Butler* relies on the assumption that a desire for sexual violence, or an orientation towards sexual violence, is not innate and pre-social but, rather, susceptible to external influences. It is contextually contingent.

While the Supreme Court of Canada also referenced changes to people's beliefs and attitudes towards women, it was clear that harm in this context meant that it "predisposes people *to act* in an antisocial manner incompatible with society's proper functioning."[18] As noted, the Court specifically identified and adopted as reasonable the conclusions of the Meese Commission that substantial exposure to sexually violent materials bears a causal relationship to anti-social acts of sexual violence.[19] The shift in the Court's approach to the harms caused by pornography, as demonstrated in *Butler*, was influenced by the feminist analysis of pornography offered by the intervener LEAF.[20] As discussed earlier, LEAF argued that the gender hierarchy between men and women is a consequence of the eroticization of sexual violence and that therefore pornographic depictions of sexual violence constitute sex discrimination.[21]

According to this constructivist account, pornography depicts sexual pleasure for women as the act of submission, and it depicts sexual pleasure for men as the act of domination. In turn, these depictions socially construct conceptions of gender. Not only do women understand sex as domination, but these portrayals also reinforce the notion that what it is to be a woman is to be sexually dominated and what it is to be a man is to sexually dominate.[22] As Kathleen Mahoney explains, "[t]he encouragement and promotion of subordination in pornography ... reinforces the systemic violence and the social harms" of rape, battery, prostitution, sexual harassment, and incest that women experience in daily life.[23] Identifying the harm of pornography as rooted in its causal relationship to sexual violence reflects an understanding of sexual violence as contextually contingent. This constructivist conception of sexual violence in *Butler* laid the groundwork for the Supreme Court of Canada's ultimate adoption of a fully contextual, harm-based test in *Labaye*.

In 2005, the Supreme Court of Canada revised the meaning of indecency (and presumably also obscenity) under the *Criminal Code*.[24] It did so by removing from the *Butler* test any reliance on community perceptions about sex – a consideration that had, in a variety of manifestations, underpinned indecency and obscenity laws in Canada for the better part of the last one hundred years. Removing consideration of the community's perceptions regarding what constitutes good sex and what constitutes bad sex from the definition of indecency meant that harm had to be identified in some other way. In *Labaye*, Chief Justice McLachlin, writing for the majority, turned to constitutional principles to do so. She reasoned that for sexual activity to be considered indecent under the criminal law the harm that it is alleged to have caused must be harm that is actually proven, whether that be through expert evidence or otherwise.[25] This is a change in the law with potentially significant implications for the role that sexual morality is to play in the criminal regulation of certain types of sexual activity. The Court's reasoning in *Labaye* reinforces the notion that the focus of criminal laws regulating sexuality should not be on sexual morality and moral harm to society but, rather, on political morality and real harm to individuals. In doing so, it leaves more space for considerations, under the law, of sexual agency and allows for greater consideration of individual subjectivities. The result, as will be discussed next, creates greater opportunity within legal reasoning for more diverse sexual narratives, and it contributes to a more constructivist conception of sexuality – a conception that better recognizes our shared interest in protecting sexual integrity.

The Constitution as Custos Morum

In *Labaye*, the majority of the Supreme Court of Canada allowed the appeal of Jean-Paul Labaye's conviction of keeping a common bawdy house on the basis that the sexual acts occurring at his establishment, Club L'Orage, did not constitute indecent ones under the *Criminal Code*.[26] Club L'Orage was a private swingers club with an annual membership fee. It was located on the top floor of a building that also housed a strip club owned by Mr. Labaye. The club was open to members and their guests only. Essentially, it consisted of "a number of mattresses ... scattered about the floor of the apartment" that served as a meeting place for individuals interested in partner swapping and group sex.[27] Labaye was charged with keeping a common bawdy house after undercover detectives observed a group of four or five men having sex with one woman, while other members of the club observed. All of the activity was, concededly on the part of the Crown, consensual.

Under the *Criminal Code*, a bawdy house is an establishment kept for the purpose of committing acts of prostitution or indecency.[28] The issue in this case was whether the activities occurring at Club L'Orage were indecent. The case turned on a matter of statutory interpretation – the interpretation of the term indecent. The majority of the Supreme Court of Canada determined that only activities that pose a significant risk of harm of the type "grounded in norms which our society has recognized in its Constitution or similar fundamental laws" – harm so serious as to be incompatible with proper societal functioning – will be considered indecent.[29] In the majority's opinion, the type of group sex occurring at Club L'Orage did not constitute harm of that nature.

Prior to the Supreme Court of Canada's decision in *Labaye,* courts used the community standard of tolerance test – developed in the obscenity context – to determine whether an act was indecent.[30] It was not necessary under this test for the Crown to lead independent evidence as to the community's standard of tolerance.[31] A judge was considered capable of determining this without independent evidence. The problem with this test was that most judges would consider themselves part of the community. As such, it would be difficult, if not impossible, to expect them to disaggregate their own subjective perception of the sexual act or depiction at issue from their subjective assessment of the community's overall subjective assessment of the sexual act or depiction at issue. In an effort to make it more objective and less susceptible to the subjective sexual morality of any given adjudicator, the test was revised in 1985.[32] *Towne Cinema Theatres v. The Queen* determined that obscenity could be established either by showing that the material violated the norm of what Canadians would tolerate other Canadians viewing or doing or by showing that the material would have a harmful effect on others in society. Later, in *Butler,* as discussed earlier, the notion of harm was incorporated directly into the community standard of tolerance. This distinction between the test in *Towne Cinema* and the test in *Butler* is significant. In *Towne Cinema,* it was still possible to find material obscene solely on the basis of community sexual morality. *Butler* ostensibly changed this approach and purported to resolve (and reject) the morality issue once and for all.

Unfortunately, *Butler* did not succeed in ridding the law of obscenity and indecency of sexual morality. The continued reliance on the community standard of tolerance test precluded such an objective, even had it been the Supreme Court of Canada's intention. Had *Butler* actually resolved (and rejected) the sexual morality issue once and for all, it is unlikely that Chief

Justice McLachlin would have thought it necessary, in *Labaye,* to reject the community standard of tolerance test altogether. What *Butler* did do was initiate the shift away from a moral concern over sex itself and towards a moral concern over power. A harm-based approach to the definition of obscenity and indecency suggests a greater concern with power. At the heart of an approach centred on a moral concern with power (a political morality-driven approach rather than a sexual morality-driven approach) is the feminist influenced social constructivist conception of sexual violence. The focus on power hierarchies in LEAF's submissions in *Butler,* and in the Court's approach in *Butler,* was underpinned by a social constructivist account of sexuality that focused more, and in a new way, on sexual integrity rather than on sexual propriety. While this change in focus itself did not complete the shift from sexual morality to political morality in the criminal regulation of obscenity and indecency, it did lay the necessary groundwork.

Labaye built on the *Butler* description of the type of harm targeted by the concept of indecent conduct under the *Criminal Code* (that being "conduct which society formally recognizes as incompatible with its proper functioning").[33] In *Labaye,* Chief Justice McLachlin determined that the harm must be both grounded in norms that our society has formally recognized in the Constitution or similar fundamental laws and be so serious as to be incompatible with proper societal functioning:

> Views about the harm that the sexual conduct at issue may produce, however widely held, do not suffice to ground a conviction. This is not to say that social values no longer have a role to play. On the contrary, to ground a finding that acts are indecent, the harm must be shown to be related to a fundamental value reflected in our society's Constitution or similar fundamental laws ... Unlike the community standard of tolerance test, the requirement of formal recognition inspires confidence that the values upheld by judges and jurors are truly those of Canadian society. Autonomy, liberty, equality and human dignity are among these values.[34]

What Chief Justice McLachlin suggests in *Labaye* is that the law, when considering or upholding social values, ought to rely on those values that the whole society agrees upon. This is why her theory of harm relies on values that have been formally recognized, such as those that are reflected in the Constitution or other fundamental laws. The social values that she identifies are autonomy, liberty, equality, and human dignity. Despite the fact that *Labaye* did not involve a constitutional challenge but, rather, a matter of statutory interpretation, the theory of harm (and definition of indecency) that Chief Justice McLachlin ultimately adopts turns on constitutional law. Instead of measuring harm based on what the community will tolerate, she suggests it ought to be measured against the Constitution. Instead of measuring it against the sexual values of the community taken as a whole, it ought to be measured against the fundamental values underpinning the Constitution. What Chief Justice McLachlin does in *Labaye* is dispose of the community standard of tolerance test by relying instead on the political morals reflected in the Constitution. In essence, she invokes constitutional principles in order to protect constitutional principles.

The structure of her reasoning is consistent with Ronald Dworkin's theory of liberal equality.[35] A definition of indecency premised on a judicial assessment of the sexual morals held by a large number of Canadians is legal reasoning based on what Dworkin describes as first-person ethics. In contrast, third-person ethics reflect those commonly held beliefs ascribed to by all or most members of a liberal democracy. A definition of indecency premised on a judicial assessment of the political morality of a large number of Canadians is legal reasoning based on Dworkin's third-person ethics. Dworkin's theory of liberal equality attempts to maintain a link between personal ethics (first-person ethics) and political values (third-person ethics) while honouring the overriding liberal principle of state neutrality between conceptions of the good. Similarly, Chief Justice McLachlin resorts to more general convictions to justify the majority's decision. In this way, she relies upon, in order to protect, the fundamental ethical and social considerations enshrined in the Constitution.

Responding to Chief Justice McLachlin's reasoning, the dissent in *Labaye* commented that "the existence of harm is not a prerequisite for exercising the state's power to criminalize certain conduct. The existence of fundamental social and ethical considerations is sufficient."[36] However, despite this statement by the dissent, the dispute between the majority and the dissent in *Labaye* is not actually over whether social values ought to play a role in making or enforcing indecency laws – both adopt reasoning that turns on an application of social values. Their disagreement is over which social values to rely upon, and what role they ought to play, in ascertaining what constitutes indecency.

While the majority's reasoning turns on what sexual restrictions and standards a society can legitimately impose on its members without compromising broader ethical convictions as articulated by the Constitution, the dissent depends on their perception and interpretation of what sexual mores the majority of Canadians have adopted. This is why the dissent endorses a strikingly quantitative approach to sexual morality and the definition of indecency in which "use can be made of factual evidence, such as surveys, reports or research regarding Canadians' sexual practices and preferences, and their attitudes toward and levels of tolerance of sexual acts in various contexts."[37] It is also the reason why the dissent suggests that, contrary to the majority's opinion, the community's standard of tolerance remains a salient consideration in identifying acts of indecency and that "serious harm is not the sole criterion for determining what the Canadian community will tolerate."[38]

The dissenting judges make this argument on two bases. First, they argue that activity that is inconsistent with the community's sexual morality, in and of itself, causes harm to the community's political morality. They assert that there is always a harm associated with transgressions of those sexual values held by most Canadians. Second, they suggest that morality for the sake of morality – and, here, they are referring to majoritarian sexual mores – should be permitted to play a role in defining the state's power to criminalize conduct, regardless of whether there is an associated harm. In fact, Chief Justice McLachlin does not actually jettison "morality for morality's sake" from the criminal law. She acknowledges that harm to values can, in and of itself, constitute the sort of harm that ought to be prohibited by the criminal law, but she strictly limits the range of values that may be subject to harm. In the end, she relies on values so cherished by Canadian society that they have been constitutionally entrenched. She rejects the community standard of tolerance test and replaces it with a new standard of tolerance: a standard required by the Constitution (of the community). Again, the values she identifies are liberty, equality, autonomy, and human dignity. She identifies three types of harm sufficient to justify coercive prohibition on the basis that acts perpetuating such harm would compromise these fundamental constitutional values.

The first includes circumstances where members of the public would, or there is a significant risk that they could, be involuntarily confronted with conduct that significantly interferes with their autonomy and liberty.[39] She is careful to point out that this is not about aesthetics. It is about being confronted with something seriously and deeply offensive such that it creates an inability to go certain places. It is about not being able to take your kids to the park for fear that they will be unwittingly exposed to people engaged in sexual activity. By definition, it refers to sexual activity occurring in public places. The second type of harm involves conduct that would, or there is a significant risk that it could, predispose others to anti-social behaviour. This, she suggests, could extend to include attitudinal harm such as conduct that undermines respect for, and the dignity of, targeted groups. She notes that it must be harm that can actually be proven. She is also careful to again include some public element in the analysis under this branch of harm: "This type of harm can only arise if members of the public may be exposed to the conduct or material in question."[40] The third type of harm identified by Chief Justice McLachlin involves conduct that would, or there is a significant risk that it could, physically or psychologically harm the persons involved.[41] She includes here both physical and psychological harm. While analysis of this sort of harm will generally be dictated by whether the participants have consented (leaving considerable space for sexual agency), she acknowledges that sometimes consent is more apparent than real. She notes that in some cases harm may be established even where there is apparent consent. The public/private distinction is not as significant under this branch of harm.

There remains an ambiguity, one that is likely inevitable, both in Chief Justice McLachlin's definition of indecency and in the argument to follow regarding the interpretation of the bawdy house provisions. It relates to the fact that it is still necessary to measure harm. What is attitudinal harm and how will it be established? How will the court assess harm to the participants? What is the line between sexual autonomy and the law's obligation to intervene in the face of obvious victimization? Will sexual morality-based reasoning not reveal itself once again when it comes time to assess harm? The answer to these questions is, at least in part, yes. Attempts to argue for the complete disaggregation of law and morality are unrealistic. Given this circumstance, the more important question becomes what order of morality ought the law to trade in.

What Chief Justice McLachlin does in *Labaye* is shift the law's focus from sexual morality to political morality. It is not a perfect answer. However, when it comes to the legal regulation of sex, it is much preferable that the law's moral compass be governed by attempts to balance constitutional values such as autonomy, liberty, equality, and dignity rather than by an assessment of what the sexual consensus at any given time in Canada might be. I said the answer was "in part" yes. The equivocation stems from an evidentiary point of distinction between *Labaye* and the community standard of tolerance test. In *Labaye*, Chief Justice McLachlin is explicit in her assertion that harm must be proven, which was not the case under the community standard of tolerance test. *Labaye* represents a shift towards a legal morality concerned more with sexual interactions than with the categorization, assessment, and judgment of specific sexual actions. By emphasizing the social factors and overall social context that produce sexual violence, an emphasis the Supreme Court of Canada has endorsed, the feminist intervention in Canada instigated a shift in the moral focus of the law from sex itself to the power dynamics and social factors constituting these dynamics.

As articulated by the Supreme Court of Canada, the language of the test for obscenity or indecency, as it stood prior to *Labaye*, was as follows:

"[W]hat would the community tolerate others being exposed to on the basis of the degree of harm that might flow from such exposure."[42] As a matter of application, the test went something more like this: "[I]ndecency laws are about what Canadians would not abide other Canadians doing."[43] As suggested, deciding "what Canadians would not abide other Canadians doing" has often been determined based on quasi-quantitative assessments of the sexual practices of most Canadians. The moral focus has been on sexual action rather than on sexual interaction. Assessing harm based on community tolerance allows for the regulation of sex based on dominant sexual morality (as reflected in community levels of tolerance) rather than on social or political morality (as reflected in instruments such as the Constitution). Historically, women (and sexual minorities) have not fared well under regimes governed by traditional sexual mores. Traditional sexual mores have been for the protection of men and male sexual propriety. A standard that is about sexual propriety is not a standard about women's interests – neither their interests regarding sexual agency and autonomy nor their interests with respect to sexual harms. A standard that is about sexual propriety is typically not a standard that is about sexual integrity.

The Supreme Court of Canada's pre-*Labaye* indecency cases demonstrate that a legal regime for the regulation of sex that is dictated by sexual morality rather than political morality is not one that deals adeptly with the complexity of sex, nor is it one that is particularly proficient at protecting the interests that sexual actors have in both their safety and their sexual integrity (broadly understood). Consider Justice Sopinka's reasoning in *R. v. Mara.*[44] Justice Sopinka, declaring lap dances to be indecent under the community standard of tolerance test, states that "it is unacceptably degrading to women to permit such uses of their bodies in the context of a public performance in a tavern. Insofar as the activities were consensual as the appellant stressed, this does not alter their degrading character."[45] He goes on to find that indecency laws are not there to protect the lap dancers but, rather, to protect the spectators. The risk of harm to the performers, he suggested, is only relevant insofar as that risk exacerbates the social harm resulting from the degradation and objectification of women. Under this reasoning, neither the safety nor the sexual agency of the women participants is relevant to the definition of indecency. Note, however, that harm to the spectators is relevant.

Justice Sopinka found that, according to the community standard of tolerance, lap dances are indecent because they desensitize sexuality and objectify women. Using the criminal law to protect the decency of sex itself, which is what it means to define acts as indecent on the basis that they "desensitize sexuality," is about sexual propriety. An analysis underpinned by this type of sexual morality is not an analysis that is particularly interested in harm to the actual women involved in a particular activity. Such reasoning is done on behalf of the decency of some monolithic notion of women as incapacitated victims of sexual objectification. Conceptualizing women's sexuality in this way is not progress for women. More importantly, it is not in the interests of those women involved in the sex trade – that is, those women who are directly affected by the legal and social implications of sex work. By finding that the issue of consent is not even a relevant factor of consideration in defining what acts, in this "adults only" establishment, constitute indecent ones, Justice Sopinka directly rejects the interests in sexual agency of the women involved as relevant to the definition. By finding that harm to these women is only relevant if harm to them results in greater harm to others, he does not focus at all on their interest in sexual safety.

His reasoning is not premised on relationships, nor is it premised on the sexual interactions at issue. It is premised on an assessment regarding the immorality of lap dances, underpinned by a moral assessment regarding the commodification of sex. Instead, legal reasoning, legal assessments, and legal definitions should be based on the understanding that the meaning of a sexual act (such as the exchange of money for a lap dance) is produced through the relationships, interactions, and context in which it occurs. Justice Sopinka's reasoning in *Mara* does not reflect a consideration of these contextual factors. The act of exchanging sex (a lap dance) for money is not, on its face, an activity that violates the types of third-person ethics (such as equality, liberty, and autonomy) reflected in legal/political instruments such as the Constitution. Under *Labaye*'s approach, a determination as to whether the lap dances at issue are harmful (indecent) would require an assessment of these factors.

Even in cases where the Supreme Court of Canada determined that a particular sexual act was not beyond the community's standard of tolerance, the application of this test often produced reasoning that maintains a moralistic, majoritarian, and essentialist approach to the regulation of sexuality. Such reasoning is evident in the Court's decision in *R. v. Tremblay*.[46] *Tremblay* concerned a charge of keeping a common bawdy house and was laid against the owner of a bar where nude dancers would perform in individual cubicles for clients who were permitted to masturbate while viewing the dancers (who were also masturbating or pretending to masturbate). In restoring the trial judge's acquittal, Justice Cory stated that

> it was entirely appropriate for the trial judge to take into account the expert testimony of Dr. Campbell in determining the community standard of tolerance. That testimony was relevant and helpful in arriving

> at an objective appreciation as to what types of sexual behaviour would be tolerated by the Canadian public. It was on the basis of the statistics provided by Dr. Campbell, which indicated that most Canadians engage in masturbation, that the trial judge concluded that the average Canadian was more likely to tolerate activities which were similar to those in which they engaged in themselves. Obviously, any perception of what would be tolerated will very properly be influenced by what is perceived as normal. What is normal will, in turn, depend upon the extent to which that same activity is engaged in by others. If the act in question is one that is performed by the majority in the community then it is impossible to say that the act itself would not be tolerated by the community ... Thus, once the act itself is found to be tolerated *then* the inquiry must shift to focus on the circumstances surrounding its performance.[47]

Now, fortunately for Mr. Tremblay, the trial judge had made a finding of fact that, based on the testimony of Dr. Campbell, the expert sexologist, 90 percent of Canadian men and 50 percent of Canadian women do indeed masturbate and so it is therefore "normal." As a result, provided that it was not occurring in a location that is overly public, it is an activity that the community will tolerate – it is not indecent.

This sort of legal reasoning is dictated by the consideration of factors (such as sexual impropriety or what most Canadians are doing sexually and what they think normal) that do not allow for diversity or the nuanced reality of many people's sexualities. Nor does this approach consider the factors that ought to matter: the context, relationship dynamics, working conditions, and potential power imbalances in which these masturbatory performances are being held. The community standard of tolerance approach – from a conceptual perspective – is a status quo approach. When it comes to sex, status quo approaches are often not good for women. Women (one in four of whom, by some accounts, will experience forced sex at least once during the course of their lifetime[48]) should not want legal definitions of what is, and what is not, decent dictated by what is, and what is not, prevalent. On a similar note, gays and lesbians (who supposedly make up less than 10 percent of the population) should not want legal definitions of what is, and what is not, decent dictated by what is, and what is not, normal. Reasoning founded on sexual morality is reasoning driven to constitute through law (as well as other social mechanisms) a particular account of sex. In fact, this is what is suggested by the notion of sexual morality. As I have already argued, the particular sexual morality that has dominated law, at least in Canada, is an essentialist, naturalized, sex-as-dangerous account of sex.

The law often purports to act out of concern for the welfare of individuals or relationships, and on one level this notion is likely true. Unfortunately, below the surface of these decisions, one can detect an underlying concern for the protection of sex itself that may be influencing or perhaps sometimes even driving the analysis in many of these cases. Such an underlying concern was exemplified by the Supreme Court of Canada's approach to the concept of sexual exploitation. Recall that obscene representations are defined as representations that unduly exploit sex. This definition, even on its face, suggests that this law is oriented towards the protection of sex itself. Its concern is directed towards ensuring that sex (not women, not children, and not visible minorities) is not exploited. However, it goes much further. Whether or not a representation is considered to unduly exploit sex is to be determined based on community standards, and, prior to *Butler,* "community standards" referred directly and explicitly to dominant sexual morality.

Reasoning based on conservative sexual morality is reasoning directed towards protecting a particular account of, or understanding about, sex. Given this, it is perhaps unsurprising that incorporating a notion of harm into the community standard of tolerance did not result in reasoning *sans* sexual morality. After all, doing so would ensure that obscenity laws would safeguard against harm to sex – that is to say, against harm to a particular account of sex – a sexual morality. An alternative, of course, would be to define exploitation based on harm to people.

As is discussed in Chapter 6 in this volume, this same observation can be made about Justice La Forest's reasoning in *Norberg v. Wynrib.*[49] In *Norberg,* Justice La Forest determined that, for the purposes of sexual battery, consent would be vitiated where the sexual relationship concerned an imbalanced and exploitative relationship between the parties. Under his analysis, a relationship would be exploitative if it contravened community standards of conduct (which intuitively must refer to sexual conduct). So instead of examining the individual and subjective perceptions and circumstances of, and risk to, the parties involved, courts are to determine whether the relationship is exploitative based on the court's assessment of what sort of sexual relationship would be approved of by the community. It will be exploitative if it transgresses the dominant account of sex – in this context, an idealized and romanticized account of sex. The inquiry, then, is focused not on exploitation to the perceived underdog but, rather, on safeguarding sex (as romantic, as procreative, as being about love and not business, and so on).

To define exploitation based on whether it transgresses dominant sexual morality is to demonstrate a concern for protecting the integrity of whatever understanding of sexuality underpins that morality rather than a concern for the harm caused by the exploitation of people – whether that be the exploitation of people working, singing, dancing, or having sex. What is needed, instead, is an approach that enables the law to accommodate the complexity that people engage with in relation to sexuality. The principles of harm and consent are not new concepts, and the reasoning in *Labaye* obviously will not serve as a panacea for what is a multi-faceted social issue. That said, *Labaye*, by removing the community standard of tolerance test from the definition of indecency, shifted the criminalization of sex (in terms of indecency) from a purely majoritarian democratic approach to a constitutional democratic approach. A legal definition that turns on political morality rather than on sexual morality will, where that political morality is anchored in values such as autonomy and equality, lend itself well to a constructivist approach. Under such an approach, power dynamics, the perspectives of all sexual actors involved, and other social factors contributing to the character of the sexual interaction would be considered.

A review of the lower court cases that have applied the reasoning in *Labaye* shows that focusing on harm more objectively (as dictated by the Constitution rather than by a quantitative assessment of the balance of a community's personally held sexual values) seems to create space for greater subjectivity in individual cases.[50] The result appears to be legal narratives that are less likely to construct an essentialist concept of women and sex – narratives that demonstrate some recognition of the diversity of women's experiences and perspectives as well as the social complexity (and production) of human sexuality. This may be an inevitable and hopeful outcome of shifting the law's focus towards harm and away from sexual morality.

The Ontario Court of Justice decision in *R. v. Ponomarev* provides one such example of the manner in which the *Labaye* approach results in reasoning and outcomes that are better able to accommodate sexual diversity and social context while avoiding the regulation of conduct based on dominant sexual morality.[51] Valeri Ponomarev, owner of a massage parlour, was charged with keeping a common bawdy house after an undercover police operation determined that the female employees of his establishment, in addition to providing full body massages, would also provide manual ejaculation if the client so desired. The manual ejaculation was included in the price of the massage. Justice Chisvin, relying on the definition established in *Labaye*, found that the activities occurring at Studio 176 were not indecent. This finding was based on the evidence that the sexual acts were not occurring in public but, rather, in private rooms, that the fee was forty dollars whether manual ejaculation occurred or not, and that the women employed at Studio 176 were there of their own volition, had accepted their position knowing what it entailed, and were not in any way coerced into accepting the job. Based on Justice Chisvin's account of the evidence, it is clear that these women were in control of the way in which the massage would proceed. In stark contrast to the reasoning in either *Mara* or *Tremblay*, the perspectives of all of the sexual actors involved in these activities were clearly considered by the judge in *Ponomarev*.

Defining indecency based on context, relationships, and power dynamics, rather than on a sense of sexual morality oriented towards maintaining a particular (essentialist) account of sex, is a good example of legal reasoning that conceptualizes issues of sexuality from a constructivist approach. Applying this constructivist approach to the interpretation of laws that criminalize sex work suggests promise for an area of law that, in terms of protecting the sexual integrity of sex workers, has been an unmitigated failure. Academic, political, and anecdotal evidence indicates that the current application and enforcement of provisions of the *Criminal Code* overseeing bawdy houses and communication for the purposes of prostitution make the lives of sex workers much worse.[52]

Curiously, while the exchange of sex for money is not, and has never been, a criminal offence in Canada, the activities associated with it have been criminalized. This has meant, in effect, that you are allowed to sell sex but that you cannot sell it in private and you cannot communicate in public in any way for the purposes of selling it. Purportedly, the rationale for prohibiting communication in public for the purposes of solicitation is to deal with the public nuisance assumed to be associated with selling sex on the street. As discussed later in this chapter, it is more likely that this law is motivated by sexual morality. The purported purpose of the bawdy house provisions, which criminalize sex work in the private sphere, has been less explicitly articulated. The Supreme Court of Canada did not have to address its legislative objective in *Reference re Prostitution* because the provision was not found to violate any section of the *Charter*.[53] Therefore, unlike with respect to the communication provision, it was not necessary to analyze whether a breach could be justified. Given that a single woman (or man) working as a sex worker out of their own home could be convicted of keeping a common bawdy house under the pre-*Labaye* interpretation of the law, its legislative objective is unlikely to be solely public nuisance.[54] The options left, it seems, are the prevention of harm or the protection of a particular sexual morality – a sexual morality that disapproves of commercial sex. *Labaye* adopts the former and rejects outright, and finally, the latter.

To understand the way in which a *Labaye* approach to the criminal regulation of sex work would better orient law's focus towards the protection of sexual actors, it is first necessary to examine what are the interpretive implications of *Labaye* for the bawdy house and communication provisions. Consider first the implications in the context of the bawdy house provision.

The principle underpinning Chief Justice McLachlin's approach in *Labaye* is that the criminal regulation of sex will only be legitimate where it is in furtherance of the political morality that we, as a society, have endorsed through the Constitution and not where it is deployed to sustain, or further, any particular sexual morality. *Labaye* establishes that an individual will not be guilty under the common bawdy house provisions unless the sexual activity occurring is of the sort that would cause the types of harm that are protected against by the values underpinning the Constitution. While *Labaye* dealt with the bawdy house laws within the context of indecency, there is nothing to suggest that this principle should not also apply to the interpretation of the provision with respect to the exchange of sex for money in a bawdy house.

To suggest this reasoning, of course, is to suggest that the exchange of sex for money is not, in and of itself, harmful. There are several examples, in addition to prostitution, where individuals legally make money by having sex or by paying other people to have sex. The actors or producers of pornography come immediately to mind. The owner of a bathhouse, post-*Labaye,* provides another example. Under the reasoning in *Labaye,* it is now no longer a criminal offence to own an establishment where patrons, for an entrance fee, can have sex (provided it is not harmful) with one another. The only difference between this establishment and one that is used for prostitution concerns how, and between whom, the money is exchanged. In the former, the participants that have engaged in sex have both (or all) paid money to a third party. It is consideration in exchange for the provision of a particular sexual opportunity and a location in which to carry it out. In the latter, the consideration is for the sex itself. Again, paying for sex is not illegal. Unless one resorts to moralistic assertions about the sanctity of sex, or the immorality of commercializing sexual acts themselves, then without some further associated harm there is nothing to distinguish these two circumstances. Protecting a particular sexual morality simply for the sake of itself – for example, a sexual morality that disapproves of commercial sex – is not, following *Labaye,* the type of harm to which the bawdy house provisions can be directed.

The exchange of sex for money that is done in a way that deprives others of their liberty and autonomy, predisposes others to anti-social conduct, or causes harm to one or both of the participants should continue to violate the bawdy house provisions. Such activity would include the exchange of money for sex in an establishment with unsafe working conditions, such as a lack of sufficient stage security or a refusal to provide condoms, for example. The proprietor of such a business would be guilty of violating section 210 of the *Criminal Code*. The exchange of money for sex, where the consent is more apparent than real (such as where it is due to coercion or intoxication), should also violate the bawdy house law. Obviously, the exchange of money for sexual activity that is otherwise prohibited by law would violate the bawdy house provisions, such as, for example, where there is no consent, where an animal is used, or where children might observe the sexual acts. In other words, the exchange of sex for money that would cause one of the types of harm identified in *Labaye* would be a violation of section 210. The exchange of money for harmless sex would not.

Consider now the implications of applying the approach in *Labaye* to the communication provisions. In *Reference re Prostitution,* the Supreme Court of Canada determined that the legislative objective of the communication provision is "to address solicitation in public places and, to that end, seeks to eradicate the various forms of social nuisance arising from the public display of the sale of sex."[55] Notably, the Court concluded that the legislation is not aimed at addressing the exploitation, degradation, and subordination of women nor at prohibiting prostitution itself. The purpose of the law, particularly the general prohibition on any communication in any manner regardless of whether it causes traffic congestions or obstruction of others, is to reduce the social nuisance caused by the sale of sex in public. The legislation is aimed at taking prostitution "out of public view."[56] The Court (with the exception of Justice Lamer) accepted the attorney-general's suggestion that "Parliament did not seek to suppress solicitation, but only to remove it from the public areas where it was creating the obvious harm."[57] *Labaye* modifies the way in which the law is to conceive of harm under criminal laws that impact sexual liberty. According to *Labaye,* concepts of harm in the criminal law context that are premised on sexual propriety and the protection of a particular sexual morality, rather than actual harm, are not consistent with the values underpinning the Constitution. *Labaye* should change the approach to the general communication provision (what is now section 213.1(c)) by modifying the notion of harm or social nuisance that can legitimately be targeted by the provision.

The social nuisance or harm identified in *Reference re Prostitution* as the object of the general communication provision relates to the "public sensitivities ... offended by the sight of prostitutes negotiating openly for the sale of their bodies and customers negotiating perhaps somewhat less openly for their purchase ... Neither prostitution nor solicitation is made illegal. But the high visibility of these activities is offensive and has harmful effects on those compelled to witness it, especially children."[58] The genre of harm referred to in this quotation falls under the first branch identified in *Labaye:* "the harm of public confrontation with unacceptable and inappropriate conduct."[59] However, as Chief Justice McLachlin notes in *Labaye* in the context of the bawdy house provisions, to be consistent with the values underpinning the Constitution the degree of harm contemplated by this genre is not "the aesthetic harm of a less attractive community, but the loss of autonomy and liberty that public indecency may impose on individuals in society, as they seek to avoid confrontation with acts they find offensive and unacceptable ... [and] live within a zone that is free from conduct that deeply offends them."[60] The disruption to "public sensitivities" by the mere sight of a sex worker soliciting money for sex or a john offering money for sex does not constitute the type of harm contemplated in *Labaye*. Communicating in a manner or location that would pose a deeply offensive affront to others, such as, perhaps, persistent and aggressive or overly graphic and sexualized communication or communication in or near a church or playground, would constitute the type of harm contemplated in *Labaye*. In the same way that, in *Labaye*, "the place in which acts take place and the composition of the audience will affect whether or not such acts cause the type of harm necessary to be considered indecent," so too will location and audience affect whether communication causes the type of harm necessary to violate section 213.1(c).[61]

There are two counter-arguments in response to this suggestion that should be addressed. The first argues that a distinction between public indecency laws and public nuisance laws ought to be made because the standards established in relation to public indecency are not appropriately applied to laws regarding public nuisance. The response to this argument is as follows. With respect to offences whose purpose relates to the social nuisance of, for instance, communicating in a manner that stops traffic or obstructs a pedestrian (such as are found under section 213.1(a) and (b)), this counter-argument is compelling. These offences are not directed towards protecting a particular sexual morality. (In *Reference re Prostitution*, the Supreme Court of Canada makes a distinction between the legislative objective of these provisions and that of the general prohibition against communication under section 213.1(c).) One could also argue that the types of harm addressed in sections 213.1(a) and (b) – interfering with traffic and obstructing pedestrians – constitute the types of harm incompatible with the proper functioning of society and would be covered under *Labaye*.

In terms of an offence such as section 213.1(c), whose purpose is to protect people from the social nuisance of seeing something that offends their own moral sensitivities (such as "the sight of prostitutes negotiating openly for the sale of their bodies"), the conception of harm established in *Labaye* is both valid and desirable.[62] Where the purpose of an offence is to prevent a moral affront, especially one that is related to matters of a sexual nature (given both its subjectivity and our tradition of intolerance in this area), it is appropriate to measure harm based on the standards established in *Labaye.* As Chief Justice McLachlin notes, "tolerance requires that only serious and deeply offensive moral assaults can be kept from public view on pain of criminal sanction."[63] Tolerance, after all, is a key ingredient to the healthy functioning of a liberal democracy.

The second counter-argument is that to consider the general communication provision as only prohibiting communication that confronts the public in a way that threatens the loss of autonomy and liberty to others – that is to say, harmful communication – will not adequately address the harm that the provision was meant to protect against – namely the social nuisance that arises when a number of sex workers tend to all work in the same area. In other words, the social nuisance to be addressed is that which is caused when a particular location becomes a stroll area. To some extent, this objection is correct. Nevertheless, the reasoning in *Labaye* suggests that objecting to the fact of a stroll area itself is not a legitimate criminal law purpose. Further, this approach will reduce some of the social nuisance caused by stroll areas by continuing to criminalize the more egregious conduct. The existence of a stroll area and the aesthetic affront experienced by some individuals by the mere sight of a sex worker plying her trade, like the fact that a particular neighbourhood might contain one or more bawdy houses, is not something that ought to be targeted by the criminal law, unless there is some associated harm of the sort contemplated in *Labaye*. Again, *Labaye* establishes that only "deeply offensive moral assaults can be kept from public view on pain of criminal sanction."[64] It does so on the basis that, in a liberal democracy, the force of the criminal law ought not to be brought down upon any one person or group merely to protect some from the thought that other Canadians are having group sex. In the same way, its force should not be deployed merely to sanitize and mask for others the reality that some (perhaps for survival, perhaps for prosperity, or perhaps due to the systemic, entrenched, and gendered disparity in economic opportunity that is existent in Canada) choose, or are compelled, to sell sex.

So why would an approach to the criminal laws regulating prostitution that does not rely on a community standard of tolerance promote legal reasoning that is better suited to protecting those sexual actors typically impacted by sex work laws? Reflecting upon the implications of *Labaye* for the common bawdy house laws and the communication law, it quickly becomes evident that most of the activities that would continue to be criminalized involve charges against johns and pimps and not against sex workers. Most likely, charges against sex workers would arise only when their conduct is actually causing a disturbance. A harm-based approach in which harm is measured against the values of the Constitution, not the community, would mean that the bar owner who coerces women into doing live sex shows should still be guilty of keeping a common bawdy house, as should the owner of a "brothel" who fails to provide security or condoms. It would mean that the john who solicits sex in exchange for money from an obviously intoxicated street worker whose consent would be "more apparent than real" should be guilty of communicating for the purposes of prostitution, as should the seriously intoxicated street worker who is aggressively propositioning passersby.

However, it would also mean that the woman who runs a sex trade out of her home should no longer be the target of the criminal law, nor should the boyfriend who lives with her. It would mean that the street worker who takes the time to properly interview a john so as to ensure her safety before climbing into a vehicle with him would not be committing a criminal offence by doing so. It would mean that neither the "massage therapist," nor the owner of Studio 176 in *Ponomarev,* would be the target of the criminal law and nor would the private dancers in adult clubs. As noted, Chief Justice McLachlin's approach in *Labaye* suggests that the criminal regulation of sex will only be legitimate where it is in furtherance of the political morality that we, as a society, have endorsed and not where it is deployed to sustain, or further, any particular sexual morality. This distinction recognizes the significance of sexual autonomy. In doing so, it permits greater space for sexual narratives that have not always been heard by the law. The Supreme Court of Canada's approach in *Labaye* is consistent with Canada's liberal democracy and the values underpinning the Constitution.

Conclusion

The Supreme Court of Canada has, in its approach to the criminal regulation of obscenity and indecency, shifted towards a more constructivist conception of sexual violence. This is a conception, as was the case with changes to sexual assault law, that better accommodates the social factors through which sexual violence is constituted. In the context of sexual assault, it has meant revisions to the meaning of sexual assault and the meaning of consent that better incorporate the perspective of all sexual actors involved. In the context of obscenity and indecency, it has meant a shift from sexual morality to political morality. In both, the result is a greater focus on sexual actors and on their sexual integrity.

Some Subjective Truths about the Objective Truth of Sex

6

> The fundamental proposition of feminism, that the personal is political, urges the displacement of all such oppositional terms, the crossing and recharting of the space between them.
>
> – TERESA DE LAURETIS

The invocation of a sexual morality concerned with sex itself is problematic. It is particularly problematic for women. This is one reason why the Supreme Court of Canada's shift towards a more constructivist understanding of sexual violence is promising. However, this feminist-inspired shift has not eliminated sexual morality-based legal reasoning. Following *R. v. Butler*, but before *R. v. Labaye* had been decided, sexual moralism, as manifested through the community standard of tolerance test, was still a part of the Court's analysis in cases involving the criminal regulation of sex work, indecency, and obscenity.[1] The reasoning in cases such as *R. v. Tremblay*, *R. v. Mara*, and *Reference re Prostitution*, discussed in the previous chapter, supported this assertion.[2] Despite the fact that during this era legal reasoning had begun to reflect aspects of the conception of sexuality suggested by feminist legal scholars, the Court's decisions persisted in perpetuating a construction of sexuality that was moralistic, at times paternalistic, and that failed to fully recognize women's sexual integrity. Unfortunately, legal approaches that incorporate a social constructivist understanding of sexual violence into a broader conceptual framework which continues to understand sexuality from a perspective imbued with sexual morality, produce problematic decisions of this type. Such results are exemplified by the majority opinion in *Norberg v. Wynrib* as well as by the decision in *Little Sisters Book and Art Emporium v. Canada (Minister of Justice)*.[3]

Desiring the Drug, Not the Doc

Norberg, a civil case involving a thirty-three-year-old woman who sued her eighty-year-old male doctor for negligence, battery, and breach of fiduciary duty, was considered a victory by feminists. It was heralded as "a milestone in the legal history of sexual abuse litigation."[4] As in *Butler*, the Women's Legal Education and Action Fund (LEAF) also intervened in this case, and, also as in *Butler*, the majority of the Supreme Court of Canada again conceptualized the sexual interactions involved through a framework of equality. They embraced concepts such as power imbalance, trust, and unconscionability to characterize the sexual relationship between the litigants.

In her early twenties, Laura Norberg became addicted to painkillers after recovering from a dental problem. Using a variety of pretexts, she obtained prescriptions for painkillers from Dr. Wynrib, an elderly medical practitioner, for some period of time until finally admitting that she was addicted to the drugs that he had been prescribing. Upon this admission, he advised her that if she was "good to him he would be good to her" and pointed upstairs to his apartment. On several occasions over the course of the following year, Norberg would allow Wynrib to fondle her and simulate intercourse with her in exchange for prescriptions. After a time, she told him that she needed help with her addiction. Instead of helping her, he advised her to "just quit."[5] Norberg eventually attended a rehabilitation centre on her own initiative and was able to resolve her addiction. She later sued Wynrib for sexual battery, negligence, breach of fiduciary duty, and breach of contract.

At trial, she admitted that she had played on the fact that he liked her in order to get drugs and that she knew throughout the relationship that he was lonely. On appeal to the Supreme Court of Canada, all members of the Court found for Ms. Norberg but on the basis of different causes of action. Justice La Forest, writing for the majority, found liability on the grounds of sexual battery. For Justice La Forest, the issue was one of consent and whether it was vitiated by Wynrib's conduct. For Justice McLachlin (as she then was), the fact that Norberg consented was irrelevant – Dr. Wynrib breached his fiduciary duty and was liable on that basis. The tort of battery consists of the intentional touching of one person by another if that touch was not consensual. Even if consent to the touch was explicitly or implicitly provided, such consent will be vitiated if it is obtained through force, the threat of force, through fraud or deceit, or if it is given under the influence of drugs.

Norberg agreed to participate in the sexual acts at issue in exchange for drugs. There was no physical force perpetrated or threatened by Wynrib, nor was Norberg found to be under the influence of the drugs to which she was addicted when her consent was provided. Justice La Forest found that, in the circumstances, the factors vitiating the consent defence should not be limited to these:

> In my view, this approach to consent in this kind of case is too limited ... "A man cannot be said to be 'willing' unless he is in a position to choose freely; and freedom of choice predicates the absence from his mind of any feeling of constraint interfering with the freedom of his will." A "feeling of constraint" so as to "interfere with the freedom of a person's will" can arise in a number of situations not involving force, threats of force, fraud or incapacity ... A position of relative weakness can, in some circumstances, interfere with the freedom of a person's will. *Our notion of consent must, therefore, be modified to appreciate the power relationship between the parties.*[6]

This is a significant finding. It is a recognition of the basic claim that sex is about power and that, as such, an inquiry into the power dynamics at play is required to accurately assess the authenticity of consent given in a particular sexual encounter. This finding is promising. Where Justice La Forest's reasoning becomes problematic is in how he structures this inquiry into the power dynamics at issue.

Justice La Forest based his decision on principles of unconscionability and inequality of bargaining position, as borrowed from the law of contract. He determined that in circumstances where two parties to a sexual encounter are not of equal bargaining position, and where the sexual relationship is exploitative, consent is vitiated. Exploitation, he determined, will be established based on community standards. He notes that contracts involving unequal parties will be considered exploitative where the transaction is sufficiently divergent from the community standards of commercial morality.[7] Drawing a direct analogy to sexual battery in the next sentence, he suggests that "if the type of sexual relationship at issue is one that is sufficiently divergent from community standards of conduct, this may alert the court to the possibility of exploitation."[8] While he does not actually specify that it is community standards of sexual morality to which he is referring, it is difficult to imagine that he is referring to anything else. In particular, this direct analogy to commercial morality and his finding that the sexual relationship in this case is exploitive because the community would find it "disgraceful" and "sordid" suggest that this is the case.[9]

Justice La Forest found that Wynrib's medical knowledge, combined with his knowledge of Norberg's drug addiction and his ability to prescribe drugs, gave him power over her. He also found, as noted, that because the community (and the medical profession) would consider the sexual conduct "disgraceful" and "sordid," the relationship was exploitive. As such, he determined that Dr. Wynrib had committed sexual battery – that is to say, the sexual relationship between the parties was not consensual under tort law. Unfortunately, despite his acknowledgment of the power dynamics at play in a sexual relationship of this sort, Justice La Forest's decision recognized the importance of protecting women's sexual integrity while simultaneously undermining it. There are three significant and interrelated difficulties with his reasoning: (1) by analogizing the sexual relationship between the parties to a contract and then using principles of contract law to develop his reasoning, he obscures the complexity of sex and ignores the important element of affectivity; (2) by concluding that the sexual relationship between the parties was non-consensual, he denies recognition of the very autonomy he is attempting to recognize;[10] and (3) by relying upon community standards of tolerance to determine whether or not a sexual relationship is exploitative, his reasoning is unduly moralistic.

Attempting to apply the principles of contract law, and the reasoning underpinning these principles, to a sexual interaction results in an account of sex that is moralistic and not reflective of many women's sexual realities. As Justice McLachlin notes in her concurrence, the doctrines of tort and contract do not "capture the essential nature of the wrong done to the plaintiff ... [T]o look at the events which occurred over the course of the relationship between Dr. Wynrib and Ms. Norberg from the perspective of tort or contract is to view that relationship through lenses which distort more than they bring into focus."[11] Justice La Forest's analogy to contract law and relationships involving an inequality of bargaining power conceals the complexity and nuance that sex can entail. Contract law, Justice La Forest notes, has developed doctrine to ensure that where contracting parties do not share equal bargaining authority the "weaker" party will be protected. As he explains, "[t]he doctrines of duress, undue influence, and unconscionability have arisen to protect the vulnerable when they are in a relationship of unequal power. For reasons of public policy, the law will not always hold weaker parties to the bargains they make."[12] He goes on to suggest that this same notion of unconscionability should be applied in the context of sexual battery.

The problem is that the rules, social mores, types of communication, criteria for evaluation, intent of the parties, social attitudes, law, interpersonal dynamics, and power imbalances involved in negotiating a sexual encounter are often different from those involved when negotiating for other things. Moreover, complex relationships involving not easily discernible, let alone easily dissected, power imbalances are likely the norm and not the exception when it comes to sexual interactions. Think, for example, of a stay-at-home mother of three who is financially and socially dependent on her husband or think about an unpopular high school girl in the back seat of the captain of the hockey team's car. Nor is gender the only salient factor implicated in these imbalances. Consider a young woman having sex with another much more experienced woman for the first time, a middle-aged gay man having sex with a much younger and more attractive man, or think about a desperately in love man negotiating sex with a girlfriend he knows is having an affair. Perhaps think about a sex worker charging $1,500 to spend the night with a lonely and sexually disabled client, then think about the drug-addicted sex worker charging $20.00 to give a blow job to a drunk college student. While it may well be possible to identify a balanced contractual relationship in other contexts, and instantiate through doctrine a determinate set of rules to govern these relationships, attempts to do so in the context of sexuality seem less plausible. Sex, even when it is not dirty, is quite often messy.

There is also something disingenuous about Justice La Forest's approach. At one point in his analysis, he indicates that "the community" would find the exchange of sex for drugs "sordid" and "disgusting." One wonders what trades – outside of love, commitment, or mutual orgasm – the community he draws on would not find to be exploitative? Adopted in its entirety, his position exposes a great number of sexual actors to tortious liability for sexual battery. This is not to suggest that the issue of power imbalances in sexual relationships is not important to the legal regulation of sex or the concept of consent. Nor obviously, is it to suggest that there cannot be legally enforced rules regulating sexual conduct in a society. Rather, it is to suggest that Justice La Forest's analysis is not a particularly helpful way to approach the issue. It is difficult to imagine a sexual interaction in which the parties are in completely the same position with respect to one another – that is to say, in which the exchange is purely an exchange of sexual goods.

Donald Dripps argues that there is, in fact, no possibility of true parallel mutuality (of this type) in sexual interactions. There is nothing to suggest, he argues, that the experience of sex for women is categorically similar to the experience of sex for men, let alone the experience of sex for any given woman or any given man: "Whether one cites feminist theorists or the judgment of Tiresius, there is no reason to believe that the exchange of a male orgasm for a female orgasm is any more symmetrical than the exchange of orgasms for money, affection, or security."[13] The hypothetical sexual scenario that he suggests most closely approximates true mutuality would be the situation of two men, unknown to each other, who have anonymous sex, no strings attached, in a bathhouse. However, he goes on to point out that, "[e]ven the bathhouse encounter is not the product of justly distributed erotic assets."[14] Even it, he argues, is constrained: "[T]he participants may diet or exercise but fundamental aspects of their bodies are unchangeable. One of them must be more attractive, or more eager for sex, or know more about the possibility of doing better by waiting, than the other."[15]

Justice La Forest's approach, by attempting to vitiate the consent that Norberg "undoubtedly gave," suggests an attempt to avoid the messy acknowledgment that sex is often, if not always, about more than the equal exchange of erotic experiences.[16] Unfortunately, to ignore this messiness is to embrace a conception of sexuality that is simplistic and that ignores both the insights of Tiresius and the lived realities of many sexual actors. While Justice La Forest's approach is consistent with radical feminist arguments – Catharine MacKinnon argues that "consent in sex ... is supposed to mean freedom of desire expressed, not compensation for services rendered"[17] – he, like MacKinnon, relies on an assumption that is at best questionable.

Why should we assume such a constricted conception of consent? Is consent really always about sexual desire? Sometimes people trade sex for drugs, money, or a warm place to sleep, especially when they are hard up for drugs, money, or a warm place to sleep. Laura Norberg was hard up for drugs. She traded some sex for drugs. As Justice McLachlin suggests, there is no doubt that she consented to the sexual activity. To engage in reasoning that attempts to show otherwise really just muddies what are already nasty waters. As Justice McLachlin notes,

> [t]ort and contract can provide a remedy for a physician's failure to provide adequate treatment. But only with considerable difficulty can they be bent to accommodate the wrong of a physician's abusing his or her position to obtain sexual favours from his or her patient. The law has never recognized consensual sexual relations as capable of giving rise to an obligation in tort or in contract. My colleagues, with respect, strain to conclude the contrary.[18]

Justice La Forest's conclusion that Norberg's consent was vitiated because her desire was for the drug, not the doc, can be directly correlated with an idealistic and moralistic account of female sexuality and sexual innocence – an account that unfortunately dichotomizes women into victims and whores, tending to protect the former and ignore, if not punish, the latter.[19] In order to address the sexual wrong that most certainly occurred in this case, without facing the perhaps not so nice fact that people sometimes trade sex for drugs, Justice La Forest constructed a woman without any sexual agency because of her less-than-ideal circumstances. Sexual agency must be an essential element of sexual integrity.

The moral implications of his reasoning are evidenced by what he identifies as the determining factor: the fact that Wynrib and not Norberg initiated the sexual exchange: "It seems to me that the determining factor in this case is that he instigated the relationship – it was he, not the appellant, who used his power and knowledge to initiate the arrangement and to exploit her vulnerability."[20] By this statement, Justice La Forest establishes a legal remedy precariously contingent on Norberg's relative sexual innocence. Under Justice La Forest's reasoning, if Laura Norberg had been the one to suggest the sex for drugs arrangement, this same doctor who undoubtedly took gross advantage of his drug-addicted patient would have escaped liability.

Alternatively, Justice McLachlin was able to acknowledge the sexual wrong and provide a remedy without denying Norberg's capacity for sexual agency or perpetuating the victim and the whore dichotomy. Under Justice McLachlin's reasoning (a finding of breach of fiduciary duty), Norberg can be a woman who traded her doctor some sex for drugs and still be entitled to compensation.[21] In order to make this finding, Justice McLachlin had to acknowledge the perhaps less-than-pleasant reality that Norberg chose to trade sex for drugs. Justice McLachlin did not question the fact that Wynrib took advantage of Norberg (and that because he did so in his capacity as a doctor he was liable), but nor did she question Norberg's sexual autonomy by suggesting that she did not have the capacity to consent.

Under Justice La Forest's reasoning, it is still necessary to inquire into the cleanliness of the claimant's hands. Had he been unable to vitiate her own sexual naughtiness, under his consent analysis he would have had to bar recovery pursuant to the doctrine of tort law which requires that claimants not rely on a claim arising in connection with their own wrongful conduct – thus, his "determining factor." Conversely, Justice McLachlin rejects outright the relevance of moral assessments regarding Norberg's sexual conduct:

> It matters not that she walked into his office in an attempt to obtain drugs to which she was addicted. Even if that purpose had not been merely symptomatic of her illness, but in some sense immoral, Dr. Wynrib's conduct in exploiting her dependency for his own ends would have in any event constituted a breach of that aspect of his fiduciary obligation enshrined, thousands of years ago, in the words of the Hippocratic Oath.[22]

The final difficulty with Justice La Forest's reasoning is his reliance on community standards to determine whether a relationship is exploitative. What does it mean to suggest that the question of whether a sexual encounter is considered exploitative depends on the community standards of morality? Why would a determination of exploitation turn on whether or not the community would consider the sexual conduct to be "sordid" and "disgraceful"? Taking into consideration the need to protect the sexual integrity of all sexual actors in a community, and the desire to protect all sexual actors from sexual harm, contrast his analysis with the harm-based approach adopted by Chief Justice McLachlin in *Labaye.*[23]

His reliance on community standards of tolerance to ascertain whether a sexual encounter is exploitative creates the possibility for a sexual morality driven inequality in the treatment of claimants. Those individuals whose sexual choices do not jive well with the sexual mores of the majority (such as, perhaps, sex workers) and those whose relationships of inequality are so entrenched in the social subconscious of dominant society that "the community" would not recognize the relationship as sexually exploitative (such as, perhaps, women in traditionally gendered marriages), will be treated differently from other claimants on the basis of sexual morality assessments regarding the nature of the relationship. Legal determinations as to which sexual interactions are exploitative and which are not should not be based on assessments as to what the majority of Canadians supposedly find sordid or disgusting.

It is not that sexual relationships of the types just suggested necessarily should be treated the same as doctor-patient – or other special dependency type – relationships. It is that if they are to be considered different under the law, the reason for the distinction ought not to be based on sexual morality. There is something deeply problematic about a legal standard for consent to sexual contact that is dependent upon a community standard of tolerance approach rather than a harm-based approach. It is the sort of reasoning that engenders discriminatory laws such as a higher age of consent for anal intercourse than for vaginal intercourse under the *Criminal Code*, a historical definition of rape that denies a wife the legal ability (under the criminal law) to refuse sexual intercourse with her husband, or, for that matter, the problematic application of the mistaken belief in consent defence to sexual assault in cases where the accused was the spouse of the complainant at the time of the offence.[24]

In the end, the manner in which Justice La Forest incorporates the ideals of radical feminism into his reasoning results in an analysis that is disempowering for some women. Theoretical approaches that make claims of objective truth regarding sexuality lend themselves to Justice La Forest's reasoning. If sexuality is always a function of unidirectional power imbalances perpetuated by systemic male dominance, it makes sense to suggest that Norberg did not have the capacity to consent. It makes sense for the same reasons that MacKinnon's theory questions the possibility that women in a sexist society can ever truly consent to sex with men.

Justice McLachlin's reasoning, by contrast, does not deny women's sexual autonomy. It does not refute Norberg's sexual agency. Under her breach of fiduciary duty analysis, Norberg's capacity to consent, as a drug-addicted woman, is affirmed. Justice McLachlin acknowledges that Norberg consented to the sexual contact. She also acknowledges that Norberg consented to the doctor-patient relationship and that she voluntarily gave power in the context of this very specific relationship. The imbalance, then, stems from her status as a patient – a status that men also hold – and not her status as a woman (or a drug addict). In fiduciary relationships, "the relation may expose the entrustor to risk even if he is sophisticated, informed and able to bargain effectively. Rather, the entrustor's vulnerability stems from the *structure* and *nature* of the fiduciary relation."[25]

The Supreme Court of Canada should recognize the fact of inequality of bargaining positions in sex. It was prudent to recognize the power imbalance that exists between a patient and a doctor. It is one thing to attach duties (and corresponding liabilities) to a specific social arrangement (such as a doctor-patient relationship), which is what Justice McLachlin does in this case. It is quite another to liken sexual interactions to contracts and then attempt to regulate them through the legal principles developed to regulate contracts. The latter, as discussed earlier, results in an idealized (and essentialist) notion of sexuality and legal reasoning based on sexual morality – reasoning that does not protect the interests of many women and that, at an analytical level, denies sexual autonomy, thus threatening, rather than protecting, the community's interest in the promotion of sexual integrity.

The differing approaches adopted by Justice La Forest and Justice McLachlin in this case raise another issue that should be addressed in this discussion. This is the issue of consent generally. The decisions in *Norberg* give some indication as to why the concept of consent cannot, alone, provide a sufficient legal theory of sexuality. A theory of sexual justice that relies solely on the concept of consent asks too much of consent. Certainly, a robust notion of consent is key to pursuing any theory of sexual justice. Nevertheless, there are sexual circumstances, interactions, and relationships that may require the law's attention, but for which a theory based solely on consent is not a sufficient tool. Justice La Forest's decision, on the one hand, reveals the limits of relying upon consent as the sole criterion by which to distinguish good sex from bad sex – doing so can paternalistically undermine the autonomy that the concept of consent is intended to protect. Justice McLachlin's reasoning, on the other hand, does not rely solely on the concept of consent. She also invokes the concept of duty. This invocation unavoidably incorporates the notion of relationship.

There are legal circumstances where even a fulsome notion of consent – such as a concept of informed consent or a relational theory of consent – may not be enough. Think, for example, of cases involving sex workers whose clients refuse to pay them after services have been rendered. It seems insufficiently cognizant of the sex worker's sexual integrity to characterize an interaction of this sort as merely a breach of contract. However, it is also not compelling to characterize it as non-consensual sex. To do so requires a legal fiction – vitiating consent post-sexual interaction. Admittedly, in some circumstances, the law does do this for policy reasons.[26] But what would be the policy justification for vitiating consent in this case – an effort to discourage post-coitus dishonesty? Surely, such a policy would cast the law's net too far.

Even a relational, contextualized account of consent is a dyadic concept. It is either present or it is not present. A concept of sexual integrity as a common interest is broader and more multi-faceted. While what should count as legitimate consent can and should be contested, just as the content of, and conditions for, sexual integrity can and should be contested, the former is bound by the confines of a binary episteme, while the latter is not. The notion of informed consent (which has difficulties of its own with respect to the legal regulation of sexuality) is probably the closest consent can come to approximating the breadth that might be accommodated by a notion of sexual integrity as a common interest. However, even reliance on a concept of informed consent would not actually avoid the sexual morality-based reasoning that is evident in Justice La Forest's reasoning, nor could it readily accommodate multi-dimensional factors such as certain duties (like those identified by Justice McLachlin in *Norberg*) and responsibilities (like the non-paying john or perhaps positive obligations placed on the government to promote shared goods such as sexual literacy). There are certain relational interests, such as duties and sexual literacy, that cannot be captured by the concept of consent.

It is important to develop a legal account of consent that recognizes its constructed character and the importance of relationships in how we define it. Legal approaches to consent should be informed by a concept of consent that recognizes the ways in which power, relationships, and norms produce perceptions of what constitutes consent and how and by whom it is given. However, theories of sexual justice that rely on panacean accounts of consent expect too much of it. A better approach is to recognize (while continuing to interrogate) the concept of consent as a necessary, but not sufficient, condition for the promotion of sexual integrity. Returning, then, to the relationship between law and sexual morality, Justice La Forest's reasoning reveals how a legal approach can incorporate a feminist perspective but continue to rely on sexual morality based reasoning. His decision also reveals the shortcomings of such an approach. The same types of shortcomings are revealed by the Supreme Court of Canada's decision in *Little Sisters.*

Taking Porn out of Context

The Supreme Court of Canada's decision in *Butler* was not well received among gay and lesbian activists and theorists.[27] Their fear was that *Butler*'s injection of the harm principle into the definition of obscenity would do nothing to prevent the discriminatory censorship of lesbian and gay erotic and pornographic materials. It turned out to be a well-founded fear. Unfortunately, as the post-*Butler* experience of businesses such as Little Sisters Book and Art Emporium in Vancouver and Glad Day Books in Toronto have demonstrated, lower courts have had no difficulty in finding that even the tamest lesbian and gay pornography does not pass the harm-based community standard of tolerance test established in *Butler.* Nor has the *Butler* test done anything to dissuade customs officials from continuing to target material imported by bookstores serving the queer community.

Recall that LEAF's argument in *Butler* was informed by MacKinnon's theory that the inequality between men and women is itself sexualized. LEAF's intervention was, of course, motivated by the individual and societal inequalities that exist between men and women. Its argument constituted a feminist analysis of pornography in which pornography, by depicting sexual violence against women, perpetuates such violence through its reinforcement of the male-female gender hierarchy. In *Butler,* Justice Sopinka's application of these ideas regarding the harm caused by pornography clearly reflected the incorporation of this feminist analysis:

> [T]here is a substantial body of opinion that holds that the portrayal of persons being subjected to degrading and dehumanizing sexual treatment results in harm, particularly to women and therefore to society as a whole ... Harm in this context means that it predisposes persons to act in an anti-social manner as, for example, the physical or mental mistreatment of women by men, or what is perhaps debatable, the reverse.[28]

Little Sisters involved a constitutional challenge to the *Butler* definition of obscenity. Little Sisters argued that the test had a discriminatory impact on sexual minorities. Justice Binnie denied the claim on the basis that the "portrayal of a dominatrix engaged in the non-violent degradation of an ostensibly willing sex slave is no less dehumanizing if the victim happens to be of the same sex, and no less (and no more) harmful in its reassurance to the viewer that the victim finds such conduct both normal and pleasurable."[29]

Why is it no less dehumanizing and, more importantly, why is it no less harmful? Is Justice Binnie's analysis in *Little Sisters* a gendered one? Does it invoke the same contextual factors at play in Justice Sopinka's feminist-influenced *Butler* decision? All of which is to ask, what harm is the Supreme Court of Canada concerned with preventing in *Little Sisters*? Is it the harm caused by the systemic hierarchical relationship between men and women and the manner in which the portrayal of sexual violence perpetuates this hierarchy and, thus, a particular social construction of gender relations and identity (as the Court accepted in *Butler*)? Alternatively, is it the potential increase in sexual violence in the gay and lesbian community perpetuated by those gays and lesbians exposed to the "portrayal of a dominatrix engaged in the non-violent degradation of an ostensibly willing [same sex] sex slave"?

Assume that the concern was with the way in which the portrayal of sexual violence perpetuates gender hierarchy. Here, the argument would be that while gay and lesbian pornography does not depict the sexual subjugation of women, it does portray the sexual subjugation of the feminine subject and that this portrayal also perpetuates attitudes of a sexualized inequality between men and women that manifests as sexual violence. A number of essentialist assumptions about sex underlie this argument. It assumes that there are feminine sexual acts and masculine sexual acts – that is to say, that men penetrate and women are penetrated or, as MacKinnon would say, man fucks woman – subject verb object.[30] The assertion would be that masculine fucks feminine. This reasoning is unavoidably heterosexist. As Bruce MacDougall notes, "domination of one gender by another is not a principal concern of gay and lesbian pornography ... Gay men for instance who are getting fucked should not be thought of as women or as representing another gender from the man who is fucking."[31] In other words, it is not masculine fucks feminine. It is man fucks man, and it is heterosexist and essentialist to superimpose upon it, or interpret it through, a male/female heterosexual paradigm.

This heterosexist reading of gay pornography was favoured by the feminist organization Equality Now, which intervened in support of the government.[32] Justice Binnie's reasoning suggests, however, that this perspective was not what he relied upon to deny Little Sisters' constitutional challenge to the *Butler* definition of obscenity as applied to gays and lesbians. Instead, he focused on the alleged harm to gays and lesbians posed by a potential increase in sexual violence in the gay and lesbian community perpetuated by those gays and lesbians exposed to sado-masochistic pornography. This is evidenced by his reliance on empirical research suggesting that the incidence of sexual violence in gay and lesbian communities equals that in heterosexual communities and by his statement that gays and lesbians are also deserving of protection against sexual violence.[33] His concern, it seems, was with how gay pornography might produce gay sexual violence.

Justice Binnie gave the following response to LEAF's argument that same sex sado-masochistic pornography is different from heterosexual sado-masochistic pornography and that the *Butler* definition fails to recognize this difference: "[V]iolence against women was only one of several concerns, albeit an important one, that led to the formulation of the *Butler* harm-based test, which itself is gender neutral."[34] This declaration that the *Butler* test is gender neutral is significant. Justice Binnie's definition of obscenity and application of the *Butler* test in *Little Sisters* assumes that gay and lesbian individuals who view sado-masochistic pornography are at risk of developing an orientation towards violent sex. *Butler* involved an equality analysis. It situated heterosexual pornography in a specific social context – a context of systemic sex and gender hierarchy. In *Butler*, the Supreme Court of Canada adopted the feminist assertion that degrading and dehumanizing depictions of women would perpetuate and sustain inequality between men and women – that such depictions would encourage sexist and misogynistic attitudes by men towards women and that such depictions risked inducing some men to behave in a sexually violent manner towards women.

Little Sisters adopts both the finding in *Butler* that pornography can induce violent anti-social behaviour and its underpinning assumption that a desire for sexual violence is socially contingent. It leaves behind, however, the contextual analysis in which the *Butler* reasoning was situated. In other words, it leaves behind the analysis of the overarching systemic gender hierarchy in which this constructivist assumption about sexual violence was originally adopted by the Supreme Court of Canada. To determine that viewing images of sexual violence perpetrated against women will, in a society systemically structured through sexuality as a gender hierarchy, influence sexual norms such that more men are oriented towards sexually aggressive behaviour directed at women suggests a socially contingent conception of sexual violence. To determine that viewing images of sexual violence will, regardless of the broader social context, promote violent sexual tendencies fails to fully account for the social contingency of sexual violence.

Contrary to Justice Binnie's position or LEAF's position, the approach to obscenity found in *Butler* should be considered neither gender neutral nor inherently gendered. The depiction of sexual aggression, sexual dominance, even sexual coercion by one muscular, hyper-masculine white man over another hyper-masculine white man should, under a constructivist conception of sexual violence, perhaps be treated differently by harm-based obscenity laws than the depiction of sexual aggression between two men, one of whom is disabled, obviously racialized, or a prisoner of war while the other is a US marine. (Asserting, without equivocation, that this is actually the case with respect to any of these examples would require further examination. The point is that an assessment of the potential harm of a sexual depiction should always be socially situated.) It is not that gay or lesbian pornography should be exempt from laws regulating obscenity. It is not that same sex depictions of dominance or degradation never pose the type of harm the Supreme Court of Canada attributed to heterosexual depictions of male-over-female sexual aggression and sexual dominance in *Butler*. It is that, if the law defines obscenity through principles of harm on the basis that sexual conduct is socially contingent, then the law in determining that harm must give recognition to the particularity of the social context from which it arises. I am not adopting LEAF's argument in *Little Sisters* that gay and lesbian pornography is just different than straight pornography.[35] I am arguing that for all pornography the broader social context in which the depictions are produced and viewed should be fully incorporated into the harm-based analysis.

Take, for example, the argument that even pornographic depictions that do not depict violence still result in the objectification of those filmed or photographed and that as such they are also harmful to society. Unless the law assumes that sexual objectification is, in and of itself, harmful – an argument that relies on sexual morality and an interest in protecting sex itself – then to assess potential harmful impact, the law must consider who is being objectified and by whom and in what social context. Perhaps, as some would argue, the sexual objectification of women is always harmful. However, if this is true, it is not because objectification is, in and of itself, inherently harmful. It is because it is harmful to objectify, through pornography, a category of people who have been oppressed and dominated in large measure by being treated as sexual objects.

Why is, as Justice Binnie suggests, the "portrayal of a dominatrix engaged in the non-violent degradation of an ostensibly willing sex slave ... no less dehumanizing if the victim happens to be of the same sex"?[36] It is only no less dehumanizing if the source of the dehumanization is purely the sexual degradation itself – that is to say, if there is some inherent harm, some essential aspect of the consensual sexual degradation itself, that makes it dehumanizing. The difficulty with the Supreme Court of Canada's approach in *Little Sisters* is not its conception of sexual violence as socially contingent. Nor is the problem the Court's continued reliance on the principle of harm established in *Butler.* The problem is its failure to fully appreciate the concept of sexual violence as socially contingent. It is a failure that, in the context of same sex pornography, results in a definition, the moral focus of which remains on protecting a particular account of sex (an account that can never involve boots, whips, and leather bustiers, let alone nipple clamps, orgasm denial, and rape fantasy). This is a circumstance that inevitably directs the law's attention towards propriety and away from integrity – an analysis that radical feminism lends itself to, despite its attempts to do otherwise. It is an approach that leaves the door wide open for discrimination on the part of homophobic customs officials and heterosexist adjudicators. It is a legal analysis that, like Justice La Forest's decision in *Norberg,* demonstrates the consequence of adopting a conception of sexuality as socially constructed within a conceptual framework that continues to rely on sexual morality in order to maintain a particular account of sex itself.

Just as the claim that the exchange of sex for money, security, or status can never constitute real consent fails to sufficiently contextualize sexual interactions, so too does a claim that sexual objectification or sexual degradation is inherently harmful. A failure to fully contextualize sexual interactions results in a conception of sexual violence as being only in part socially constructed. If sexual violence is only in part a function of context, then it must also be in part a function of some element inherent in the individuals who perpetuate it. That is to say, there must be something essential about it. Essentialist assumptions about sex – being that they are essentialist – tend to assume a particular account of sexuality. A particular account of sexuality suggests a particular sexual morality. As suggested in Chapter 5 of this volume, laws oriented towards protecting a particular sexual morality tend to focus more on sexual acts than on sexual actors. This is a tendency that does not promote further inquiry into the social factors, relationships, and power dynamics that constitute sexual norms, orientations, and behaviours. It is self-perpetuating. Essentialist conceptions promote essentialist conceptions.

Recall that the notion of sexual integrity articulated in Chapter 4 in this volume included not only freedom from sexual violation – in other words, the freedom to say no – but also the "conditions for" a community of sexual actors with the capacity for sexual integrity. These conditions would include a broad but not unrestrained freedom to say yes. Cases such as *Little Sisters* and *Norberg,* as well as cases such as *Mara, Tremblay,* and *Reference re Prostitution* discussed in the previous chapter, demonstrate how a constructivist conception of sexual violence that remains rooted in sexual morality does not sufficiently protect this particular aspect of sexual autonomy (and thus sexual integrity as a whole).

Just as the liberty interest in the freedom to say no should be steadfastly protected, legal conceptions of sexuality must also recognize the important interest in the ability, and freedom, to say yes. That said, the "conditions for" sexual integrity cannot be reduced only to notions of sexual liberty – whether that be the freedom to say no or the freedom to say yes. There should be something more to the notion of integrity. Integrity includes the quality of being principled. To have sexual integrity requires sexual principles – to have sexual principles is to make distinctions between good sex and bad sex. As demonstrated in *Labaye*, this determination can be done based on sexual morality (first-person ethics) or political morality (third-person ethics).

Drawing Moral Distinctions

An Ontario Court of Appeal decision from 1999 reveals how legal reasoning based on political morality can articulate limits on sexual autonomy and still be conducive to promoting the "conditions for" sexual integrity – including the production of a community of sexual actors with the capacity for lived sexualities that promote sexual integrity as a social good. *R. v. B.E.* dealt with an appeal from the conviction of a father for "participating in sexual immorality thereby endangering the morals" of his children under section 172 of the *Criminal Code*.[37] The Crown in *B.E.* argued that placing sexually explicit advertisements in newspapers, engaging in group sex, possessing sexually suggestive photos, pornographic videos, vibrators, and "other sexual devices," videotaping sexual acts with one's spouse, and participating in "lesbian sexual activity" constituted "immoral sexual activity" for the purposes of section 172.[38] With the exception of the evidence that one of the children was either present when the appellant and his wife videotaped him masturbating and ejaculating on her or that the child had seen the videotape, there was no evidence (or allegation) that any of the supposed "sexual immorality" occurred with, or in front of, the children. The trial judge failed to draw a distinction between labelling conduct sexually immoral such that it endangers the morals of a child where the child is involved in some way in the conduct – that is, the context in which the act occurs makes it immoral – and identifying certain acts as sexually immoral and then discerning whether they succeeded in endangering the morals of a child. Accepting that a particular sexual behaviour is immoral simply on its face and absent evidence of a problematic context – which is what the crown argued and the jury accepted – is an example of making assessments about good sex and bad sex based on assumptions about the moral essence of a particular sexual act.

Instead of focusing on the morality of a particular sexual act, the Ontario Court of Appeal determined that the provision should be interpreted to prohibit conduct that could impede a child's ability to develop the values needed for a free and democratic society. They defined the harm at issue under section 172 as a matter of political, and not sexual, morality: "[C]onduct that endangers the morals of a child is that which poses a real risk that the child will not develop those values which are essential to the operation of a free and democratic society."[39] According to the Ontario Court of Appeal, the moral assessment required under section 172 should turn on the context in which the sexual acts occurred (rather than identifying certain acts as immoral and then discerning whether or not they had endangered the child's morality). The Court found that the trial judge erred by not properly explaining to the jury that the morals of a child could only be endangered by conduct of which the child was aware and capable of appreciating. Such an approach balances sexual liberty and sexual autonomy. It is an approach oriented towards producing a community of sexual actors whose values include "an appreciation that exploitive or non-consensual sexual activity is wrong; an appreciation that conduct which dehumanizes or degrades women is wrong; an appreciation by the children of their own self worth and personal autonomy; and an appreciation of the responsibility of parents to protect and nurture their children."[40] This reasoning seems a good start towards a legal approach that promotes the conditions for a community of sexual actors possessed with sexual integrity.

Unavoidably, principles such as those identified by the Ontario Court of Appeal – the protection of bodily integrity and the promotion of equality, autonomy, sexual liberty, and positive duty – draw moral distinctions between legally acceptable and unacceptable sexual conduct. They make distinctions between good sex and bad sex. The distinctions, however, are not premised on essentialist claims or first-person sexual moralities. Nor are they premised on claims of objective truth about sex and/or gender. There is no overarching or underpinning assertion of truth about power in any of the principles the Court relies upon. None of these principles are conceptually static nor do they require a static analysis. None of them draw on a judicial perception of the first-person sexual moralities held by most members of the community and none of them need be hegemonic. To adopt a legal theory of sexuality that is disaggregated from sexual morality requires the rejection of the possibility that there are objective truths regarding sex, gender, and sexuality. That is to say, it requires an analysis that can and will apply its constructivist insights to its own claims. Improving the law's ability to protect and promote sexual integrity as a social good depends upon at least the theoretical possibility of open-ended, fully contextual, and infinitely re-articulated conceptions about sex, gender, and sexuality.

Underpinning the theoretical claim that sexuality, sex, and gender, as well as the structures in which, and through which, we understand these concepts, are socially constructed – that is to say, only ever open-ended, fully contextual signifiers – is the postmodern assertion that the formation of all meaning occurs through an infinite process of exclusion in which meaning is never complete.[41] The building blocks of social constructivist theories are found in the toolbox of postmodernism. Unlike modern thought, which assumes the existence of, and therefore seeks to discover, measure, and characterize, universal meaning and objective truth (or, in the context of sexuality, inherent or natural meaning and objective truths about sex),[42] postmodernism focuses on the particular. It challenges the possibility of any universal/pre-discursive meaning, asserting, rather, that meaning, because it is formed through a (social) process of exclusion and is therefore permanently unstable, can never be complete or universal. The brief discussion in Chapter 1 in this volume examines how queer theory, for example, has relied upon postmodern accounts of meaning to critique binary modes of knowledge and identity.

In this way, postmodernism helpfully destabilizes identity groups including, most importantly, those categories of subjects whose identities have served to unjustly privilege some and oppress others. Mary Joe Frug's *Postmodern Legal Feminism*, for example, concludes by stating "only when the word 'woman' cannot be coherently understood, will oppression by sex be fatally undermined."[43] The "death of the subject" is also a key theme in queer theories. Judith Butler describes this notion of the incomplete subject as "the failure of any particular articulation to describe the population it represents."[44] She contends that "every subject is constituted differentially, and that what is produced as the 'constitutive outside' of the subject can never become fully inside or immanent."[45] In response to these postmodern claims about the subject, liberal and radical feminists as well as gay and lesbian rights activists have understandably asked "how can we build a political coalition to advance the position of women [or sexual minorities] in law if the subject that drives our efforts is 'indeterminate' 'incoherent' or 'contingent'?"[46]

One response is that a postmodern or queer understanding of the subject does not necessarily preclude the pursuance of political agendas and social justice movements. Think, for example, of Michel Foucault's discussion regarding the production of identity through "reverse discourses." Foucault notes that the same discourse that made possible "a strong advance of social controls into the area of perversity ... also made possible the formation of a reverse discourse: homosexuality began to speak on its own behalf, to demand that its legitimacy or 'naturality' be acknowledged, often in the same vocabulary, using the same categories by which it was medically disqualified."[47] Foucault's observation is revealed by the paradoxical use of essentialist reasoning in the Supreme Court of Canada's decision in *Egan v. Canada,* discussed in Chapter 3 in this volume.[48]

Postmodernists do not claim that there is no meaning but, rather, that all meaning is socially contingent. Meaning is in constant movement through time and space, and it is constituted through infinite reiterations of, and deviations from, norms. (This is why Butler suggests that this type of thought does not take a position but, rather, is "a critical interrogation of the exclusionary operations by which 'positions' are established."[49])This claim about meaning is critically necessary for justifying any legal theory of sexuality that calls for an infinite process of normative re-evaluation. It is the basis upon which queer and feminist postmodern theories help us to understand how deviation is constituted, how power is produced through meaning, how that power operates, and how sexual actors are constituted and regulated as a result of the manner in which deviation is formed and power operates.

Queer theorists and postmodern feminists have used these insights to demonstrate how the subversion of hegemonic sex and gender norms can be emancipatory. Gayle Rubin, for example, challenges the sexual taxonomies that draw distinctions between good sex and bad sex in ways that privilege some by oppressing others.[50] Eve Kosofsky Sedgwick challenges the reliance on diacritical modes of knowing and distributing power in order to constitute some subjects in an effort to stabilize the hegemony of other subjects.[51] Frug offers a feminist legal methodology that seeks to promote women's equality by destabilizing gendered subjectivity.[52] Janet Halley develops a queer legal methodology that aims to reveal justice interests that are not otherwise apparent.[53] Teresa Ebert relies on the notion of resistance in postmodern feminism to suggest a feminist rewriting of patriarchy.[54] The justice projects pursued by these (and other) postmodern thinkers avoid both the assumption of objective truths about sexuality (such as those assumed by Justice La Forest in *Norberg*) and the failure to fully contextualize sexual practices (such as is evident in Justice Binnie's *Little Sisters* decision).

This is not to suggest, however, that with postmodern thought the pursuit is over. A legal theory of sexuality still requires more: "Unless postmodernism can claim exemption from what it reveals about other discourses it has to allow for large areas of the discursive terrain where it simply" is not enough.[55] To suggest otherwise would be to take part in a "striking performative contradiction ... that both criticizes 'theoretical centralism' and simultaneously tries to enact it."[56] Such a statement, of course, leads one to ask: in what sense is postmodernism not enough – which parts of the discursive terrain require more? If everything is particular, then there is no non-arbitrary way to reject the anti-social practices of others.[57] Sexual justice requires moments of closure, of decidability. By destabilizing all meaning, the insights of postmodern thought, without something more, cannot justify criteria by which to judge between good sex and bad sex. The problem with this is that the law needs judgment to be operationalized. Its reforming, preventative, and distributive functions all require judgment. And for law to be just, this judgment must not be arbitrary. To avoid arbitrary judgment requires meaningful criteria. It requires moments of closure.

Think of this point in terms of legal impediments to sexual liberty. Organizations such as the North American Man/Boy Love Association provide the most obvious and well-trodden example. It is likely not possible to deploy postmodern constructivist arguments to normatively distinguish between the claims of different sexual minorities. Coherent legal distinctions between the constructivist claims of men oriented towards sexual interactions with other men and those of men oriented towards sexual interactions with boys requires resort to some principles that are beyond the principle of particularity. Whether it be harm, consent, equality, dignity, or community, the justification relied upon will require the invocation of a principle with content and with the possibility of stable meaning.

Similarly, think of the example of sex work. Constructivist arguments based on principles of particularity work well to destabilize the normative distinctions that radical feminism makes between the exchange of sex for erotic pleasure and the exchange of sex for anything else. However, legal arguments that distinguish between trading sex for survival and trading sex for success, for example, do not tend to be based on principles of particularity. If we are to meet the demands of, and to regulate, individuals and groups with conflicting interests, it is necessary to appeal to some more general principles.[58] If the notion of sexual integrity is to contribute to the pursuit of a legal theory of sexuality it has to have some content – some meaning. It needs moments of closure.

Radical feminist theories regarding sexuality ably provide this moment of closure. In the Canadian context, they were successfully relied upon by feminist scholars and activists to shift the Supreme Court of Canada's conception of sexual violence. In litigation, such as the proceedings in which LEAF has intervened, a party (or intervener) must take a position – they must make some assertion of truth. Feminists active in the work of pushing Canadian courts towards a constructivist account of sexual violence in the 1990s would have met with little success had their argument not been put forth as an accurate, coherent, complete, and stable description of the problematic social context that produces sexual violence. A legal claim requires a moment of closure.

That said, any moment of closure, any concession of decidability, unavoidably closes off other possibilities – such as the possibility that there are other accounts of the relationship between power, sexuality, and gender that speak other, even contradictory, "truths." Radical feminist theories, for example, do not typically leave much space for accommodating female heterosexual desire and sexual pleasure.[59] If sexuality is always and only understood as a function of gender hierarchy, it also becomes, always and only, a story about danger.[60] As postmodern feminists have observed, rarely in this story is "the diminishment or marginalization of women's sexual pleasure invoked as a reason, albeit one among others, to oppose particularly odious social practices."[61] A legal approach that starts from the theoretical premise that issues regarding sexuality should always be understood through the lens of systemic male sexual subordination over women is an approach that tends not to allow for the possibility (or advisability) of multiple contextually contingent narratives about sexuality. It is the kind of approach that presumes that because of social realities such as economic deprivation, social conditioning, or false consciousness women can never truly consent to, for example, loveless sex, involvement with pornography, consensual sado-masochism, or commodified sex. A radical feminist-influenced conception of sexuality leaves space for the Supreme Court of Canada to ascribe to a more constructivist understanding of sexual violence without rejecting the possibility that there are objective truths – essences – about sexuality. The possibility that there are objective truths about sexuality, in turn, leaves generous conceptual space for legal reasoning premised on sexual morality and on the need to protect sex itself. In this way, the Court was perhaps able to incorporate the constructivist insights of arguments informed by radical feminism without eliminating legal reasoning underpinned by sexual morality.

Radical feminism provided the theoretical underpinnings for an important moment of closure that supported one of the objectives of the feminist intervention in Canadian courts and law reform in the 1980s and 1990s. Radical feminist thought did not avoid, and cannot logically be expected to have avoided, the implications of taking a position, demanding a moment of judgment, and refusing the possibility of a fully contextual, open-ended understanding of sexuality. I should also note the distinction between the strategic invocation of an idea or argument and the theoretical underpinnings driving that idea or argument.[62] One objective of the feminist intervention in Canadian courts and law reform in the 1980s and 1990s was to challenge the assumption that sexual violence is a function of biology and arousal. This challenge was made in order to encourage the Supreme Court of Canada to recognize a particular relationship between power and sexual violence so that it might accept that rape is an equality issue. To fault this movement for its failure to simultaneously provide an argument that could accommodate the infinite number of other relationships between sexuality and power – in other words, for its failure to provide *the* answer – would be to fault it for failing to do precisely what neither radical feminist theory (with its inevitable exclusions) nor postmodern thought (with its "process over position" perspective) should purport to do.

Conclusion

Law needs borders. Justice requires dissent. A theoretical approach to sexuality and its regulation with the capacity to handle law and concepts of justice requires an ability to judge (to take a position) as well as a recognition of the need, and a space for, constant tension, deviation, and subversion (or what might also be called dissent).

7

Trouble Ahead
An Iconoclastic Approach to Sexual Integrity in the Law

I am in trouble. I have argued that legal conceptions of sexuality as socially constructed are to be preferred over essentialist conceptions of sexuality. I have suggested that constructivist conceptions promote legal reasoning that is more focused on sexual integrity and less likely to understand and measure every sexual act, desire, or identity through a heterosexual paradigm. Constructivist accounts of sexuality are better able to accommodate the relational, contextual, and institutional factors that contribute to the regulation and production of sexuality (by not overemphasizing biology, heterosexual arousal, romance, and sexual morality). I have also argued that constructivist approaches that remain inhered to sexual morality fail to remain open to perfection – they lack what Jacques Derrida would refer to as hospitality – and, as a result, do not fully shift the law's focus away from sexual acts and towards sexual actors.[1] Queer theory, and postmodernism more broadly, avoids this inhospitableness. They demonstrate the need for any just system or social structure to recognize that its fairness depends on its ability to continually redefine and reinterpret itself and the social context in which it operates. My problem is that I have also suggested that while queer theory and postmodernism are invaluable, these fully constructivist, open-ended theories do not meet the law's need to identify or establish criteria by which to judge. It seems to me that these claims I have made are quite in tension.

The Space between Derrida/s and the Promise of Sexual Integrity

Is it possible to adopt a legal theory of sexuality that allows for meaning, judgment, and perpetual openness? Derrida asks a similar question:

> How are we to distinguish between the force of law of a legitimate power and the supposedly originary violence that must have established this authority and that could not itself have been authorized by any anterior legitimacy, so that, in this initial moment, it is neither legal nor illegal – or, others would quickly say, neither just nor unjust?[2]

Derrida's question identifies for democracy the same analytical paradox that queer theory, and postmodernism more generally, poses for "sexual justice" – that is, the paradox between a legal recognition that (sexual) meaning is socially constructed and acknowledgment that law needs moments of closure – judgment (between good sex and bad sex) – if it is to be operationalized. In other words, is there an approach that can identify some content in sexual integrity without sacrificing the need to recognize and maintain its social contingency?

Derrida claimed that "for a decision to be just and responsible, it must, in its proper moment if there is one, be both regulated and without regulation: it must conserve the law and also destroy or suspend it enough to have to reinvent it in the reaffirmation and the new and free confirmation of its principle."[3] As a result, to experience the paradox "in which the decision between just and unjust is never insured by a rule" is to experience justice.[4] For this reason, "justice remains, is yet to come, à-venir, it has an, it is à-venir, the very dimension of events irreducibly to come. It will always have it, this à-venir, and always has ... 'Perhaps,' one must always say perhaps for justice."[5] The paradox for law presented by the deconstruction of sexuality and sexual integrity resembles the paradox revealed in Derrida's description of justice.

Derrida's "democracy to come" has been described as the promise of an authentic democracy that will never be embodied in any structure, institution, or system that we call democracy.[6] Derrida suggests that the structure of a promise is inscribed in the idea of democracy because internal to the concept of democracy is the notion of an endless or infinite process of improvement and perfectibility.[7] By infinite, he means unavoidably incomplete, and by perfectibility, he must mean "just." His argument is that no political system, principle, or law (or meaning) can by itself be called just (in other words, be universally just) because any system or law – in other words, all institutionalized power – arises out of, and is instituted by or through, an ultimately unjustifiable violence. This is premised on the notion that any rule formation, any attempt at a closed meaning, and, therefore, any content to a system, principle, or rule will inevitably involve a process of exclusion – an "inhospitableness," a violence. Democracy as a concept has to remain open to perfection – to a reality in which there is not the violence of excluding some (meaning) and favouring others (other meanings).

To harbour simultaneously meaning and its negation is impossible. The difficulty with conceptualizing justice (or identity or sexual integrity) in this manner is not that it is nihilistic. It is that it is a ceaseless and infinite struggle ending always and only in exclusion. Despite this circumstance, the theory of justice claimed by Derrida should still be understood as being other than futile because tucked neatly inside the space between Derrida/s is one little nugget of normativity – a nugget of normativity that is also helpful in pursuing a theory of sexual justice. Derrida argues that because democracy is a promise, and will remain a promise, it keeps the meaning of fundamental terms such as freedom and equality open-ended. The structure of a promise opens up a space between democracy's actual condition and its future, and it is in this space between the present and the future to come – delineated by the concept of democracy to come – where the meaning of fundamental terms such as freedom and equality (and sexual integrity) can remain open-ended. The normative shift in Derrida's argument is at that point where this space between the present and the future to come enters his analysis. He gives us a sense of what ought to transpire in this space. He suggests that the promise of repetition and the open-endedness of the future to come keeps social values and institutional structures open to different interpretations of what democracy means, thus allowing multiple voices to clash and negotiate with one another. It is in this "space" that such clashes can and will occur. This repetition may keep the law open to different interpretations of what sexual integrity means and what conditions are necessary for the promotion of sexual integrity as a common interest.

The open-endedness of this space between the present and the future to come applies to the identities of the subjects engaged in modern discussion as well as the topics of modern discussion. The identity of people is not fixed. It can only be determined by the interpretations and continuous re-identifications of people themselves. This is why identity is inherently unstable, internally and infinitely differentiated, and open to never-ending contestation. It is why Derrida focuses on notions of hospitality. It is also why Mary Joe Frug asserts that it is only when the category of woman has been utterly destabilized that oppression based on sex will be undermined.[8]

Derrida's polemical space of democratic decision making is opposed to a notion of deliberative democracy that specifies normative criteria in advance.[9] His rejection of all normative criteria, a refusal to lay down even a basic set of rules for what goes on in "the space," or to even understand what happens within the space must stem from a belief that to do so would limit access to the space. It must be tied to the value he identifies in avoiding inhospitality and unfriendliness. However, in taking such a position, Derrida has specified normative criteria in advance – he has laid down at least one rule: access for everyone to the space, the place, and the medium or forum where clash occurs and where meaning is contested. Derrida's space is not merely the public arena of political discourse. It is a radical space of struggle, violence, and contestation where there are no rules. The first (and only) rule of Derrida's fight club is that there are no rules in fight club. In this way, everyone gets to join. His rule is meant to pursue, if not to achieve, his concept of hospitality – unconditional openness to "other," which is a successful accommodation of singularity (or what Ernesto Laclau would call particularity).[10] His rule, which is that there be no rules, is consistent with his underlying reason for having no rules, but it nonetheless results in just the sort of double bind in which he seems to delight. Yet what can his aporetic account of friendship tell us about sexual integrity?

Recall Derrida's definition of justice – that being those "moments in which the decision between just and unjust is never insured by a rule."[11] Recall also that I have said law requires closure. It may be that law (with its inevitable but inhospitable closures) is a performative negation of justice in the same way that queer is a performative negation of identity. To identify as queer is to identify with a norm of deviating from the norm. To do so is either an act of negation or of infinite regression. Either way, the closure necessitated by the act of identification is impossible. Think of it in terms of discursive performativity. In the same sense that the statement "I am out" is performative (in and by its declaration, it constitutes that which it is), the statement "I am queer" is a performative negation (in and by its declaration, it deconstitutes that which it declares to be).

Justice, perhaps, is the infinite repetition of these negations. Justice is what happens in the space between now and the future to come. What is just about this? Where is the nugget of normativity? Perhaps it is in the open-endedness – the hospitality and friendship – found in that space between the present and the future to come. By his introduction of this space and his assertion that it is a hospitable one, Derrida has made a normative claim. Whether it is called democracy, justice, equality, hospitality, or friendship, there is hope in the space created by this futural promise. Perhaps the possibility of some criteria by which to judge is found in the desirability of recognizing and sustaining the open-ended process of conflict through which identity and meaning is unendingly contested. One of the infinite processes of meaning formation that might occur in Derrida's space would be an iconoclastic process in which meaning (such as the content of sexual integrity) is repeatedly constituted and then reconstituted. As explained in the paragraphs to come (no pun intended), there may be possibility for successes – for moments of sexual justice – to occur in the space between failures to achieve sexual justice.

This, however, still leaves at least two theoretical problems. First, how, in the context of sexuality, does any system, institution, or social structure ensure access to that space between now and the future to come where meaning is constituted and reconstituted continually? Second, by what criteria and through what method are the meanings attached to sexual integrity accepted or rejected at any given moment? In accepting the need to judge, as is necessary for law, is there a way to stay open to perfection without arriving at the paradox that law faces when presented with such openness?

Sexual Integrity and Iconoclasm

Assume it is true that the law ought to conceptualize sexuality as a social construct and that, more specifically, the law ought to concern itself with the promotion and protection of sexual integrity where law and sexuality intersect. (The reason being, as was demonstrated by the Supreme Court of Canada's newly constructivist conception of sexual violence, that this will better enable legal approaches that focus on the affective, interactional, and contextual character of sexuality.) Assume it is also correct to say that the law should be oriented towards not only ensuring freedom from violations of sexual integrity but also promoting and protecting the "conditions for" sexual fulfillment, sexual diversity, sexual literacy, the safety necessary for sexual exploration, the freedom within bounds to say "yes," and the capacity to gain sexual benefit (whether that benefit be physical, emotional, financial, or social). These "conditions for" would require the need for a community of sexual actors with intact sexual integrities, so that each of its members might have access to the relational aspects of sexual integrity. This aim, in turn, suggests that sexual integrity is in part relational, and the fact that it is in part relational suggests that it could be understood as a common good – a common good that individuals need in order to be autonomous.

What does it mean to suggest that people require certain relational components to their lives – such as a community with the "conditions for" sexual integrity – to be autonomous? Joseph Raz identifies certain conditions for autonomy.[12] According to him, a person must have certain cognitive and affective capacities as well as a certain degree of health and physical ability. An autonomous person must be free from coercion or manipulation by others and must have a range of valuable comprehensive goals available from which to choose. An autonomous person is one who is of sound mind, capable of affectivity, rational thought, and action (the conditions for autonomy), and whose life circumstances have included a sufficient range of significant options at different stages of life, some of which that person has willingly embraced. Raz argues that freedom or autonomy is valuable only if it is exercised in pursuit of valuable projects.[13] At first glance, this idea might seem contradictory. What he means is that freedom is morally valuable or intrinsically good, but it does not mean that any activitiy – including sexual activity – becomes valuable simply because it is chosen freely. For Raz, the overarching ethical conviction of individuals and society ought to be to foster individual well-being. The well-being of individuals is constituted by the pursuit of their relationships and projects but only of those relationships and projects that are actually valuable.

Setting aside for the moment the question of how to assess what is valuable, I think that Raz's autonomous sexual actor would be one who has the physical and affective capacities and social options to willingly pursue a lived sexuality that is valuable such that it is in keeping with his or her sexual integrity. For Raz, morality, both political and personal, is about the promotion of well-being – the pursuit of value. He proposes that there is a duty on the state to promote well-being, to facilitate its citizens' pursuit of their worthwhile goals – to promote, produce, and protect those social forms that are necessary for autonomy. That is to say, our well-being depends on our ability to pursue valuable goals, and our ability to pursue valuable goals is limited by the social forms of our society. Autonomy requires the existence of a range of options for the pursuit of valuable projects and relationships. These options are derived from the social practices that define activities and relationships – the existence of certain social conditions.

My argument is that sexual integrity (on a community or a societal level) constitutes one of those necessary social conditions or social forms. A community, society, and legal system that promote the conditions for sexual integrity are necessary to ensuring that individuals can "exercise all the capacities human beings have an innate drive to exercise, as well as to decline to develop any of them."[14] So, for example, a society that refuses to support or provide the forum for an artistic or literary endeavour solely on the grounds that it contains too much sexual expression fails to promote well-being by failing to protect or provide for certain social forms necessary for sexual integrity, as does a society that denies birth control to unmarried women.

Raz argues that the state has an obligation to adopt policies that promote and encourage personal autonomy – not because autonomy is an individual right but, rather, because it is a social good (that is, it furthers well-being). If well-being is attained through the achievement of worthwhile projects and the state's role is to promote conditions for the well-being of all of its citizens, then the state has an obligation to create social forms, including sexual social forms, that make such projects and relationships available. For Raz, political morality cannot be founded simply on individual rights to autonomy. There are certain collective goods that cannot be expressed in terms of individual rights because individuals cannot claim a right to a particular social form.[15]

Some values that are important at the individual level are also important at the societal level and cannot be conceptualized within a rights' framework. For example, "there is no right to have friends or be loved, and none of the virtues can be understood in terms of rights."[16] Similarly, a community of sexual actors with sexual integrity is necessary for autonomy, but I cannot really argue that I have a "right" to my neighbours' sexual integrity. (I would, of course, assert that I have a right to many aspects of my own sexual integrity, such as bodily autonomy and freedom from discrimination.)

Take the example of sexual literacy and consider it in conjunction with the suggestion that sexuality be thought of as a social product, like language. One of the conditions necessary to promote and protect the common good of sexual integrity would be sexual literacy. It should be incumbent on the state and individuals to promote and support sexual literacy. So I would argue that a sexually literate community of sexual actors is necessary for my autonomy, but I would not necessarily suggest that I have a right to a sexually literate community. The point is not to suggest that rights are anything other than indispensable. The point is that political morality cannot be reduced simply to an account of rights. Political morality must also contain duties regarding our responsibility towards others and principles concerning the well-being of people. Much like how the notion of sexual integrity requires a robust concept of consent but is not sufficed by consent alone, rights are a necessary, but not sufficient, component of political morality.

According to Raz, this approach could still avoid freeing the state to impose its will and infringe civil liberties to attain perfectionist goals, provided it recognizes the existence of, and the need for, value pluralism. Value pluralism recognizes that many of the choices available to individuals are both valuable and incompatible. How then, if this is the case, does his liberal perfectionism avoid the imposition of majoritarian morality in the inevitable eventuality of competing values? He does so by adopting a version of John Stuart Mill's harm principle. He suggests that a theory that values autonomy highly can justify restricting the autonomy of one person for the sake of the greater autonomy of others or even of that person himself in the future, but it cannot justify restricting autonomy on the basis of incommensurate values. However, Raz extends the principle beyond the concepts of negative freedom. Since autonomy is an intrinsic good and since autonomy requires a range of valuable options, state inaction can also cause harm. That is to say, a government's failure to provide individuals with a range of valuable options also constitutes an interference with autonomy. Raz defines harm as including not only pain and offence but also the deprivation of valuable options and the frustration of one's pursuit of the projects and relationships necessary for one's well-being. The harm principle serves not as a restraint on the promotion of moral goals by the state but, rather, as providing the state with guidance and criteria regarding the right way to promote the well-being of people. This assertion, of course, is a significant departure from the traditional harm principle proposed by Mills.

There are two points arising from this aspect of Raz's work that are particularly relevant to this discussion. The first is his suggestion that individual autonomy requires certain social forms. The second is his account of a harm principle in which a state's failure to act – to create certain social forms or support aspects of community – also causes harm, and states therefore have an obligation or duty to create or promote certain social forms. I have suggested that sexual integrity be thought of as a social form that is in the common good. Raz makes a distinction between public interests and common goods. While both are a function of individual interests, the common good is a good that is in the interests (albeit perhaps to varying degrees) of everyone in a given society, while the public interest is based on a resolution of the conflicting interests of various citizens. He uses the examples of the existence of pollution-free air and the existence of a network of railway tracks to illustrate the distinction. There may be a public interest in a system of railway tracks. It is an interest possessed not only by railway users but also by other members of the public, such as consumers. That said, some people may derive no benefit from this good, and others may actually be adversely affected by the railway's existence. For instance, the railway may cause them to endure noise or air pollution, or it may cause a decline in the value of their property. This does not mean that there is any less of a public interest in the existence of a viable railway. Raz contrasts this public interest with a common good such as the existence of clean air: "Everyone has a health interest which benefits from unpolluted air. The benefit is noncompetitive (one person's enjoyment is not at the expense of anyone else) and it is similar in nature for everyone."[17]

Is sexual integrity more like a railroad system or clean air? Is its benefit non-competitive, and is it similar in nature for everyone? Recall that I characterized sexual integrity as including not just freedom from bodily violation but also the conditions for sexual benefit, fulfillment, diversity, literacy, and exploration. Sexual integrity is more like clean air. It is a common good. However, what of the individual who receives gratification by violating the bodily integrity of another sexual actor? Does the fact of this gain to them suggest that sexual integrity is not a common interest, that its benefit is competitive? A common good is one in which one person's enjoyment of that good is not at the expense of anyone else. A polluter may well receive financial benefit from dumping toxins into the air rather than spending the resources to ensure a more environmentally friendly manufacturing process.

This does not mean that that polluter has less of an interest in inhaling clean air into his lungs when he steps out of his office. The fact that someone may take action (including action from which they derive a benefit) that threatens something that is in the common good does not make it less of a common good. A sexual actor who commits acts or behaves in ways that deprive others of their capacity for sexual pleasure, their sense of sexual self, their ability to relate in a sexually beneficial way to others in their community does threaten the common good of sexual integrity. That person's actions do not change the nature of this common interest or even this particular sexual actor's interest in its benefit. An individual who behaves in this manner is not enjoying the common interest in sexual integrity because they are not acting with sexual integrity. A conflict in interests is not created. An individual may enjoy chain smoking in a confined space with non-smokers present or hot boxing their parents' car without their parents' consent. This does not mean that by doing so they have transformed a common interest in clean air into a competitive benefit not enjoyed similarly by everyone. It simply means they are not breathing clean air.

Social forms can only be created through the collective – through community. Some social forms originate from common goods (interests) and others from public interests. Raz says that there are certain social forms, which are necessary for individual well-being, that the state has a duty to provide. Presumably, where a duty to provide a social form exists, what must be at issue is a social form related to a common good rather than a public interest. The state (and a just system of law) has a duty to act in a manner that is consistent with common goods. To do otherwise is to fail to maintain the value of community and the collective. Conversely, particular social forms related to public interests rather than common goods are not necessarily duty-based. The state may choose to pursue a particular public interest or not, and, regardless of what it chooses, it may still act in a manner that maintains the value in community, provided whatever political process of balancing they conduct is done fairly. In other words, there may be a common interest in a fair balancing process that gives rise to a duty on the part of the state to serve the public interest with integrity, but there is not a duty on the state to serve any specific public interest. However, where a common good is at stake, the state must act in pursuance of it, or consistently with it, in order to maintain value in the community and sustain its political legitimacy as a liberal democracy.

Assume it is correct to say that sexual integrity is a common good – that it is necessary for autonomy – and that therefore the law (as an institution of the state) ought to promote and protect the conditions for a community possessed of sexual integrity (because it is necessary for the well-being of individuals). Further assume, as suggested in Chapter 4 in this volume, that the range of valuable options necessary to create this common interest includes as well as bodily integrity, the conditions for sexual fulfillment, sexual literacy, sexual diversity, the safety necessary for sexual exploration, and sexual benefit. Raz would say that "one particularly important type of common good is the cultivation of a culture and a social ambience which make possible a variety of shared goods, that is, a variety of forms of social association of intrinsic merit."[18] The common good referred to here is the availability of an adequate range of shared goods. (Shared goods are goods whose benefit for people depends on people enjoying the good together and thereby contributing to each other's good.)

Some reference ought to be made in this context to the distinction between laws that criminalize an activity, laws that decriminalize an activity, and laws that actually promote an activity. In terms of the promotion of social forms, decriminalizing, for example, group sexual activity through the redefinition of indecency cannot be equated with, say, offering tax incentives to swingers clubs or the legal recognition of polyamorous relationships. However, due to the unique character of law itself as a social form or potential good, the redefinition of a legal concept that regulates sexuality in a manner that makes some sexual association legally available does increase the range in the availability and the variety of shared goods. In terms of the intersection between law and sexuality, coercively prohibiting, regulating, remaining neutral towards, manipulating, and/or promoting particular sexual associations do not reside within distinct categories but, rather, on a spectrum.

In the context of sexual integrity the cultivation of a social ambience that makes possible a variety of shared goods would require the autonomy to choose one's forms of social (sexual) association and the capacity for sexual benefit. This is not simply an argument in favour of sexual diversity, tolerance, or sexual liberty. First, recall that for Raz autonomy requires the availability of a range of meaningful options. Promoting a common interest in sexual integrity (so as to protect individual autonomy) does not require the cultivation of a social ambience that makes possible *all* social forms of sexual association. It requires a social ambience that makes possible forms of sexual association that are themselves valuable. Second, a community of sexual actors with the capacity for sexual benefit depends as much on legal regulation and prohibition as it does on sexual liberty. It, of course, requires freedom from violation (both affective and corporeal). It also requires a sexually literate community, which in turn requires an open, articulated discourse on sexual pleasure and desire but also on sexual harm.

The difficulty with these suggestions is in ascertaining (1) which forms of sexual association are of intrinsic merit; (2) which conditions are necessary for a community of sexual actors possessed of sexual integrity; and (3) what substantive concept of sexual integrity the law should be operating under. By what criteria should the law distinguish between the social forms it is meant to promote and those it is meant to discourage or prohibit? Can a legal theory of sexuality accept the possibility of the intrinsic merit of some sexual social forms and still maintain a constructivist conception of sexuality? If law ascribes to a constructivist account of sexuality – which understands sexuality as a socially contingent product of norms and practices – by what criteria is sexual benefit to be identified and assessed? All of which is to ask, how can law stay open to perfection in the Derridean sense while pursuing excellence in the Razian sense? My answer is that it cannot. Yet here is what it can do. It can try and fail. More importantly, it can fail over and over and over and over again – and in the space between failures, we will find discrete moments of success (such as radical feminism's intervention into sexual assault law) and finite moments of meaning formation and then reformation (such as the inchoate valuing of sexual minorities under section 15 of the *Canadian Charter of Rights and Freedoms*).[19]

However, to fail over and over and over again – thus creating for a moment that potentially hospitable space between failures – is a necessary, but not sufficient, condition. Discrete moments of success as well as finite moments of meaning formation and then reformation require, by their very definition, closure – that originary violence that is the constitution of meaning. In each of these moments and in every failed attempt to stay open to perfection while at the same time pursuing excellence that comes both before and after each of these moments, there is a need to judge – to say and to know what constitutes sexual integrity. As suggested in the previous chapter, law needs judgment to be operationalized. Law cannot escape this requirement. What law can do is drive itself, or be driven, to try (over and over and over again) to stay open to perfection while it pursues excellence. A conception of sexual integrity measured against political morality rather than sexual morality – using the aspirational principles of the Constitution rather than those of God or nature – should drive law to keep trying (and failing). Think, for example, of the approach that Chief Justice McLachlin takes in determining the definition of indecency in *R. v. Labaye*.[20] A relational standard of valuation, which evaluates social forms based not only on how well a sexual association fits within the standards of excellence for its genre but also on how it relates to its genre, should help to keep the space between failures hospitable. Consider the argument in Chapter 3 in this volume regarding family status as a relational category and the promise of subverting or deconstructing the categorical approach to equality from within the categories themselves.

I should explain further what I mean by a relational standard of valuation and genre-based evaluation. Raz suggests that specific social forms belong to a kind. He notes that two elements determine how items or activities can be evaluated: the definition of the kinds of goods to which they relate (including the constitutive standards of excellence for each kind) and the way in which each item relates to that kind. To put it another way, something may be evaluated not only based on how neatly it fits within the standards of excellence for its genre but also based on how it relates to its genre:

> Genre-dependent evaluation is marked by the fact that objects are evaluated by reference to kinds, to genres. But there are different relations they can bear to the genre. Straightforward membership or exemplification of the kind is only one of them. Two elements determine how items can be evaluated. First is the definition of the kinds of goods to which they relate, which includes the constitutive standards of excellence for each kind. Second are the ways the item relates to the kinds. It may fall squarely within them. Or it may, for example, relate to them ironically, or iconoclastically, or as a source of allusions.[21]

As Raz suggests, one way in which an item, activity, or law can relate to its genre is iconoclastically. An iconoclast is one who challenges traditional or popular ideas or institutions on the basis that these beliefs or institutions are wrong. Iconoclasm is not the same as subversion or deconstruction. Iconoclasm, unlike subversion, is about meaning formation. This is because the site of its transgression is expressly and concededly within a cultural construct and not external to it. It is the intentional destruction within a culture of one of the culture's own icons, symbols, or meanings. Unlike subversion, which aims simply to deconstruct, iconoclasm's purpose is to attack a cherished belief by relying on a new or different cherished belief. This is why it has the capacity to be a shared value. It is about the collective – often done for political (or, in the past, religious) reasons. Illuminating the distinction between iconoclasm and the notion of queer theory (because of its reliance on the concept of subversion) helps to illustrate how iconoclasm accommodates new meaning rather than simply disrupting old meaning.

Queer – the notion of a positionality in deviation from the norm – does not allow for the notion of genre-based evaluation. Judgment in kind necessitates the identification and affirmation of categories and is antithetical to queer theory and to deconstruction generally. The distinction between an iconoclastic approach and a queer approach is real. An iconoclast dissents against a popular belief or tradition on the grounds that it is in error. To disrupt cherished beliefs about sex, or to dissent against traditional sexual mores on the basis that they are wrong, is not to contest the existence of categories, the possibility of standards of excellence, or the ability to judge – quite the opposite, in fact. An iconoclastic approach to the legal regulation of sexuality, unlike a queer approach, acknowledges the inevitability of judgment. It recognizes the social fact that an icon once shattered will undoubtedly and expediently be replaced by a new icon. For this reason, it is better able to account for, contest, and at times work within the liberal political context in which the legal regulation of sexuality operates in Canada's constitutional democracy.

The legal contest over same sex marriage provides a good example. Certainly, gay and lesbian marriages operate within the particular cultural construct of marriage (which is why queer activists have opposed a social movement focused so heavily on this issue). However, this very fact reveals its iconoclastic potential. In Canada, marriage no longer means the legal union of one man and one woman. Some argue that same sex marriage does not change the meaning of marriage but merely expands the scope of relationships to which it applies. Given that "marriage" is the description of a particular type of relationship, it is not a persuasive argument. It is true that the exclusionary character of marriage as a mechanism of social and financial benefit distribution remains intact. Gay and lesbian marriages did not deconstruct the institution of marriage in Canada – but they did change, to some degree, its icon.

If, in the context of legal regulation, the evaluation of a given sexual act is based on whether, and the way in which, it challenges traditional or popular ideas about sex, then the benefit or detriment (the good or bad) of it is in its effect – it is relational. It is dependent on there being a genre and the existence of a standard of evaluation for that genre, but it is not dependent on what that standard is. Its benefit or detriment is in the process of reconsideration that its transgression perpetuates. This does not mean that every transgression, every new meaning formation, will promote the common interest in sexual integrity. It means only that the space between failures will be preserved, and it will be preserved in a manner that allows for the possibility of those finite moments of meaning formation and then reformation.

This reasoning entails making two interrelated normative assumptions. First, it entails an assumption that there exists substantive meaning to the concept of sexual integrity – albeit meaning that is constantly evolving and shifting and, due to its relational nature, potentially plural in form.[22] In other words, there need not be (nor could be) one account of what constitutes the standards of excellence for sex. That said, in any and all sexual contexts, there will be criteria constitutive of sexual integrity. Given that the focus of this discussion is on the potential good of iconoclastic jurisprudence, a standard under this account cannot be static. While it is not possible to assume one standard of excellence for sex, it is possible to assume that in any sexual act there is always a standard. The suggestion that a standard can be objective yet unstable in this way may create a certain degree of unease. The objective element of this assertion stems from Raz's observation that, while a given value may not be universal, the fact that people value *is* universal. Raz argues that the fact of this universalism suggests that, through reason, pluralism can be accommodated. The normative element at play in my claim is an assumption that judgment is both necessary and legitimate. Law needs judgment to be operationalized. For law to be just, this judgment must not be arbitrary. To avoid arbitrary judgment requires meaningful criteria. It requires standards of excellence.

Second and correspondingly, it entails an assumption that some sexual dissent, some challenges to social forms such as human sexuality, and some degree of this process of openness is required. Dissent is an essential criteria for the progress of any community. This is no less true with respect to sexual dissent than with respect to political dissent. Indeed, to disaggregate sexual dissent from political dissent is in many respects a false distinction. Provided an ability to judge is maintained (which is what the first normative assumption I articulated achieves), it can fairly be said that sexual dissent is presumptively in the common interest. Both a standard, achieved through practice, argument, and reason, and dissent are necessary to accommodate pluralism. Evaluating how much, and when, dissent would be good – because dissent too is a relational concept – can be determined by resorting to an external standard, such as a harm principle or the promotion of community tolerance. This determination avoids requiring reliance on a standard of excellence that is internal to the genre itself. In this way, it is possible to articulate an impermanent content or meaning to what constitutes sexual integrity without attempting to articulate a coherent account of what constitutes excellent sex.

Revisiting the Supreme Court of Canada's approach to the *Criminal Code*'s definition of indecency outlined in *Labaye* reveals how the approach just described might be applied when the law intersects with issues of sexuality. It also demonstrates how the concept of iconoclasm might be deployed to evaluate the Court's reasoning. Recall that *Labaye* involved the reinterpretation of the definition of indecency under the bawdy house provisions such that the community standard of tolerance test was no longer part of the analysis. The majority of the Court determined that only activities that pose a significant risk of harm – of the type "grounded in norms which our society has recognized in its Constitution or similar fundamental laws," harm so serious as to be incompatible with proper societal functioning – will be considered indecent.[23] There are two interrelated aspects of the common interest in sexual integrity that one might argue are served by the majority's revised definition of indecency in *Labaye*. They are tolerance and the iconoclastic legal recognition of sexual desire.

The first, tolerance, is related to another type of good that Raz discusses: shared goods. As noted, "shared goods are goods whose benefit for people depends on people enjoying the good together and thereby contributing to each other's good."[24] It is certainly the case that the sorts of sexual activities occurring at Club L'Orage and Coeur à Corps would be of this shared character. At issue, after all, was the decency or indecency of "orgies," to use the term employed by Chief Justice McLachlin.[25] Shared goods are not to be confused with common goods. Common goods are those that serve the same interest of every person in a non-competitive way. The ability to legally engage in group sex in a semi-public setting does not serve the interests of every person in Canada. While it is a shared good among those who desire to engage in group sex in semi-public settings, it is not a common good. There is, however, a common interest at issue in this case. The common good referred to in this case is the availability of an adequate range of shared goods – in the context of indecency and obscenity, the common interest in cultivating an ambience of eclectic sexual associations (which is needed for autonomy).

This is the common good of toleration. It is a common good to live in a sexually tolerant society. We all benefit from living in a tolerant and non-discriminatory society. This point becomes clearer when we think about the consequences of intolerance.[26] Raz uses the example of an apartheid society and the ways in which such a system detrimentally affects the lives of all of its members by colouring "the nature of the social relations each can have" and imposing "duties actively to fight prejudice and discrimination in one's own society in order not to be tainted by its failures through membership in it."[27] These same duties ought to pertain in every society in which intolerance exists. The common good of living in a Canadian society that is not operating under a system of apartheid seems obvious. To think of an extreme example that is analogous to an apartheid society, in the context of sexual intolerance and repression, one might consider the fictional, futuristic theocracy of Margaret Atwood's sexually repressed Republic of Gilead in *The Handmaid's Tale:*

> What's going on in this room, under Serena Joy's silvery canopy is not exciting. It has nothing to do with passion or love or romance or any of those notions we used to titillate ourselves with. It has nothing to do with

> sexual desire, at least for me and certainly not for Serena. Arousal and orgasm are no longer thought necessary; they would be a symptom of frivolity merely, like jazz garters or beauty spots.[28]

The common good of living in a Canadian society that has not relegated the female orgasm to the status of unnecessary trend from a bygone era seems obvious. Less clear for some is the common good of living in a society that tolerates sexual practices that the majority of Canadians find disgusting, depraved, repulsive, and immoral. However, as Raz notes, tolerance is not the approval of many incompatible forms of life. Tolerance and pluralism are not synonymous: "Toleration is a distinctive moral virtue only if it curbs desires, inclinations and convictions which are thought by the tolerant person to be in themselves desirable."[29] One is not really exercising sexual tolerance simply by tolerating a particular sexual act even though it is an act that one would never engage in. One is only exercising sexual tolerance where one tolerates a sexual act of which one disapproves.

Chief Justice McLachlin's definition of indecency and obscenity requires that we not criminalize as indecent or obscene any sexual act or depiction without an associated harm even if most people find it repulsive, disgusting, immoral, and of no intrinsic merit. Contrast this notion with the dissent's approach to the definition of indecency and obscenity: "Social morality, which is inherent in indecency offences and is expressed through the application of the standard of tolerance, must still be allowed to play a role in all situations where it is relevant."[30] To criminalize sexual conduct purely on the basis that it is, from a majoritarian perspective, immoral (as in it is harmless to others but would nonetheless be considered immoral by most citizens' first-person ethics) cannot be an act of tolerance. To tolerate sexual conduct and depictions despite considering them immoral is to act out of toleration – it is to protect the common good of a tolerant society. To limit such tolerance to within the bounds of harmlessness is to act in promotion of the community's interest in sexual integrity. Chief Justice McLachlin rejects the traditional "community standard of tolerance" and, in doing so, instead sets a standard of tolerance for the community – a standard that our Constitution dictates is necessary so as to avoid being tainted by membership in an intolerant society. Her definition makes a demand for a standard of tolerance for the community that is in the common good or interest of each of us to pursue and that it is incumbent upon any state dedicated to acting in the interests of the community to maintain.

A consideration of the jurisprudential context in which this case was decided provides another way of thinking about this case in relation to the positive obligation born by the state to create certain social forms – in this instance, the promotion of some sexual relationships. Any modicum of legal realism recognizes that laws are never made, and cases are never decided, in a contextual vacuum. In considering *Labaye,* one ought to recall that the Supreme Court of Canada was making its determination in the context of a post-*Charter* wealth of jurisprudence defining which sorts of sexual relationships will be recognized, valued, and promoted in Canadian society.[31] Both legislative and adjudicative branches of the Canadian state have focused a great deal of attention in the last twenty years on debating, redefining, and, with respect to certain forms of sexual relationships (particularly same sex and non-married ostensibly monogamous heterosexual relationships) formalizing and privileging through legal recognition particular types of sexual associations – that is to say, making available certain social forms that the state has recognized as valuable. This is consistent with Raz's suggestion that the state ought not to coercively prohibit undesirable or valueless options that do not cause harm but most certainly should endeavour to promote through incentive and preferential treatment those life options that are valuable and desirable and therefore promote well-being. The Court decided *Labaye* in an era in which some would argue that, as a society, we have actually increased the role of law and government in the definition, regulation, and control of human relating (albeit through positive mechanisms such as tax incentives and property rights rather than through negative legal mechanisms such as the criminal law). This may be a context that makes it "safe" for the Court (and the community) to withdraw regulation in areas that in a previous legal era might have seemed at least desirable if not necessary.[32] It is, as suggested, also consistent with Raz's assertion that the state ought to encourage, through incentive, certain common goods (for example, social forms such as marriage) that promote well-being by increasing individual autonomy rather than prohibiting undesirable, but harmless, life choices.

However, does Chief Justice McLachlin's decision offer value beyond the common interest a society has, and each of its members have, in promoting tolerance? Recall that one way in which to evaluate the worth of an item or activity is to assess how it relates to its genre. The reasoning adopted by Chief Justice McLachlin in *Labaye* could be evaluated based on an assessment of the iconoclastic effect the decision may have on the legal regulation of human sexuality or sexual expression. Such an evaluation would ask whether the decision produces an iconoclastic impact such that it serves the common interest in a community of sexual actors possessed with sexual integrity? In fact, given that an iconoclastic decision is one that challenges and replaces cherished beliefs, one could consider the Supreme Court of Canada's decisions in *Labaye* and *R. v. Kouri* to be some of the most iconoclastic jurisprudence to date regarding the legal regulation of sexuality in Canada.[33] In their outcome, these decisions challenge two of what are the most significant pillars of the legal regulation of sex in this society: they transgress the heavily fortified sexual boundary of the public/private realms, and they challenge the taboo against the commodification of sex – most significantly, they do so without using claims of anti-subordination, identity, privacy, or safety.

Jeffrey Weeks suggests that our culture too often justifies erotic activity on some basis other than desire, such as reproduction or the consummation of relationships.[34] The same could be said with respect to the law's relationship to sexuality. The law typically adopts an approach to sexual desire and erotic activity that focuses on rights, responsibilities, and personal morality. Legal analyses concerning issues of sexual activity and human sexuality are most frequently framed as either claims to safety, claims to privacy,[35] claims to expressive rights,[36] or claims of identity (or anti-subordination claims more generally).[37] As discussed in Chapter 3 in this volume, in the case of sexual minorities, legal arguments and analyses typically focus on claims of identity or relationship recognition. In the case of sexual liberty more broadly, the emphasis is usually on claims that reify the public sphere/private sphere division or on claims premised on the expressive rights held by individuals. Legal recognition of the bodily pleasures beyond, behind, or outside of an identity, relationship, or sanctuary – of the significance of autonomously held and experienced sexual arousal – is infrequently claimed and less frequently, if ever, granted. That said, neither privacy rights, expressive rights, nor identity claims aptly characterize the arguments or reasoning involved in these cases. Both *Labaye* and *Kouri* involve sexual activity in semi-public.[38] Neither *Labaye* nor *Kouri* involve a group of sexual actors that could reasonably be described as a sexual minority, and neither *Labaye* nor *Kouri* involve claims regarding freedom of expression.

The jurisprudential construction of sexuality – what sex means in the context of its relationship to law – has taken different forms. At different times and in different legal contexts, sex has been about morality, religion, identity, privacy, and class. It has been about health, gender, expression, violence, family, and love. It has even been about communism![39] But it has never really been about the recognition of pleasure or desire. This is not something that the Supreme Court of Canada has typically done, and having done it in *Labaye* changes, at least to some degree, the meaning of the legal regulation of sexuality in Canada. It is an example of the formation and reformation of meaning, achieved at a discrete moment, in a discrete context, and as measured against the political morality underpinning the Constitution. In *Labaye,* Chief Justice McLachlin states that "sexual activity is a positive source of human expression, fulfillment and pleasure."[40] A review of prior case law defining obscenity demonstrates that legal recognition of the significance of sexual pleasure was not the focus (or even a focus) of analysis prior to *Labaye.* In 1962, when the Court first grappled with the British common-law definition of obscenity in a case involving the novel *Lady Chatterley's Lover,* the analysis focused on the merits and demerits of legal censorship.[41] The Court in *R. v. Brodie* did not concern itself with the sexual fulfillment and pleasure of Lady Chatterley, her lover, or the book's readers. In 1985 and 1992, when the Court revisited the definition of obscenity, the focus was on incorporating a notion of harm into the Court's analysis of the community's attitude towards a particular sexual act or depiction.[42] Desire, pleasure, and fulfillment were not taken into account.

Claims about pleasure and desire were actually made by Little Sisters Book and Art Emporium and certain of the interveners in *Little Sisters Book and Art Emporium v. Canada (Minister of Justice),* but these claims were not endorsed by the Supreme Court of Canada.[43] *Little Sisters,* as discussed in Chapter 5 in this volume, involved a constitutional challenge to obscenity laws based on the discriminatory manner in which they were applied by customs officials to gay and lesbian material imported by the Little Sisters bookstore. The challenge was brought on the basis of freedom of expression as well as on an equality claim based on sexual orientation. Underpinning the equality argument in *Little Sisters* (which was premised on the assertion that pornography figures differently in gay and lesbian communities than in straight ones) was a claim about desire – same sex desire specifically. The equality claim was rejected by the Court.

It may be that, for doctrinal reasons, the Supreme Court of Canada was not well situated in any of these pre-*Labaye* cases to give recognition to the significance of desire and sexual pleasure. Take *Little Sisters,* for example. Given the other section 15 jurisprudence regarding sexual orientation developing at the time that *Little Sisters* was decided, it is not surprising that the Court was unwilling to accept arguments suggesting that the sexual needs (for pornography or for particular sexual depictions) or the sexual acts of gays and lesbians were different from those of heterosexuals. More generally, it may be that until the Court had rejected the community standard of tolerance test there was not conceptual space for considerations of desire. Considerations regarding desire and sexual pleasure are more easily incorporated into a definition of indecency centred on actual, proven harm to sexual participants or other members of society as measured against the values of liberty, dignity, equality, and autonomy. They are not so easily accommodated where harm is measured by the community's standard of tolerance.

As is the case with respect to the prior case law regarding obscenity, the prior Supreme Court of Canada cases defining indecency cannot be said to have given rise to a legal recognition of sexual desire. The lap-dancing trilogy of the 1990s, including *R. v. Tremblay, R. v. Mara,* and *R. v. Pelletier,* involved charges against tavern owners whose performers gave lap dances or private shows of some sexual variety.[44] None of these decisions appear to take into consideration, as Chief Justice McLachlin did in *Labaye,* that sexual activity is a source of pleasure, which may be due in part to the factual patterns that gave rise to the indecency charges in these cases. All of them involved the explicit exchange of money for sexual contact of some type. It would perhaps be surprising to find reasoning that suggested a legal recognition of sexual desire in cases involving the exchange of money for sexual contact – where the sexual desire is presumably not mutually experienced by both or all of the sexual participants.

While *Labaye* also involved an exchange of money for sex, the interrelationship between sex, money, and desire in *Labaye* is different than it is in any of these cases. Unlike these older cases, *Labaye* involved reciprocal, rather than unilateral, sexual desire, and unlike these older cases it involved people paying money to have a sexual interaction but the money was paid by *all* of the sexual actors to a third party. Money was not the motivating factor for any of the sexual participants. Presumably, mutual desire to engage in the sexual activity at issue was the motivating factor. It is for this reason – the mutual desire of the individual sexual actors – that Chief Justice McLachlin determined that the commercial element of these activities was not a factor suggesting that the activities were indecent. She stated that "on the present set of facts, the commercial aspect of the respondent's operation is hardly relevant to this type of harm. The entrance fee was not paid by some to secure the sexual services of others. It merely enabled all the customers to gain access to the bar and to equally participate in the activities taking place therein."[45] It may be that, in part, what distinguished the exchange of sex for money in *Labaye* from the exchange of sex for money in the lap-dancing trilogy (where the exchange of sex for money was most certainly a determining factor – albeit under the community standard of tolerance test) was the role of (or the type of) desire.

Labaye and *Kouri* represent Supreme Court of Canada decisions stipulating that, absent an associated and provable harm, the law ought not to interfere with the exercise of a sexual desire – in particular, a sexual desire that takes place in semi-public settings and that includes a commercial element. The intrinsic worth of the shared goods occurring at Club L'Orage and Coeur à Corps is manifested through the Supreme Court of Canada's decisions. The fact that this desire may be beyond reason and rationality, and therefore not susceptible to valuation, does not suggest that the social forms that stem from drives or capacities that exceed the limits of reason cannot be evaluated based on arguments regarding the standards of excellence for those social forms or their iconoclastic implications for those standards. The recognition of desire is a recognition, by law, of something outside of itself – something outside of law. Further, a legal recognition of desire is itself *prima facie* iconoclastic because the law's legitimacy is premised on reason. The iconoclastic effect of these social forms is reflected in the legal recognition that these pleasure-seeking activities received from the highest court in the country. It is not simply that these forms of human relating transgress dominant sexual norms – many forms of human relating do so and may possess intrinsic worth (or be detrimental) for reasons of their own. It is that the fact of their existence resulted in a change or shift in the law's relationship to human sexuality. In *Labaye* and *Kouri,* the Court shattered a long held and stridently protected legal (and social) belief that, either directly or indirectly, sexual morality is a proper object of the criminal law power. In doing so, the Court recognized the value of desire, if not for the first time, then in a novel way.

However, while the legal recognition of desire changes the law's relationship to sexuality and, as such, could be described as iconoclastic, that does not alone make it a common good. What makes this particular iconoclastic jurisprudence an aspect of the common interest in sexual integrity? Why is changing the relationship between law and sexuality, such that it recognizes the value and significance of sexual pleasure, an iconoclastic effect of benefit and not a detriment? Francisco Valdes identifies the defence of desire as the next strategic move in the pursuit of "sex/gender reform and equality."[46] He notes that "sexual and affectional intimacy, driven by erotic desires, is integral to humanity and society because both intimacy and desire are affirmations of life and therefore are diametrically opposed to dogmatic regimes such as the dominant Euro-American sex/gender system."[47] As such, he suggests that human intimacy and desire are neither frivolous nor legally insignificant.[48] Whether it is cross-sex or same sex desire, he argues that the defence of desire may be the most significant contribution that queer theory[49] has to offer:

> [B]ecause desire is not rational in the Western sense, this tactic also commits Queer legal theory to engaging the law beyond the limits of (legal) rationality. This tactic or method calls forth a joy in and for humanity that is distinct, though not separate, from the notions (and the limits) of reason or logic that characterize the very culture of the law ... defending desire effectively calls for us to "come out of the closet" with respect to human pleasure and its worth.[50]

What common interest (that has not already been met through a rights paradigm) is served when the meaning of sexuality within the context of its legal regulation changes in this way? When law comes out of the closet with respect to human pleasure and its worth, a common interest in human flourishing is served. A focus on desire and pleasure (in conjunction with harm) locates well-being and human flourishing as central to the law's concern in this context. It allows for legal analysis that takes as one of its primary considerations the quality of people's lives. In this way, it serves our common interest in sexual integrity, similar to the way that a re-conceptualization of the harm caused by sexual violence allows legal analysis to take as one of its primary concerns the perspective of all sexual actors involved in a sexual interaction.

Incorporating concepts of pleasure and desire into the law's conception of sexuality reveals a more nuanced and truthful account of this human activity – an activity the ubiquity of which is matched only by the historical degree to which it has been socially and legally regulated. This portrayal matters because legal analysis that recognizes sex as having the capacity to be positive, pleasurable, and fun reflects a reality about sex that the law has tended not to reveal. This is significant for a number of reasons. It is significant not simply for its celebration of one of the very positive aspects of our humanity but also because the law's capacity to better recognize, account for, and reflect the good of sex might also lend itself to a capacity to better account for, and reflect, the bad of sex. That is to say, it might better highlight the very real harms related to, or caused by, certain sexual behaviours (particularly for women, children, and sexual minorities). A legal capacity to better reflect these sexual realities facilitates a greater ability to handle those complex and difficult legal circumstances in which pain and pleasure and desire and fear intersect, overlap, and at times blur. Issues such as consensual sado-masochism and certain types of sex work, for example, reveal circumstances where the law has, to date, failed to develop a coherent theory or theories of sexuality that can account for the infinite complexity that arises when human beings interact sexually. Issues such as access to birth control and abortion have been framed almost exclusively as necessary to protect against gendered dependency rather than women's interests in enjoying their own bodies.[51] Legal analysis capable of accommodating concepts of sexual pleasure (if done in a context informed by principles of substantive equality) offers opportunities to develop further arguments aimed at protecting women's sexual integrity.

The decisions of the Supreme Court of Canada in *Labaye* and *Kouri* establish an understanding of the regulation of public sex that is based on political morality, that acknowledges the value of community, and that reveals a moment where law was hospitable to a meaning reformation. Chief Justice McLachlin's reasoning, far from relegating Canadian values to the private domain, invokes our generally agreed upon fundamental ethical convictions for the very purpose of protecting them, and she does so in a manner that continues to recognize the importance of community and common interests without subjugating minority desires to majoritarian sexual morality. *Labaye* and *Kouri* are not premised on claims of identity, privacy, or expression and, as such, actually represent the potential for a more significant shift in the jurisprudence. The iconoclastic implications of her reasoning illuminate a shift in the legal regulation of sexuality towards an accommodation of concepts of pleasure and the significance of sexual desire. Such reasoning protects our common interests in tolerance and human flourishing, achieved through the recognition and affirmation of sexual pleasure, bounded by both sexual dissent and liberal judgment.

In this way, the legal recognition of desire in *Labaye* and *Kouri* reveal a moment of meaning formation and then reformation. Of course, the legal recognition of desire (even when confined by the principles of the Constitution) will not solve every issue of sexual liberty, any more than equality rights for gays and lesbians will give the law a complete answer to the social conflict that inevitably arises from sexual diversity or than re-conceptualizing the harm of sexual violence will resolve the many other tensions evident in sexual assault law (such as the tension between the right to a fair trial and a complainant's right to privacy). The iconoclastic impact of the reasoning in *Labaye* reveals a moment of success. It is a moment of success that is at the same time, inevitably, a failure to stay open to perfection. It is also a moment of success that fails to answer any of the following questions. What does desire mean? What types of desire should be valued and protected by the law? Can equality claims be made based on desire? How does the legal recognition of desire change what desire is? Nonetheless, the legal recognition of desire is nonetheless a moment of success, if for no other reason than because it raises these questions. In doing so, it makes the space between failures more hospitable, if only for a moment.

Conclusion

Legal approaches to sexuality that understand sexuality as a product of social context, norms, and regulative practices tend, as demonstrated in the context of sexual assault law and obscenity and indecency laws, to promote legal reasoning that is more concerned with sexual actors and sexual integrity than with sexual acts and sexual propriety. Legal reasoning that identifies sexual integrity as the interest at stake when law and sexuality intersect is legal reasoning that will focus on sexual interactions, on context, on power dynamics, on affectivity – not just bodily autonomy – and on the perspectives of all sexual actors involved in an interaction. Where the notion of sexual integrity that the courts adopt is understood as a social form that is in the common good, legal reasoning will reflect a concern over the social conditions that produce whatever issue of sexuality has come before the court. This may be reflected in, for example, the development of remedies that are attuned to the regulatory norms that perpetuate the use of sexual hostility in the workplace or the legal recognition that it is not only social categorizations such as "family" that can evolve, shift (or shatter and reconstitute!) as social contexts change but also the legal categories that reflect, regulate, and in fact at times constitute these social categories.

Where a common interest in sexual integrity is understood as necessary for individual autonomy, then there should be space to recognize a community's role in producing this social form by relying on reasoning based on political morality rather than resorting to legal reasoning that is reliant on sexual morality. Unavoidably, when law intersects with sexuality, morality will come into play. Where sexuality is understood as a pre-social, essential element of humanity and subjectivity, the law will be more likely to rely on sexual morality (so as to protect a particular account of sex). Where law conceptualizes sexuality as a function of interactions, relationships, power, and social practices and institutions, the law is more likely to rely on political morality (so as to reflect those constitutional values that have already been agreed upon as fundamental to the way we govern our broader relationships). It is true that political morality is equally as susceptible to Derrida's critique regarding the originary violence – the exclusionary character – of all meaning.[52] There is a closure, an inhospitality, in every constitutional choice to value, for example, liberty, equality, or tolerance. Of course, Derrida would say that the political choice even to have a constitution – let alone moments of closure regarding the substance of what that constitution is meant to value and protect – constitutes an originary violence. Political morals constitute as much of a closure – an inhospitableness – as do sexual morals. Yet perhaps broad concepts such as liberty and equality also possess, at the least, the potential for more moments of success, in the space between these failures, to stay open to perfection. They are relational and therefore more hospitable to interpretation, struggle, recalculation, and iconoclastic moments than are the principles of sexual morality.

Where it is recognized that sexuality is socially constructed through social practices, norms, and discursive regimes, it should also be recognized that law constitutes one of the discursive regimes through which this construction occurs. This creates a tension, given that with law must come judgment, that for judgment not to be arbitrary there must be criteria by which to judge, and that the criteria by which to judge are as socially constructed as are the subjects of law's judgment. There may not be a way to maintain a constructivist legal theory of sexuality that can reconcile this tension. But then, there may not need to be. In likening postmodern legal feminist methodology to premenstrual and post-menopausal blues, Mary Joe Frug comments: "Sometimes the 'PMs' that label my notes remind me of female troubles ... Maybe I am destined to do exactly what my title prescribes; just note the discomfort and keep going."[53] Both her discomfort and her perseverance resonate with me. While it is impossible for a legal conception of sexual integrity (or a legal approach to protecting and promoting sexual integrity) to remain open to perfection, the pursuit of sexual justice might be found in law's infinite and repetitive attempts to try. Perhaps there will always be trouble up ahead, and perhaps so long as this is the case we are (always and only) on the right track towards a legal theory of sexuality.

Notes

Introduction

1 Jeffrey Weeks, *Sexuality*, 2nd edition (London: Routledge, 2003) at 21.

2 Glad Day Bookshop, http://www.gladdaybookshop.com/.

3 See Brenda Cossman, *Sexual Citizens: The Legal and Cultural Regulation of Sex and Belonging* (Stanford, CA: Stanford University Press, 2007).

4 Mary Joe Frug, *Postmodern Legal Feminism* (New York: Routledge, 1992).

5 See Janet Halley, *Split Decisions: Taking a Break from Feminism* (Princeton, NJ: Princeton University Press, 2006).

6 See Carol Smart, "Desperately Seeking Post-Heterosexual Woman" in Janet Holland and Lisa Adkins, eds., *Sex, Sensibility and the Gendered Body* (London: Macmillan Press, 1996) 222.

7 *Criminal Code*, R.S.C. 1985, c. C-46.

8 See Peter Hogg and Allison Bushell, "Charter Dialogue between Courts and Legislatures" (1997) 35 Osgoode Hall L.J. 75.

9 *Vriend v. Alberta*, [1998] 1 S.C.R. 493 at para. 138.

10 *Canadian Charter of Rights and Freedoms*, Part 1 of the *Constitution Act, 1982*, being Schedule B to the *Canada Act 1982* (U.K.), 1982, c. 11.

11 *R. v. Butler*, [1992] 1 S.C.R. 452.

12 *R. v. Labaye*, [2005] 3 S.C.R. 728.

Chapter 1: Essentialism and Constructivism in Law

1 Gayle Rubin, "Thinking Sex: Notes for a Radical Theory of the Politics of Sexuality" in Henry Abelove and Michele Aina Barale, eds., *The Lesbian and Gay Studies Reader* (Routledge: New York, 1993) 3 at 9.

2 *Ibid*. at 149.

3 See, for example, Brenda Cossman, *Sexual Citizens: The Legal and Cultural Regulation of Sex and Belonging* (Stanford, CA: Stanford University Press, 2007); Bruce MacDougall, *Queer Judgments: Homosexuality, Expression, and the Courts in Canada* (Toronto: University

of Toronto Press, 2000); Jeffrey Weeks, *Sexuality*, 2nd edition (London: Routledge, 2003); Eve Kosofsky Sedgwick, *Epistemology of the Closet* (Berkeley and Los Angeles: University of California Press, 1990).

4 Jeffrey Weeks, *Against Nature* (London: Rivers Oram Press, 1991) at 87.

5 As early as 1949, Simone de Beauvoir argued that "one is not born, but rather, becomes a woman." Simone de Beauvoir, *The Second Sex* (New York: Knopf, 1953) at 1.

6 Gayle Rubin, "The Traffic in Women: Notes on the 'Political Economy' of Sex" in Rayna R. Reiter, ed., *Toward an Anthropology of Women* (New York: Monthly Review Press, 1975) 157.

7 Catharine MacKinnon, "Feminism, Marxism, Method and the State: An Agenda for Theory" (1982) 7 Signs 515; "Feminism, Marxism, Method and the State: Towards a Feminist Jurisprudence" (1983) 8 Signs 635.

8 Janet Halley, "Sexual Orientation and the Politics of Biology: A Critique of the Argument from Immutability" (1994) 46 Stan. L. Rev. 503 at 558.

9 *Ibid.* at 558.

10 *Ibid.* at 560.

11 Judith Butler, *Gender Trouble: Feminism and the Subversion of Identity*, 2nd edition (New York: Routledge, 1999) at 11.

12 Jeffrey Weeks describes this common conception in Jeffrey Weeks, *The World We Have Won* (New York: Routledge, 2007).

13 Michel Foucault, *The History of Sexuality, Volume I: An Introduction* (New York: Vintage Books, 1978); Jeffrey Weeks, *Coming Out: Homosexual Politics in Britain from the Nineteenth Century to the Present* (London: Quartet Books, 1977); Weeks, *supra* note 4; Ken Plummer, *Sexual Stigma: An Interactionist Account* (New York: Routledge, 1975).

14 My use of the word "positionality" to reflect the relational nature of queer is borrowed from Adam Romero, "Methodological Descriptions: 'Feminist' and 'Queer' Legal Theories: Book Review of Janet Halley's *Split Decisions: How and Why to Take a Break from Feminism*" (2007) 19 Yale J.L. & Fem. 227 at 228.

15 Foucault, *supra* note 13 at 35.

16 *Ibid.* at 43. See also David Halperin, *One Hundred Years of Homosexuality: And Other Essays on Greek Love* (New York: Routledge, 1990); David Halperin, *How to Do the History of Homosexuality* (Chicago: University of Chicago Press, 2002).

17 Rubin, *supra* note 1 at 16.

18 Sedgwick, *supra* note 3 at 10.

19 *Ibid.* at 81.

20 Ernesto Laclau, *Emancipation(s)* (London: Verso, 1996) at 14.

21 Kenji Yoshino, "The Epistemic Contract of Bisexual Erasure" (2000) 52:2 Stan. L. Rev. 353.

22 Elaine Craig, "Trans-phobia and the Relational Production of Gender" (2007) 18:2 Hastings Women's L.J. 101 at 154.

23 Weeks, *supra* note 4 at 4.

24 See, for example, John Finnis, "Law, Morality, and Sexual Orientation" (1994) 69 Notre Dame L. Rev. 1049, where he draws on natural law principles to argue against equality for sexual minorities. The work of early sexologists such as Havelock Ellis, Magnus Hirchfield, and Richard Kraft Von-Ebbing or the work of Alfred Kinsey all constitute examples of what I mean by sexual science.

25 Weeks, *supra* note 4 at 4.

26 *Ibid.*

27 *Criminal Code*, R.S.C. 1985, c. C-46.
28 Weeks, *supra* note 12 at 5.
29 *Ibid.* at 7.
30 The Second World War and the post-Second World War era offer an example. During this period, large numbers of young adults left their sheltered, supervised, and confining rural settings in order to join same sex environments to serve their countries and then, upon return, find employment in cities. This phenomenon is often attributed with creating new opportunity for same sex sexual exploration and creating, for the first time, gay and lesbian communities. These communities allowed greater possibilities for gay and lesbian sexual identities and contributed to the commencement of the gay and lesbian rights movement, at least in North America. See Allan Berube, *Coming Out under Fire: The History of Gay Men and Women in World War Two* (New York: Free Press, 1990). He demonstrates that the development of same sex sexual identity was contingent not only on societal factors but also on the particular same sex sexual practices in which people engaged. See George Chauncey, *Gay New York: Gender, Urban Culture and the Making of the Gay Male World, 1890-1940* (New York: Basic Books, 1994).

Chapter 2: Legal Conceptions of Sexual Nature and Natural Sex

1 Michel Foucault, *The History of Sexuality, Volume I: An Introduction* (New York: Vintage Books, 1978) at 32.
2 *Ibid.*
3 Robin West, *Caring for Justice* (New York: New York University Press, 1997) at 272.
4 *Ibid.* at 273.
5 This is the notion that there is no doer behind the deed – all there is the deed. Judith Butler, borrowing from Nietzsche, makes this suggestion in Judith Butler, *Gender Trouble: Feminism and the Subversion of Identity*, 2nd edition (New York: Routledge, 1990) at 33.
6 See North American Man/Boy Love Association, http://www.nambla.org.
7 See, for example, *R. v. Dick, Penner and Finnigan*, [1965] 1 C.C.C. 171 at para. 39, where the Court refers to the accused's animal lust in describing his rape of an adult woman.
8 *R. v. Handy*, [2002] 2 S.C.R. 908 at para. 40 [*Handy*].
9 G.R. Hibbard, ed., *Hamlet* (Oxford: Oxford University Press, 1987) at 188.
10 *R. v. Smith* (1915), 84 L.J. K.B. 2153.
11 *Makin v. Attorney-General for New South Wales* (1893), [1894] A.C. 57 [*Makin*].
12 *R. v. Horwood*, [1970] 1 Q.B. 133; *D.P.P. v. Boardman*, [1975] A.C. 421 (C.A.).
13 *R. v. D.(L.E.).* (1989), 71 C.R. (3d) (S.C.C.); *B.(C.R.).*, *infra* note 21; *C.(M.H.).*, *infra* note 21; *B.(F.F.), infra* note 21; *Handy, supra* note 8.
14 See Marc Rosenberg, "Similar Fact Evidence," in *Special Lectures 2003: The Law of Evidence* (Toronto: Irwin, 2003) 391 at para. 41.
15 Hamish Stewart, "Rationalizing Similar Facts: A Comment on *R. v. Handy*" (2003) 8 Can. Crim. L. Rev. 113 at 114.
16 *Handy, supra* note 8. See Rosenberg, *supra* note 14; Stewart, *supra* note 15.
17 *Handy, supra* note 8 at para. 55.
18 As cited in John Sopinka, Sidney Lederman, and Alan Bryant, *The Law of Evidence in Canada*, 2nd edition (Toronto: Butterworths, 1999) at 524.
19 The cases that are of particular significance for this discussion are those in which the factual issue in dispute essentially comes down to credibility as to the *actus reus*. This line of cases can, and should, be distinguished from cases in which the factual issue in dispute concerns the identity of the perpetrator. The analysis in identity cases understandably

focuses almost exclusively on the similarity in *modus operandi* and on the evidence of signature type behaviour rather than on evidence of the accused's sexual propensity.

20 See Lee Stuesser, "Similar Fact Evidence in Sexual Offence Cases" (1996) 39 Crim. L.Q. 160; Stewart, *supra* note 15.

21 *R. v. B.(C.R.)*, [1990] S.C.J. no. 31 [*B.(C.R.)*]; *R. v. B.(F.F.)*, [1993] 1 S.C.R. 697 [*B.(F.F.)*]; *R. v. C.(M.H.)*, [1991] 1 S.C.R. 763 [*C.(M.H.)*].

22 *B.(C.R.), supra* note 21 at para. 2.

23 *Ibid.* at para. 24.

24 *Ibid.* at para. 42.

25 *C.(M.H.), supra* note 21 at para. 20.

26 *B.(C.R.), supra* note 21 at para. 24.

27 *Ibid.* at para. 27.

28 *C.(M.H.), supra* note 21 at para. 22.

29 *Ibid.* [emphasis added].

30 *Ibid.* at para. 25.

31 *C.(M.H.), supra* note 21 at para. 22.

32 *B.(F.F.), supra* note 21.

33 R.J. Delisle, "Annotation, *R. v. B.(F.F.)*" (1993) 18:4 C.R. 261; Lynn Hanson, "Sexual Assault and the Similar Fact Rule" (1993) 27 U.B.C. L. Rev. 51.

34 *B.(F.F.), supra* note 21 at para. 23.

35 *Handy, supra* note 8 at para. 78 [emphasis added].

36 *R. v. R.B.*, [2005] O.J. No. 3575 at para. 15.

37 *R. v. Finelli*, [2008] O.J. No. 2242 at para. 4.

38 *Escobar, infra* note 41; *E.S., infra* note 41.

39 *R. v. Shearing*, [2002] 3 S.C.R. 33.

40 *Ibid.* at para. 54.

41 For further examples of this tendency, see *R. v. Escobar*, [2008] O.J. No. 264 [*Escobar*], where similar fact evidence was admitted to show that the accused has a "situation specific propensity to abuse sexually young children with whom he is in contact as a result of his relationship with a particular person" (at para. 55). See *R. v. E.S.*, [2006] O.J. No. 1750 [*E.S.*], where similar fact evidence involving the accused's seven daughters and one sister-in-law was admitted. See also *R. v. R.C.*, [2003] O.J. No. 3919; *R. v. K.M.*, [2008] O.J. No. 198; *R. v. Kennedy*, [2006] O.J. No. 4976.

42 See, for example, *R. v. J.M.H.*, [2003] O.J. No. 5511 at para. 41: "The accused, in the similar fact evidence, was in a relationship of trust ... a stepdaughter he had known for years in a home they shared. In the case at bar, it was a random encounter [*sic*] neither of them know the other." See *R. v. Blake* (2005), 68 O.R. (3d) 75.

43 *R. v. F.L.*, [2003] O.J. No. 4040.

44 *R. v. Cormier*, [2009] O.J. No. 2937.

45 See *R. v. R.W.D.*, [2004] O.J. No. 3091 at para. 75.

46 *R. v. M.B.*, [2008] O.J. No. 2521.

47 *R. v. R.W.D.*, [2004] O.J. No. 3091 at para. 75.

48 *Ibid.* at para. 75.

49 See *R. v. T.B.*, [2009] O.J. No. 751, where the court found that "in short, toward his step-nieces the respondent was a sexual predator." For other cases involving child complainants, and in which the court characterized those who sexually offend against children as sexual predators, see *R. v. D.I.*, [2008] O.J. No. 1823; *R. v. Wadel*, [2001] O.J. No. 4248.

50 *Makin, supra* note 11.
51 It seems as if in adult cases where the power imbalance is assumed (due to the nature of the relationship), relationship dynamics play a similar analytical role to the role they play in child complainant cases. See *R. v. Gavrilko,* [2007] B.C.J. 2154 at para. 31; *G.(J.R.I.) v. Tyhurst,* [2003] 6 W.W.R. 402; *R. v. Stewart,* [2004] B.C.J. No. 195.
52 See, for example, *R. v. J.G.E.S.,* [2005] B.C.J. No. 3161; *R. v. Yusufi,* [2007] O.J. No. 2321; *R. v. Whitehead,* [2004] O.J. No. 4030.
53 *Handy, supra* note 8 at para. 35.
54 *R. v. G.G.,* [2003] N.W.T.J. No. 88..
55 *Ibid.* at para. 14.
56 See, for example, *R. v. C.P.K.,* [2002] O.J. No. 4929. *Handy, supra* note 8, itself may also substantiate this point.
57 See *R. v. Butler,* [1992] 1 S.C.R. 452 [*Butler*]; *Little Sisters Book and Art Emporium v. Canada (Minister of Justice),* [2002] 2 S.C.R. 1120 [*Little Sisters*].
58 *R. v. Sharpe,* [2001] 1 S.C.R. 45 [*Sharpe*].
59 *Criminal Code,* R.S.C. 1985, c. C-46.
60 *Canadian Charter of Rights and Freedoms,* Part 1 of the *Constitution Act, 1982,* being Schedule B to the *Canada Act 1982* (U.K.), 1982, c. 11 [*Charter*].
61 Section 2(b) of the *Charter, ibid.,* provides constitutional protection for freedom of expression in Canada. Section 1 creates a saving provision under which, in some circumstances, the government can justify laws that infringe the rights and freedoms guaranteed under the *Charter.* Section 163.1(4)'s prohibition of material created and used solely by the accused and material created by an accused teenager with another teenager depicting otherwise lawful activity was not saved under section 1. In upholding the provision, the Court carved out these exceptions to the general prohibition on possession of child pornography.
62 *Sharpe, supra* note 58 at 87.
63 *Butler, supra* note 57; *Little Sisters, supra* note 57.
64 *Sharpe, supra* note 57 at para. 88 [emphasis added].
65 *Butler, supra* note 57 at para. 108; *Little Sisters, supra* note 57 at para. 60.
66 *Sharpe, supra* note 57 at para. 89
67 *R. v. Morelli,* [2010] 1 S.C.R. 253.
68 *Ibid.* at para. 85. The majority and the dissent in *Morelli* differed with respect to the definition of possession – whether it required downloading the images or merely having them in one's computer cache. Justice Fish's other reason for quashing the conviction was that because the warrant was not based on any evidence that the accused had actually downloaded images off the Internet onto his computer the charge should have been accessing child pornography, not possessing child pornography.
69 *Ibid.* at para. 86.
70 *Ibid.* at paras. 51, 86.
71 *Ibid.* at paras. 63, 70, 73, 76, 80, 96.
72 For a discussion of this characterization, see Eric S. Janus, "'Don't Think of a Predator': Changing Frames for Better Sexual Violence Prevention" (2007) 8:6 Sex Offender Law Report 81, Social Sciences and Research Network, http://papers.ssrn.com/sol3/papers.cfm?abstract_id=1084921.
73 Statistics Canada, *Family Violence in Canada: A Statistical Profile,* edited by Catherine Trainor and Karen Mihorean (Ottawa: Canadian Centre for Justice Statistics, 2001).
74 *Criminal Code, supra* note 59.

75 There are some examples where the law does attempt to penetrate this circle. One would be the exception to spousal privilege found under section 4(2) of the *Canada Evidence Act*, R.S.C. 1985, c. C-5. Section 4(2) stipulates that a husband or wife is a competent and compellable witness against a spouse charged with an offence under any of sections 151, 152, 153, 155, or 159, subsection 160(2) or (3), or sections 170 to 173, 179, 212, 215, 218, 271 to 273, 280 to 283, 291 to 294, or 329.
76 *Tackling Violent Crime Act*, S.C. 2008, c. 6.
77 *Ibid.*, preamble.
78 *House of Commons Debates*, 39th Parl., 2nd Sess., No. 9 (26 October 2007).
79 *R. v. Legare*, [2009] 3 S.C.R. 551 at para. 25.
80 See Susan Estrich, *Real Rape: How the Legal System Victimizes Women Who Say No* (Cambridge, MA: Harvard University Press, 1987).
81 This should not be taken as a wholehearted endorsement of the Court's decision in *Butler*, *supra* note 57. While the more constructivist approach to sexuality that it adopts seems correct, there is another element to the case that remains problematic. This is the Court's failure to reject the "community standards of tolerance test" used to establish harm. For a discussion on this point, see Chapter 5 in this volume.

Chapter 3: Natural Categories and Non-Categorical Approaches to Law and Sexuality

Short excerpts from the first section of Chapter 3 in this volume were previously published in Elaine Craig, "Family as Status in *Doe v. Canada:* Constituting Family under Section 15 of the Charter" (2007) 20 N.J.C.L. 197.

1 *Canadian Charter of Rights and Freedoms*, Part 1 of the *Constitution Act, 1982*, being Schedule B to the *Canada Act 1982* (U.K.), 1982, c. 11 [*Charter*].
2 These include the provincial human rights codes; the *Canadian Human Rights Act*, R.S.C. 1985, c. H-6; and the entrenched equality guarantee under section 15 of the *Charter, supra* note 1.
3 *Egan v. Canada*, [1995] 2 S.C.R. 513 at para. 5 [*Egan*]. Justice La Forest adopted the same essentialist understanding of sexual orientation in the refugee claimant context two years earlier in *Canada (A.G.) v. Ward*, [1993] 2 S.C.R. 689.
4 See, for example, Jeffrey Weeks, *Against Nature* (London: Rivers Oram Press, 1991).
5 See, for example, Douglas Kropp, "Categorical Failure: Canada's Equality Jurisprudence – Changing Notions of Identity and the Legal Subject" (1997) 23 Queen's L.J. 201; Carl Stychin, "Essential Rights and Contested Identities: Sexual Orientation and Equality Rights Jurisprudence in Canada" (1995) 8 Can J.L. & Jur. 49; Didi Herman, *Rights of Passage: Struggles for Lesbian and Gay Legal Equality* (Toronto: University of Toronto Press, 1994); Nitya Iyer, "Categorical Denials: Equality Rights and the Shaping of Social Identity" (1993) 19 Queen's L.J. 179.
6 See, for example, Ruthann Robson, "Assimilation, Marriage and Lesbian Liberation" (2002) 75 Temp. L. Rev. 709; Stychin, *supra* note 5; Brenda Cossman, "Lesbians, Gay Men, and the *Canadian Charter of Rights and Freedoms*" (2002) 40 Osgoode Hall L.J. 223; Michael Warner, *The Trouble with Normal* (Glencoe, IL: Free Press, 1999); Jody Freeman, "Defining Family in *Mossop v. D.S.S.*: The Challenge of Anti-Essentialism and Interactive Discrimination for Human Rights Litigation" (1994) 44 U.T.L.J. 41.
7 See Lise Gotell, "On Law's Categories" (2002) 17:1 C.J.L.S. 89; Kathleen A. Lahey, *Are We 'Persons' Yet? Law and Sexuality in Canada* (Toronto: University of Toronto Press, 1999).
8 Claire F.L. Young and Susan B. Boyd, "Challenging Heteronormativity? Reaction and Resistance to the Legal Recognition of Same-Sex Partnerships" in Dorothy E. Chunn,

Susan B. Boyd, and Hester Lessard, eds., *Reaction and Resistance: Feminism, Law and Social Change* (Vancouver: UBC Press, 2007) 262; Paula Ettelbrick, "Since When Is Marriage a Path to Liberation?" in Suzanne Sherman, ed., *Lesbian and Gay Marriage: Private Commitments, Public Ceremonies* (Philadelphia: Temple University Press, 1992) 20; Shane Phelan, *Sexual Strangers: Gays, Lesbians, and Dilemmas of Citizenship* (Philadelphia: Temple University Press, 2001).

9 For example, Young and Boyd, *supra* note 8, have noted that changes to the definition of spouse to include gays and lesbians under various laws have actually had a detrimental financial impact on lower income lesbian couples. Kathleen Lahey, *supra* note 7, makes a similar point. See also Brenda Cossman, "Family Feuds: Neo-Liberal and Neo-Conservative Visions of the Reprivatization Project" in Brenda Cossman and Judy Fudge, eds., *Privatization, Law and the Challenge to Feminism* (Toronto: University of Toronto Press, 2002) 169.

10 Iyer, *supra* note 5 at 186.

11 Stychin, *supra* note 5 at 53.

12 Young and Boyd, *supra* note 8 at 278.

13 See Diana Fuss, *Essentially Speaking: Feminism, Nature and Difference* (New York: Routledge, 1989); Carl Stychin, *Law's Desire: Sexuality and the Limits of Justice* (New York: Routledge, 1995).

14 *Civil Marriage Act,* S.C. 2005, c. 33.

15 *Old Age Security Act,* R.S.C. 1985, c. O-9.

16 *Egan, supra* note 3 at 536. Justice Sopinka agreed with the outcome of Justice La Forest's judgment. This meant a majority of the Court denied Egan's claim.

17 *Halpern v. Canada (Attorney-General),* [2003] O.J. No. 2268 [*Halpern*].

18 *Layland v. Ontario (Minister of Consumer and Commercial Relations)* (1993), 104 D.L.R. (4th) 214. In *Bliss v. Canada,* [1979] 1 S.C.R. 183, the Court denied a *Canadian Bill of Rights* challenge to provisions of the *Unemployment Insurance Act,* 1971, 1970-71-72 (Can.), c. 48, ss. 30, 46, arguing that the provisions discriminated on the basis of sex by providing different benefits for pregnant women than for other claimants under the insurance scheme. The challenge was denied on the basis that "inequality between the sexes in this area is not created by legislation but by nature." He determined that the provisions do not distinguish between men and women but, rather, between those who are pregnant and those who are not pregnant. This line of reasoning was rejected by the Court ten years later in *Brooks, infra* note 33.

19 Cossman, *supra* note 6 at 236.

20 *Mossop v. Canada (Attorney General),* [1993] 1 S.C.R. 554.

21 *Vriend v. Alberta,* [1998] 1 S.C.R. 493; *Trinity Western University v. British Columbia College of Teachers,* [2001] 1 S.C.R. 772; *Little Sisters Book and Art Emporium v. Canada (Minister of Justice),* [2002] 2 S.C.R. 1120.

22 *Halpern, supra* note 17; *M. v. H.,* [1999] 2 S.C.R. 3; *Chamberlain v. Surrey School District No. 36,* [2002] 4 S.C.R. 710; *Susan Doe v. Canada (Attorney General)* (2006), 79 O.R. (3d) 586, aff'd 276 D.L.R. (4th) 127 (C.A.) [*Susan Doe*].

23 *Susan Doe, supra* note 22. The constitutional validity of the *Processing and Distribution of Semen for Assisted Conception Regulations,* S.O.R./96-254 [*Semen Regulations*], was originally challenged in an earlier case *Jane Doe v. Canada (Attorney General),* [2006] O.J. No. 191. *Jane Doe* was dismissed after the claimant successfully conceived through home insemination.

24 *Semen Regulations, supra* note 23 at s. 1.

25 The cost is measured both in dollars and in lowered conception rates. The Court in *Susan Doe, supra* note 22, made a finding of fact that frozen semen has a lower rate of conception than does fresh semen. The *Semen Regulations* impose an additional barrier to accessing assisted conception procedures for those women who are not in a sexual or spousal relationship with their known donor and whose known donor is gay or over forty years of age. For these donors, a physician must acquire a special government authorization before using their semen to perform assisted conception procedures.

26 The claimant also unsuccessfully challenged the *Semen Regulations* under section 7 of the *Charter, supra* note 1.

27 *Susan Doe, supra* note 22 at para. 83.

28 Marital status has been recognized as an analogous prohibited ground of discrimination under section 15 of the *Charter* (*Miron v. Trudel,* [1995] 2 S.C.R. 418). Family status is recognized as a prohibited ground under human rights codes in Canada (including the *Canadian Human Rights Act, supra* note 2). While the Supreme Court of Canada has not yet spoken on whether family status is an analogous ground under section 15, it is not unreasonable to suggest that were they asked to do so they would likely find that it is.

29 Elaine Craig, "'I DO' Kiss and Tell: The Subversive Potential of Non-Normative Social Sexual Expression from within Cultural Paradigms" (2004) 27 Dal. L.J. 403; Elaine Craig, "Laws of Desire: The Political Morality of Public Sex" (2009) 54 McGill L.J. 1.

30 Jacques Derrida, *Rogues: Two Essays On Reason* (Stanford, CA: Stanford University Press, 2005).

31 *Janzen v. Platy Enterprises Ltd.*, [1989] 1 S.C.R. 1252 [*Janzen*, S.C.].

32 *Janzen v. Platy Enterprises Ltd.*, [1987] 1 W.W.R. 385 (Man. C.A.) at para. 29.

33 *Brooks v. Canada Safeway Ltd.*, [1989] 1 S.C.R. 1219 [*Brooks*]. *Brooks* was released the same day as *Janzen*, S.C., *supra* note 31.

34 *Janzen*, S.C., *supra* note 31 at paras. 64 and 65.

35 *Ibid.* at para. 57.

36 *Ibid.*

37 See, for example, Colleen Sheppard, "Systemic Inequality and Workplace Culture: Challenging the Institutionalization of Sexual Harassment" (1995) C.L.E.L.J. 249.

38 Katherine Franke, "What's Wrong with Sexual Harassment?" (1997) 46 Stan. L. Rev. 691.

39 For a discussion on this point, see Catharine A. MacKinnon, *Sexual Harassment of Working Women: A Case of Sex Discrimination* (London: Yale University Press, 1979). While the Court in *Janzen*, S.C., *supra* note 31, cited Catharine MacKinnon's definition of sexual harassment, it did not adopt MacKinnon's analysis of power or MacKinnon's constructivist account of sexuality and gender.

40 See *Jubran*, C.A., *infra* note 42, discussed later in this chapter; *MacDonald, infra* note 49, discussed later in this chapter; *Smith v. Menzies Chrysler Inc.*, [2008] O.H.R.T.D. No. 35; *Selinger v. McFarland,* [2008] O.H.R.T.D. No. 48; *R. (on behalf of her son) v. Squamish School District No. 48 (c.o.b. Myrtle Philip Community School),* [2003] B.C.H.R.T.D. No. 49. For a well-known American example, see *Oncale v. Sundowner Offshore Services,* 118 S. Ct. 998 (1998), and Janet Halley's discussion of *Oncale* in *Split Decisions: Taking a Break from Feminism* (Princeton, NJ: Princeton University Press, 2006) at 290.

41 See Michael Messner, "The Triad of Violence in Men's Sports" in Emilie Buchwald, Pamela Fletcher, and Martha Roth, eds., *Transforming a Rape Culture,* revised edition (Washington, DC: Milkweed Editions, 2005) 23, for a discussion of the way in which young male athletes use sexuality not only to bond with each other but also to bully those teammates with less social status. His research reveals that the more aggressive the sport and the

higher the social status of that sport in a particular community the more likely the higher status members of the team are to be sexually aggressive.

42 *North Vancouver School District No. 44 v. Jubran*, [2005] B.C.J. No. 733 (C.A.) [*Jubran*, C.A.].

43 Taken from the Supreme Court of British Columbia's description. *North Vancouver School District No. 44 v. Jubran*, (2003), 9 B.C.L.R. (4th) 338 (S.C.) (rev'd [2005] B.C.J. No. 733 (C.A.)) at para. 5 [*Jubran*, S.C.].

44 *North Vancouver School District No. 44 v. Jubran*, [2002] B.C.H.R.T.D. No. 10 at para. 10.

45 *Ibid.* at para. 13.

46 *Jubran*, S.C., *supra* note 43 at para. 5.

47 Maura Jette, "Sticks and Stones: Jubran v. Board of Trustees and the relationship between Homophobic Harassment and Sex Discrimination" (2003) J.L. & Equality 2.

48 *Jubran*, C.A., *supra* note 42 at para. 50.

49 *MacDonald v. Brighter Mechanical Ltd.*, [2006] B.C.H.R.T.D. No. 326.

50 *Ibid.* at para. 21.

51 *Mercier v. Dasilva*, [2007] B.C.H.R.T.D. No. 72 at para. 27.

52 *Janzen*, S.C., *supra* note 31 at para. 49.

53 As Jette argues, *supra* note 47 at 301, framing these types of claims as discrimination on the basis of sex makes the claimant's actual sexual orientation and the harasser's perception of the claimant's sexual orientation, irrelevant. See also Fransisco Valdes, "Queers, Sissies, Dykes and Tomboys: Deconstructing the Conflation of Sex, Gender and Sexual Orientation in Euro-American Law and Society" (1995) 83 Cal. L. Rev. 3.

Chapter 4: Socially Constructed Conceptions of Sexual Violence

1 See, for example, *R. v. Dick, Penner and Finnigan*, [1965] 1 C.C.C. 171 at para. 39; *R. v. Phelps*, [1983] B.C.J. No. 1387 at para. 3. For further discussion on the essentialist reasoning in these older cases, see Constance Backhouse, *Carnal Crimes: Sexual Assault Law in Canada 1900-1975* (Toronto: Irwin Law, 2008).

2 *R. v. Butler*, [1992] 1 S.C.R. 452 [*Butler*].

3 *Norberg v. Wynrib*, [1992] 2 S.C.R. 226 [*Norberg*]; *M.K. v. M.H.*, [1992] 3 S.C.R. 6.

4 See, for example, *R. v. Osolin*, [1992] 2 S.C.R. 313 [*Osolin*]; *R. v. Litchfield*, [1993] 4 S.C.R. 333 [*Litchfield*]; see *R. v. R.A.*, [2000] 1 S.C.R. 163, where the Court relied on the power imbalance between employer and employee as an aggravating factor in sentencing an accused convicted of sexually assaulting his employee. Justice L'Heureux-Dubé incorporated a power analysis of sex into her dissenting and concurring opinions before the majority of the Court began to adopt this position. See, for example, her reasoning in *R. v. Seaboyer*, [1991] 2 S.C.R. 577 [*Seaboyer*].

5 See, for example, Lorenne Clark and Debra Lewis, *Rape: The Price of Coercive Sexuality* (Toronto: Women's Press, 1977); Christine Boyle, *Sexual Assault* (Toronto: Carswell, 1984); Elizabeth Sheehy, "Canadian Judges and the Law of Rape: Should the Charter Insulate Bias?" (1989) 21 Ottawa L. Rev. 741; Julianne Roberts and Renate Mohr, eds., *Confronting Sexual Assault: A Decade of Legal and Social Change* (Toronto: University of Toronto Press, 1994); Patricia Hughes, "Pornography: Alternatives to Censorship" (1985) 9 Can. J. Pol. & Soc. Theory 96.

6 Kathleen Lahey, *Implications of Feminist Theory for the Direction of Reform of the Criminal Code* (unpublished study of the Law Reform Commission of Canada, Ottawa, 1984) at 2.

7 For Canadian feminist work on sexual violence during this period, which demonstrates how the historical context for rape laws was not the protection of women's sexual integrity

but, rather, systemic sexism oriented towards the protection of a male proprietary interest in female sexual property, see Clark and Lewis, *supra* note 5; Constance Backhouse and Leah Cohen, *The Secret Oppression: Sexual Harassment of Working Women* (Toronto: MacMillan, 1978); Constance Backhouse, "Nineteenth-Century Canadian Rape Law 1800-1892" in David H. Flaherty, ed., *Essays in the History of Canadian Law* (Toronto: Osgoode Society, 1983) 200; Christine Boyle, "Married Women beyond the Pale of the Law of Rape" (1981) 1 Windsor Y.B. Access Just. 192; Lucinda Vandervort, "Enforcing the Sexual Assault Laws: An Analysis for Action" (1985-86) 44:4 Resources for Feminist Research 14.

8 See, for examples of this tension, Sheila McIntyre, "The Charter: Driving Women to Abstraction" (1985) 6 Broadside 5; Brettel Dawson, "Legal Structures: A Feminist Critique of Sexual Assault Reform" (1984) 13 Resources for Feminist Research 40. See also Susan Boyd and Elizabeth Sheehy, "Feminist Perspectives on Law: Canadian Theory and Practice" (1986-88) 2 C.J.W.L. 1, for a discussion of feminist work exploring this tension.

9 Sheila McIntyre, "Redefining Reformism: The Consultations That Shaped C-49" in Roberts and Mohr, *supra* note 5, 293 at 295. McIntyre was, of course, borrowing from Audre Lorde's "The Master's Tools Will Never Dismantle the Master's House" in N. Bereano, ed., *Sister Outsider: Essays and Speeches* (Berkeley: Crossing Press, 1984) 110.

10 See, for example, Clark and Lewis, *supra* note 5. In the American context, see Susan Brownmiller, *Against Our Will: Men, Women and Rape* (New York: Bantam, 1975). See also Robin Morgan, *Going Too Far: The Personal Chronicle of a Feminist* (New York: Vintage, 1978).

11 Taken from Boyle, *supra* note 5 at 53.

12 *Criminal Code*, R.S.C. 1985, c. C-46.

13 *R. v. Bernard*, [1988] 2 S.C.R. 833 at para. 84.

14 Diana Marjury, "*Seaboyer* and *Gayme:* A Study In Equality" in Roberts and Mohr, *supra* note 5; Lahey, *supra* note 6; Constance Backhouse and Leah Cohen, "Desexualizing Rape: A Dissenting View on the Proposed Rape Amendments" (1980) 2:4 Canadian Women's Studies 99.

15 Kathleen Mahoney, "The Canadian Constitutional Approach to Freedom of Expression in Hate Propaganda and Pornography" (1992) 55 Law & Contemp. Probs. 77.

16 Christine Boyle, "The Judicial Construction of Sexual Assault Offences" in Roberts and Mohr, *supra* note 5, 136 at 137.

17 *Ibid.* at 138.

18 Catharine A. MacKinnon, "Feminist Approaches to Sexual Assault in Canada and the United States: A Brief Retrospective" in Constance Backhouse and David Flaherty, eds., *Challenging Times: The Women's Movement in Canada and the United States* (Montreal and Kingston: McGill-Queens University Press, 1992) 186 at 191; Catharine A. MacKinnon, *Toward a Feminist Theory of State* (Cambridge, MA: Harvard University Press, 1989); Catharine A. MacKinnon, *Feminism Unmodified: Discourses on Life and Law* (Cambridge, MA: Harvard University Press, 1987).

19 See, for example, *Osolin, supra* note 4.

20 MacKinnon is cited in numerous factums by the Women's Legal Education and Action Fund (LEAF) (including their submissions in *Butler, supra* note 2; *Norberg, supra* note 3; and *R. v. Ewanchuk*, [1999] 1 S.C.R. 330 [*Ewanchuk*]). Sheila McIntyre suggested that LEAF's recommendations for the substantive changes to sexual assault law in 1992 were

based on MacKinnon's and Ronald Dworkin's anti-pornography work (McIntyre, *supra* note 8).

21 MacKinnon was cited approvingly by Justice Cory for the majority in *Osolin, supra* note 4, and by Justice L'Heureux-Dubé in her concurring decision in *Ewanchuk, supra* note 20, her dissent in *Symes v. Canada*, [1993] 4 S.C.R. 695, and her partial dissent in *Seaboyer, supra* note 4. She was cited approvingly by Chief Justice Dickson in *Janzen v. Platy Enterprises Ltd.*, [1989] 1 S.C.R. 1252, for her definition of sexual harassment (see Chapter 3 in this volume for a discussion of how the Court's conception of sexual harassment in *Janzen* still relied on essentialist assumptions about sexuality). In both *Seaboyer* and *Ewanchuk*, the Court cited Elizabeth Sheehy, "Canadian Judges and the Law of Rape: Should the Charter Insulate Bias?" (1989) 21 Ottawa L. Rev. 741. Christine Boyle's book, *Sexual Assault, supra* note 5, has been cited repeatedly by the Court in cases developing the Court's sexual assault doctrine.

22 *R. v. Chase*, [1987] 2 S.C.R. 293 [*Chase*].

23 *R. v. M.(M.L.)*, [1994] 2 S.C.R. 3 [*M.(M.L.)*]; *Ewanchuk, supra* note 20.

24 *Criminal Code*, R.S.C. 1970, c. C-34, s. 143 [repealed 1980-81-82, c. 125, s. 6].

25 *R. v. Swietlinski*, [1980] 2 S.C.R. 956.

26 See, for example, *R. v. Hay*, [1959] M.J. No. 4 at para. 7.

27 See *R. v. Louie Chong* (1914), 23 C.C.C. 250, where the Court upheld the trial judge's conviction on the basis that the appellant seized hold of the complainant and offered her money for "an immoral purpose."

28 See, for example, *R. v. Collins*, [1985] O.J. No. 51, where an accused's conduct amounted to an indecent assault not because repeatedly forcing his tongue into the complainant's mouth violated her sexual integrity or dignity as a human being but, rather, because of it "being morally offensive, violating prevailing notions of decency, and being committed in circumstances that, viewed objectively, involved the sexual gratification of the appellant."

29 See, for example, *R. v. Moore*, [1955] A.J. No. 1, where based on 1950s community standards of tolerance a woman making a pass at another woman constituted circumstances of indecency where the same action by a man would not.

30 The three tiers adopted include (1) sexual assault; (2) sexual assault with a weapon, threats to a third party, or causing bodily harm; and (3) aggravated sexual assault. *An Act to Amend the Criminal Code in Relation to Sexual Offences and Other Offences against the Person*, S.C. 1980-81-82-83, c. 125, s. 19. For a comprehensive discussion of the evolution of these early legislative reforms, see Boyle, *supra* note 5. There were further reforms in 1987 (S.C. 1987, c. 34, ss. 1-8), 1992 (S.C. 1992, c. 38, ss. 1-3), and 1997 (S.C. 1997, c. 30, ss. 1-3).

31 *Chase, supra* note 22.

32 *R. v. Chase*, (1984), 13 C.C.C. (3d) 187 (C.A.).

33 *Chase, supra* note 22 at para. 11.

34 See *R. v. Robicheau*, [2002] S.C.J. No. 50, overturning the Nova Scotia Court of Appeal in *R. v. Robicheau*, [2001] N.S.J. No. 113.

35 See, for example, *R. c. Archontakis*, [1980] J.Q. no. 196 [*Archontakis*].

36 See, for example, *R. v. G.B.*, [1982] N.W.T.J. No. 40 at para. 6.

37 *Archontakis, supra* note 35 at para. 9.

38 *Chase, supra* note 22 at para. 10.

39 See, for example, *R. v. Alderton*, [1985] O.J. No. 2419.

40 See Jennifer Nedelsky, "Reconceiving Autonomy: Sources, Thoughts and Possibilities" (1989) Yale J.L. & Fem. 7 at 8.
41 See Nicola Lacey, "Unspeakable Subjects, Impossible Rights: Sexuality, Integrity, and Criminal Law" (1998) 11 Can. J.L. & Jur. 47.
42 Lacey, *supra* note 41 at 49.
43 *R. v. Spence*, [1994] O.J. No. 981.
44 *R. v. Crowe*, [1987] O.J. No. 1671.
45 *Litchfield*, *supra* note 4.
46 *Ibid.* at HN [emphasis added].
47 *Ibid.* at para. 13.
48 *Ibid.*
49 Lacey, *supra* note 41.
50 *R. v. Clarence* (1988), 22 Q.B.D. 23 at 44. In *Clarence*, the husband's failure to disclose that he had gonorrhea did not vitiate his wife's consent because "the only sorts of consent which so far destroy the effect of a woman's consent ... are frauds as to the nature of the act itself, or as to the identity of the person who does the act."
51 *Bolduc v. The Queen*, [1967] S.C.R. 677.
52 *Ibid.* at para. 2.
53 *R. v. Cuerrier*, [1998] S.C.J. No. 64 [*Cuerrier*, S.C.].
54 *R. v. Cuerrier* (1996), 83 B.C.A.C. 295.
55 *Cuerrier*, S.C., *supra* note 53 at para. 108. The issue was the definition of "fraud" as it pertains to consent under section 265(3)(c) of the *Criminal Code*. When the *Criminal Code* amendments in 1982 were enacted the definition dropped these words. The provision now states that consent is vitiated where it is given pursuant to a fraud.
56 Recent cases have explored the standard for "significant risk" in the context of viral loads and condom usage. See, for example, *R. v. Mabior*, [2010] M.J. No. 308 (leave to appeal granted) [*Mabior*]; *R. v. J.A.T.*, [2010] B.C.J. No. 1024. For a discussion regarding the arguments for and against the use of criminal law to regulate the failure to disclose HIV status to sexual partners, see Isabel Grant, "The Boundaries of the Criminal Law: The Criminalization of the Non-Disclosure of HIV" (2008) 31 Dal. L.J. 123.
57 *Mabior*, *supra* note 56.
58 *R. v. Nicolaou*, [2008] B.C.J. No. 1331 [*Nicolaou*].
59 *Ibid.* at para. 23.
60 *Ibid.* at para. 31.
61 *R. v. Larue*, [2003] 1 S.C.R. 277.
62 *R. v. Larue*, [2002] B.C.J. No. 3045 at paras. 33-36.
63 See Jeffrey Weeks, *The World We Have Won* (Routledge: New York, 2007).
64 *Ewanchuk*, *supra* note 20. The word affirmed is used here because many of the changes with respect to the doctrine of consent recognized in *Ewanchuk* had already been adopted in earlier concurrences or dissents and in lower court decisions. See, for example, *R. v. Park*, [1995] 2 S.C.R. 836 [*Park*]; *R. v. Esau*, [1997] 2 S.C.R. 777 [*Esau*]; *R. v. M.(L.M.)*, [1994] 2 S.C.R. 3. My description of the change to the definition of consent established by *Ewanchuk* appeared in an earlier article discussing the mistaken belief in consent defence. Elaine Craig, "Ten Years after *Ewanchuk* – The Art of Seduction Is Alive and Well: An Examination of the Mistaken Belief in Consent Defence" (2009) 13 Can. Crim. L. Rev. 3.
65 *Ewanchuk*, *supra* note 20. Both at common law and under sections 265.3 and 273.1 of the *Criminal Code*, consent must be freely given in order to be legally effective. Fear, duress, incapacity, abuse of trust, fraud, and coercion all vitiate consent to sexual touching.

66 *Ewanchuk*, *supra* note 20 at para. 39.

67 This was supported by sections 265.3 and 273.1 of the *Criminal Code*, both of which are framed in the negative. Did the complainant submit or not resist (section 265.1)? Did the complainant express a lack of consent (section 273.1)?

68 The Court had earlier affirmed the rather significant point that passivity or silence did not constitute consent in an unremarkable one-paragraph decision overturning the Nova Scotia Court of Appeal (*M.(M.L.)*, *supra* note 23). In addition, section 265.3 of the *Criminal Code* stipulates that no consent is obtained where the complainant submits or does not resist by reason of the application of force, threats or fear of the application of force, fraud, or the exercise of authority.

69 Lucinda Vandervort, "Mistake of Law and Sexual Assault: Consent and *Mens Rea*" (1987-88) 2 C.J.W.L. 233. *Park*, *supra* note 64; *Esau*, *supra* note 64.

70 *R. v. J.R.*, [2006] O.J. No. 2698.

71 See Craig, *supra* note 64.

72 MacKinnon, "Feminist Approaches," *supra* note 18 at 189.

73 Gavin Lust, "Advances Less Criminal Than Hormonal: Rape and Consent in *R. v. Ewanchuk*" (1999) 5 Appeal 18 at 23.

74 For example, in all of the reported American criminal cases, the term "sexual integrity," at the time of writing, had only been used nine times (as compared to 551 times in Canada). It has never been used in the sense that it has been used in Canadian cases since 1987. This is all the more remarkable given that the number of Canadian cases each year is vastly outnumbered by the number of American cases each year.

Chapter 5: A Moral Shift

Aspects of the arguments advanced in the first and second parts of this chapter were initially explored in Elaine Craig, "Re-interpreting the Criminal Regulation of Sex Work in Light of *Labaye*" (2008) 1 Can. Crim. L. Rev. 327, and Elaine Craig, "Laws of Desire: The Political Morality of Public Sex" (2009) 54 McGill L.J. 3. Some excerpts from these articles have been revised and included in this chapter.

1 See, for example, *R. v. B. and S.*, [1957] C.C.S. No. 921; *R. v. P.*, [1968] M.J. No. 12 at para. 63; *R. v. J.*, [1957] A.J. No. 78 at para. 20.

2 *R. v. Butler*, [1992] 1 S.C.R. 452 [*Butler*].

3 *R. v. Labaye*, [2005] 3 S.C.R. 728 [*Labaye*].

4 *Little Sisters Book and Art Emporium v. Canada (Minister of Justice)*, [2002] 2 S.C.R. 1120.

5 See, for example, Varda Burstyn, "Political Precedents and Moral Crusades: Women, Sex and the State" in Varda Burstyn, ed., *Women against Censorship* (Toronto: Douglas and McIntyre, 1985) 4; Kathleen Lahey, "The Canadian Charter of Rights and Pornography: Toward a Theory of Actual Gender Equality" (1984-85) 20 New Eng. L. Rev. 649; Sheila Noonan, "Pereira-Vasquez: Obscenity – For the Sake of Dirt" (1988) 64 C.R. (3d) 277.

6 See, for example, June Callwood, "Feminist Debates and Civil Liberties" in Burstyn, *Women against Censorship*, *supra* note 5, 121. However, see also Susan Cole, "Book Review: *Women against Censorship*" (1985) 1 C.J.W.L. 226.

7 Carol Smart, *Feminism and the Power of Law* (London: Routledge, 1989) at 120.

8 See, for example, Catharine A. MacKinnon, *Only Words* (Cambridge, MA: Harvard University Press, 1993).

9 See, for example, Maryann Ayim, "Pornography and Sexism: A Thread in the Web" (1985) 23 U.W.O. L. Rev. 189; Susan Cole, "The Minneapolis Ordinance: Feminist Law-Making"

(1985) 14 Resources for Feminist Research, Special Issue "Women and the Criminal Justice System" 30.

10 *Butler, supra* note 2, remains the leading precedent on the definition of obscenity in Canadian criminal law. Kathleen Mahoney, "The Canadian Constitutional Approach to Freedom of Expression in Hate Propaganda and Pornography" (1992) 55 L. & Contemp. Prob. 77; Kathleen Mahoney, "Obscenity, Morals, and the Law: A Feminist Critique" (1985) 17 Ottawa L. Rev. 33.

11 *Butler, supra* note 2 at paras. 8 and 31 (factum of the intervener Women's Legal Education and Action Fund (LEAF)). *Canadian Charter of Rights and Freedoms,* Part 1 of the *Constitution Act, 1982,* being Schedule B to the *Canada Act 1982* (U.K.), 1982, c. 11 [*Charter*].

12 *Charter, supra* note 11 at section 1, which provides a balancing function between constitutionally protected rights and broad societal interests. It gives the government the opportunity to justify a law that has been found to violate a provision of the *Charter* by demonstrating that it is a well-tailored, measured approach to pursuing a legitimate government objective.

13 *Butler, supra* note 2 at para. 21.

14 *Ibid.* at para. 59.

15 *Towne Cinema Theatres v. The Queen,* [1985] 1 S.C.R. 494 [*Towne Cinema*]. In *Towne Cinema,* Chief Justice Dickson stated that "it is harm to society from undue exploitation that is aimed at by the section, not simply lapses in propriety or good taste" (at para. 30).

16 *Butler, supra* note 2 at para. 103.

17 *Ibid.* at para. 108. The Meese Commission (United States, *Attorney General's Commission on Pornography: Final Report,* Washington, DC, US Department of Justice, 1986) was constituted by President Ronald Reagan to conduct a comprehensive investigation into the purported harms of pornography.

18 *Ibid.* at para. 61 [emphasis added].

19 *Ibid.* at para. 108.

20 For example, the Court in *Butler* quoted the same passages from the MacGuigan Report as those provided to them in LEAF's factum. (*Butler, supra* note 2 at para. 85; LEAF factum, *supra* note 11 at para. 16). The MacGuigan Report, an investigation of the Standing Committee on Justice and Legal Affairs, identified pornography as causing clear behavioural and psychological harms (*Report of the Standing Committee on Justice and Legal Affairs,* 1978).

21 LEAF factum, *supra* note 11 at para. 7. See also *Butler, supra* note 2 at para. 22, where LEAF argues that "pornography is a systematic practice of exploitation and subordination based on sex that differentially harms women."

22 Catharine A. MacKinnon, *Feminism Unmodified: Discourses on Life and Law* (Cambridge, MA: Harvard University Press, 1987) at 160.

23 Mahoney, "Canadian Constitutional Approach," *supra* note 10 at 97.

24 *Criminal Code,* R.S.C. 1985, c. C-46.

25 *Labaye, supra* note 3 at para. 57.

26 *Labaye, ibid.,* and *R. v. Kouri,* [2005] 3 S.C.R. 789, were heard by the Court on the same day. The revised legal test for indecency established by the majority in *Labaye* was relied upon to uphold the acquittal in *Kouri.* The Court dealt with these cases as companion cases. Except where otherwise indicated, references to *Labaye* can be assumed to also refer to the analysis in *Kouri.*

27 *Labaye, supra* note 3 at para. 7.

28 *Criminal Code*, *supra* note 24 at s. 197.
29 *Labaye*, *supra* note 3 at para. 29.
30 *R. v. Brodie*, [1962] S.C.R. 681.
31 See, for example, *R. v. Dominion News & Gifts (1962) Ltd.*, [1964] S.C.R. 251; *R. v. Provincial News Co.*, [1974] S.C.J. No 140.
32 *Towne Cinema*, *supra* note 15.
33 *Butler*, *supra* note 2 at para. 59.
34 *Labaye*, *supra* note 3 at para. 33.
35 Ronald Dworkin, *Is Democracy Possible Here?* (Princeton, NJ: Princeton University Press, 2006); Ronald Dworkin, "Foundations of Liberal Equality" in S. Darwall, ed., *Equal Freedom* (Ann Arbor, MI: University of Michigan Press, 1995) 190; Ronald Dworkin, "Liberalism" in S. Hampshire, ed., *Public and Private Morality* (Cambridge: Cambridge University Press, 1978).
36 *Labaye*, *supra* note 3 at para. 104.
37 *Ibid.* at para. 86.
38 *Ibid.* at para. 97.
39 *Ibid.* at para. 62.
40 *Ibid.* at para. 47.
41 *Ibid.* at para. 62.
42 *Butler*, *supra* note 2 at para. 61.
43 This is taken from the dissent of Justices LeBel and Bastarache in *Labaye*, *supra* note 3 at para. 101.
44 *R. v. Mara*, [1997] 2 S.C.R. 630.
45 *Ibid.* at para. 35.
46 *R. v. Tremblay*, [1993] 2 S.C.R. 932.
47 *Ibid.* at para. 71 [emphasis added].
48 J. Brickman and J. Briere, "Incidence of Rape and Sexual Assault in an Urban Canadian Population" (1984) 7:3 Int'l J. Women's Studies 195. Between 80 percent and 85 percent of all victims of sexual assault are girls and women. A 1993 Statistics Canada survey found that one out of every three Canadian women have experienced at least one incident of sexual or physical violence. Almost 60 percent of these women were the targets of more than one such incident. H. Johnson and V. Stacco, "Researching Violence against Women: Statistics Canada's National Survey" (1995) 27 Can. J. Crim. 281.
49 *Norberg v. Wynrib*, [1992] 2 S.C.R. 26.
50 *R. v. Ellison*, [2006] B.C.J. No. 3241; *Latreille c. R.*, [2007] J.Q. no. 11274 (Que. C.A.); *R. v. Ponomarev*, [2007] O.J. No. 2494 [*Ponomarev*].
51 *Ponomarev*, *supra* note 50.
52 See Standing Committee on Justice and Human Rights, *The Challenge of Change: A Study of Canada's Criminal Prostitution Laws*, written by Art Hanger and John Maloney (Ottawa: Communication Canada, Publishing, 2006); Special Committee on Pornography and Prostitution in Canada, *The Challenge of Change* (Ottawa: Department of Supply and Services, 1985). The applicants in two ongoing constitutional challenges to the communications provision and the bawdy house provision, in Ontario and in British Columbia, are arguing that these provisions violate the *Charter* because of the indirect harm they cause to sex workers. See *Bedford v. Canada*, [2010] O.J. No. 4057 [*Bedford*] (in which the Ontario Superior Court of Justice found the provisions unconstitutional – this decision has been appealed); *Downtown Eastside Sex Workers United against Violence Society*

v. Attorney-General (Canada), Vancouver docket no. S075285 (public interest standing has been granted in this case, and the trial is scheduled to proceed in 2011) [*Downtown Eastside Sex Workers*].

53 *Reference re Prostitution*, [1990] 1 S.C.R. 1123. Analyzing whether a law can be saved under section 1 of the *Charter, supra* note 11, requires identifying its legislative objective. The Court in *Bedford, supra* note 52, did do a section 1 analysis of the bawdy house provision. Justice Himel identified public nuisance and safety as its objective.
54 *R. v. Worthington* (1972), 10 C.C.C. (2d) 311 (Ont. C.A.).
55 *Reference re Prostitution, supra* note 53 at para. 2.
56 *Ibid.* at para. 2.
57 *Ibid.* at para. 123.
58 *Ibid.* at para. 120.
59 *Labaye, supra* note 3 at para. 40.
60 *Ibid.* at para. 40.
61 *Labaye, supra* note 3, citing *R. v. Tremblay*, [1993] 2 S.C.R. 932.
62 *Reference re Prostitution, supra* note 53 at para. 128. This quote is from Justice Wilson's dissent, but the majority adopts her reasoning on this point.
63 *Labaye, supra* note 3 at para. 41.
64 *Ibid.* at para. 41.

Chapter 6: Some Subjective Truths about the Objective Truth of Sex

1 *R. v. Butler*, [1992] 1 S.C.R. 452 [*Butler*]; *R. v. Labaye*, [2005] 3 S.C.R. 728 [*Labaye*].
2 *R. v. Tremblay*, [1993] 2 S.C.R. 932 [*Tremblay*]; *R. v. Mara*, [1997] 2 S.C.R. 630; and *Reference re Prostitution*, [1990] 1 S.C.R. 1123.
3 *Norberg v. Wynrib*, [1992] 2 S.C.R. 226 [*Norberg*]; *Little Sisters Book and Art Emporium v. Canada (Minister of Justice)*, [2000] 2 S.C.R. 1120 [*Little Sisters*].
4 Jan Cowie, "Difference, Dominance, Dilemma: A Critical Analysis of *Norberg v. Wynrib*" (1994) 58 Sask. L. Rev. 357 at 358.
5 *Norberg, supra* note 3 at para. 6.
6 *Ibid.* at para. 27 [emphasis added].
7 *Ibid.* at para. 37.
8 *Ibid.* at para. 40.
9 *Ibid.* at para. 44.
10 Certainly, Justice La Forest's reliance on tort evidences his intention to recognize the importance of (women's) autonomy. As he notes, "the concept of consent as it operates in tort law is based on a presumption of individual autonomy and free will" (*ibid.* at para. 27). The purpose of the tort of battery is to protect the personal autonomy of the individual. *Non-Marine Underwriters, Lloyd's of London v. Scalera*, [2000] 1 S.C.R. 551 at para. 15. Another critique of his decision is to suggest that it protects a conception of autonomy that is inadequate. It protects a conception of autonomy as "freedom from." From either a Razian or relational feminist perspective, his understanding of autonomy is impoverished.
11 *Norberg, supra* note 3 at para. 60.
12 *Ibid.* at para. 28.
13 See Donald Dripps, "Beyond Rape: An Essay on the Difference between the Presence of Force and the Absence of Consent" (1992) 92 Colum. L. Rev. 1780 at 1790. Tiresius is a male figure in Greek mythology who was, for seven years, transformed into a woman. Upon being questioned as to whether sex is more pleasurable for men or women, he

replied with the following: "Of ten parts a man enjoys only one; but a woman's sense enjoys all ten in full." Hesiod, *Homeric Hymns, Epic Cycle, Homerica*, translated by Hugh G. Evelyn-White (New York: G.P. Putnam and Sons, 1922).

14 Dripps, *supra* note 13 at 1791.

15 *Ibid.* at 1789.

16 *Norberg, supra* note 3 at para. 57 (this is taken from Justice McLachlin's concurrence, acknowledging the finding of the trial judge).

17 Catharine A. MacKinnon, *Feminism Unmodified: Discourses on Life and Law* (Cambridge, MA: Harvard University Press, 1987) at 11.

18 *Norberg, supra* note 3 at para. 73.

19 It should be noted that MacKinnon's assertion that consent is supposed to mean freedom of desire expressed is not premised on an idealized and romantic account of sex. No one would accuse her of that. See, for example, Leo Bersani, "Is the Rectum a Grave?" (1987) 43 October 197, where he discusses MacKinnon's very unromantic and not idealized account of sex.

20 *Norberg, supra* note 3 at para. 46.

21 Doctrinally, this move is significant. While there was, at this point in the law of fiduciaries, no question that a doctor-patient relationship could give rise to fiduciary obligations (*McInerney v. MacDonald*, [1992] 2 S.C.R. 138), the law was still unsettled as to what the nature of such obligations would be. In *LAC Minerals Ltd. v. International Corona Resources Ltd.*, [1989] 2 S.C.R. 574, Justice Sopinka, writing for the majority, held that fiduciary obligations "must be reserved for situations that are truly in need of the special protection that equity affords." He suggests that the duty ought to be reserved for matters akin to the duty of confidentiality. Preferring instead Justice Wilson's earlier opinion in *Frame v. Smith*, [1987] 2 S.C.R. 99, Justice McLachlin holds that the principles of fiduciary obligation should not be restricted to such narrow legal and economic interests but, rather, should also be used to defend fundamental human and personal interests. Justice McLachlin's approach to fiduciary duty in the context of sexual contact was adopted by the majority less than a year later in *M.K. v. M.H.*, [1992] 3 S.C.R. 6, where the Court, with Justice La Forest writing for the majority, found a father liable for breach of fiduciary duty based on incestuous sexual abuse he perpetrated against his daughter. The issues that arise in *Norberg* regarding a finding that consent was vitiated would not arise in *M.K.*, in which the child lacked capacity to consent to sexual contact with the father.

22 *Norberg, supra* note 3 at para. 90. Although unnecessary to her analysis, Justice McLachlin did still feel compelled to note that she did not consider her to be a "sinner" in any event.

23 *Labaye, supra* note 1. See Chapter 5 in this volume for a discussion of this decision.

24 Trial judgments reflect a trend of misapplying the test for this defence in cases involving complainants who are in an ongoing relationship with the defendant. This ongoing discrepancy in how trial judges approach spousal complainants reflects a problematic historical sentiment regarding the sexual accessibility of wives. See Elaine Craig, "Ten Years after *Ewanchuk* – The Art of Seduction Is Alive and Well: An Examination of the Mistaken Belief in Consent Defence" (2009) 13 Can. Crim. L. Rev. 3; *Criminal Code*, R.S.C. 1985, c. C-46.

25 *Norberg, supra* note 3 at para. 60 [emphasis added].

26 *R. v. Jobidon*, [1991] 2 S.C.R. 714; *R. v. Cuerrier*, [1998] 2 S.C.R. 371. In these cases, the policy justification for vitiating consent involved protecting against non-trivial bodily harm.

27 See Brenda Cossman, "Lesbians, Gay Men, and the *Canadian Charter of Rights and Freedoms*" (2002) 40 Osgoode Hall L.J. 223; Bruce MacDougall, *Queer Judgments:*

Homosexuality, Expression, and the Courts in Canada (Toronto: University of Toronto Press, 2000); Leslie Green, "Men in the Place of Women, from *Butler* to *Little Sisters*," reviewing *Gay Male Pornography: An Issue of Sex Discrimination,* by Christopher Kendall, (2005) 43 Osgoode Hall L.J. 473; Brenda Cossman et al., *Bad Attitude/s on Trial: Pornography, Feminism, and the* Butler *Decision* (Toronto: University of Toronto Press, 1997).

28 *Butler, supra* note 1 at paras. 52 and 61.

29 *Little Sisters, supra* note 3 at para. 60.

30 Catharine MacKinnon, "Feminism, Marxism, Method, and the State: An Agenda for Theory" (1982) 7 Signs 515 at 541.

31 MacDougall, *supra* note 27 at 50.

32 For an articulation of this argument, see Janine Benedet, "*Little Sisters Book and Art Emporium v. Canada (Minister of Justice):* Sex Equality and the Attack on *R. v. Butler*" (2001) 39 Osgoode Hall L.J. 187.

33 *Little Sisters, supra* note 3 at para. 199. He quoted with approval from Neil M. Malamuth: "There are studies suggesting that within homosexual interactions the frequency of sexually coercive acts as well as non-sexual aggression between intimates occurs at a frequency quite comparable to heterosexual interactions" (at para. 63). He also noted that "Equality Now took the view that gay and lesbian individuals have as much right as their heterosexual counterparts to be protected from depictions of sex with violence or sexual conduct that is dehumanizing or degrading in a way that can cause harm that exceeds community standards of tolerance" (at para. 63).

34 *Ibid.* at para. 99.

35 See Lara Karaian, "The Troubled Relationship of Feminist and Queer Legal Theory to Strategic Essentialism: Theory/Praxis, Queer Porn, and Canadian Anti-discrimination Law" in Martha Albertson Fineman, Jack Jackson, and Adam Romero, eds., *Feminist and Queer Legal Theory: Intimate Encounters, Uncomfortable Conversations* (New York: Ashgate Press, 2009) 375, for a discussion highlighting the essentialism implicit in Little Sisters' argument.

36 *Little Sisters, supra* note 3 at para. 60.

37 *R. v. B.E.*, [1999] O.J. 3869 at para. 1.

38 *Ibid.* at para. 10.

39 *Ibid.* at para. 40.

40 *Ibid.* at para. 80.

41 Postmodern, like many other terms used to connote broad concepts or areas of thought, is a contested term and a label that many theorists whose work is commonly characterized as postmodern have rejected. As Linda Alcoff explains, "[p]ostmodernism is no more nor less an accurate representation of reality than ... are words such as 'thing,' 'self,' 'truth' indeed even 'word.' Like these other terms, however, there are productive uses to which the term postmodern can be put." Linda Alcoff, "The Politics of Postmodern Feminism, Revisited" (1997) 36 Cultural Critique 5 at 7.

42 Recall, for example, the discussion in Chapter 5 in this volume of Justice Cory's reliance in *Tremblay, supra* note 2, on Dr. Campbell, the expert sexologist, in an effort to determine whether masturbation was common enough (and thus a naturally occurring behaviour) not to be indecent.

43 Mary Joe Frug, *Postmodern Legal Feminism* (New York: Routledge, 1992) at 153.

44 Judith Butler, Ernesto Laclau, and Slavoj Žižek, *Contingency, Hegemony, Universality: Contemporary Dialogues on the Left* (London: Verso, 2000) at 12.

45 *Ibid.* at 12.
46 Frug, *supra* note 43 at 131, notes this query of radical and liberal feminists.
47 Michel Foucault, *The History of Sexuality, Volume I: An Introduction* (New York: Vintage Books, 1978) at 101.
48 *Egan v. Canada*, [1995] 2 S.C.R. 513.
49 Judith Butler and Joan Scott, eds., *Feminists Theorize the Political* (New York: Routledge, 1992) at xiv.
50 Gayle Rubin, "Thinking Sex: Notes for a Radical Theory of the Politics of Sexuality" in Henry Abelove and Michele Aina Barale, eds., *The Lesbian and Gay Studies Reader* (Routledge: New York, 1993) 3.
51 Eve Kosofsky Sedgwick, *Epistemology of the Closet* (Berkeley and Los Angeles: University of California Press, 1990).
52 Frug, *supra* note 43.
53 Janet Halley, *Split Decisions: Taking a Break from Feminism* (Princeton, NJ: Princeton University Press, 2006).
54 Teresa Ebert, "The 'Difference' of Postmodern Feminism" (1991) 53:8 College English 886.
55 *Ibid.* at 888.
56 *Ibid.*
57 Ernesto Laclau, *Emancipation(s)* (London: Verso, 1996) at 26. Ernesto Laclau acknowledges that, in its efforts to deconstruct the totalizing meta-narratives of modernity, the postmodernists have created a paradox.
58 *Ibid.*
59 See Katherine Franke, "Theorizing Yes: An Essay on Feminism, Law and Desire" in Martha Fineman, Jack Jackson, and Adam Romero, eds., *Feminist and Queer Legal Theory: Intimate Encounters, Uncomfortable Conversations* (Burlington, VT: Ashgate Publishing Company, 2009) 29, for a discussion on this point.
60 Carole S. Vance, ed. *Pleasure and Danger: Exploring Female Sexuality* (London: Pandora Press, 1989).
61 Franke, *supra* note 59 at 39.
62 I am grateful to Rebecca Johnson for drawing this point to my attention.

Chapter 7: Trouble Ahead

An earlier version of my discussion of Joseph Raz's theory, its application to the Supreme Court of Canada's reasoning in *R. v. Labaye*, [2005] 3 S.C.R. 728, and the promise of iconoclasm appeared in Elaine Craig, "Laws of Desire: The Political Morality of Public Sex" (2009) 54 McGill L.J. 3.

1 Jacques Derrida, *Rogues: Two Essays on Reason* (Stanford, CA: Stanford University Press, 2005).
2 Jacques Derrida, "Force of Law" (1989) 11 Cardozo L. Rev. 919 at 927.
3 *Ibid.* at 961.
4 *Ibid.* at 947.
5 *Ibid.* at 969.
6 Matthias Fritsch, "Derrida's Democracy to Come" (2002) 9:4 Constellations 574. Derrida, *supra* note 1 at 86.
7 See Fritsch, *supra* note 6.
8 Mary Joe Frug, *Postmodern Legal Feminism* (New York: Routledge, 1992) at 153.

9 Fritsch, *supra* note 6. This might be contrasted with Jürgen Habermas' theory of communicative action as developed in *Between Facts and Norms* (Cambridge, MA: MIT Press, 1998).
10 Ernesto Laclau, *Emancipation(s)* (London: Verso, 1996) at 27.
11 Derrida, *supra* note 2 at 947.
12 Joseph Raz, *The Morality of Freedom* (Oxford: Clarendon Press, 1986).
13 *Ibid.* at 381.
14 *Ibid.* at 375.
15 *Ibid.* at 207.
16 Joseph Raz, "Rights and Politics" (1995) 71 Ind. L.J. 27 at 31.
17 Raz, *supra* note 12 at 420.
18 Raz, *supra* note 16 at 35.
19 *Canadian Charter of Rights and Freedoms,* Part 1 of the *Constitution Act, 1982,* being Schedule B to the *Canada Act 1982* (U.K.), 1982, c. 11.
20 *R. v. Labaye,* [2005] 3 S.C.R. 728 [*Labaye*].
21 Joseph Raz, *The Practice of Values* (Oxford: Oxford University Press, 2003) at 41.
22 I am indebted to Leslie Green for observing that under the argument I am making it must be the case that any standards of excellence for sex be plural in form.
23 *Labaye, supra* note 20 at para. 29.
24 Raz, *supra* note 16 at 36.
25 *Labaye, supra* note 20 at para. 69.
26 Raz, *supra* note 16 at 38.
27 *Ibid.*
28 Margaret Atwood, *The Handmaid's Tale* (Toronto: McClelland Books, 1985) at 89.
29 Raz, *supra* note 12 at 401.
30 *Labaye, supra* note 20 at para. 103.
31 See, for example, *Halpern v. Canada (Attorney-General),* [2003] O.J. No. 2268 [*Halpern*]; *Nova Scotia v. Walsh* [2002] 4 S.C.R. 325 [*Walsh*]; *M. v. H.,* [1999] 2 S.C.R. 3; *A.A. v. B.B.,* [2007] O.J. No. 2.
32 This observation contradicts to some extent the argument suggested by queer theorists such as Michael Warner. Warner opposed the gay and lesbian rights movement's focus on recognition of same sex marriage and other equality rights of this nature on the basis that acquiring these rights would intensify the legal regulation of sexual practices that did not conform to the monogamous, binary relationship norm. See Michael Warner, *The Trouble with Normal: Sex, Politics and the Ethics of Queer Life* (New York: Free Press, 1999).
33 *R. v. Kouri,* [2005] 3 S.C.R. 789 [*Kouri*].
34 Jeffrey Weeks, *Sexuality,* 2nd edition (London: Routledge, 2003).
35 See, for example, *Bowers v. Hardwick,* 478 U.S. 186 (1986), challenging Georgia's anti-sodomy laws on the basis of a liberty interest in sexual privacy; *Lawrence v. Texas,* 539 U.S. 558 (2003), striking anti-sodomy law on the basis of a constitutional right to privacy under the due process clause of the American Bill of Rights. In the Canadian context, this right to sexual privacy has more frequently been acquired legislatively (as in Parliament's decriminalization of sodomy in 1967) or through equality claims (see, for example, *R. v. M.(C.)* (1995), 30 C.R.R. (2d) 112). This may be, in part, due to the comparatively greater emphasis on equality in the Canadian constitutional context than is the case in the American constitutional context.

36 See, for example, the claims in obscenity cases such as *R. v. Butler*, [1992] 1 S.C.R. 452 [*Butler*], and *Little Sisters Book and Art Emporium v. Canada (Minister of Justice)*, [2000] 2 S.C.R. 1120 [*Little Sisters*].

37 The two most obvious examples being claims of discrimination based on sexual orientation (*Egan v. Canada*, [1995] 2 S.C.R. 513; *Vriend v. Alberta*, [1998] 1 S.C.R. 493) and claims for relationship recognition made by same sex and common-law couples (*Halpern*, *supra* note 31; *M. v. H*, *supra* note 31; *Walsh*, *supra* note 31).

38 Given its facts (which involved a publicly accessible dance bar in which up to one hundred people at a time would engage in sexual acts together on the dance floor), *Kouri*, *supra* note 33, in particular, can hardly be described as a case driven by privacy interests.

39 In the 1950s and 1960s in Canada (and elsewhere), gays and lesbians were perceived by the government to be security risks due to purported close ties to communism (in addition to their supposed susceptibility to blackmail). Hundreds of gays and lesbians were purged from the Royal Canadian Mounted Police and other public servant positions. By 1967, the government had a list of 9,000 "suspected homosexuals" in Canada. See Gary Kinsman, "Challenging Canadian and Queer Nationalisms" in T. Goldie, ed., *In a Queer Country: Gay and Lesbian Studies in the Canadian Context* (Vancouver: Arsenal Pulp Press, 2001) 209 at 220.

40 *Labaye*, *supra* note 20 at para. 48.

41 *R. v. Brodie*, [1962] S.C.R. 681.

42 *Towne Cinema Theatres v. The Queen*, [1985] 1 S.C.R. 494; *Butler*, *supra* note 36.

43 *Little Sisters*, *supra* note 36.

44 *R. v. Tremblay*, [1993] 2 S.C.R. 932; *R. v. Mara*, [1997] 2 S.C.R. 630; *R. v. Pelletier*, [1999] 3 S.C.R. 863.

45 *Kouri*, *supra* note 33 at para. 22.

46 Francisco Valdes, "Queers, Sissies, Dykes and Tomboys: Deconstructing the Conflation of Sex, Gender and Sexual Orientation in Euro-American Law and Society" (1995) 83:1 Cal L. Rev. 1 at 368.

47 *Ibid.* at 368.

48 Valdes was writing from an American legal context that was prior to *Lawrence v. Texas*, 539 U.S. 558 (2003), and more specifically within a claim to the right to sexual privacy.

49 Borrowing Valdes' focus on the regulation of desire ought not to be taken as a reliance on queer theory itself. While Valdes' project is substantive – it imagines queer theory as the substantive work of subverting sex and gender norms – recent writers argue that queer legal theory is not a substantive project but, rather, a methodology for critique. See generally Janet Halley, *Split Decisions: Taking a Break from Feminism* (Princeton, NJ: Princeton University Press, 2006). As suggested earlier, queer theory, unlike iconoclasm, is less able to accommodate theories of justice, reflect legal struggles as they actually transpire, or operate within a liberal framework that operationalizes law through judgment.

50 Valdes, *supra* note 46 at 369.

51 Katherine Franke, "Theorizing Yes: An Essay on Feminism, Law and Desire" (2001) 101 Colum. L. Rev. 181.

52 Derrida, *supra* note 2.

53 Frug, *supra* note 8 at 125.

Bibliography

Legislation

An Act to Amend the Criminal Code in Relation to Sexual Offences and Other Offences against the Person, S.C. 1980-81-82-83, c. 125

Canadian Charter of Rights and Freedoms, Part 1 of the *Constitution Act, 1982*, being Schedule B to the *Canada Act 1982* (U.K.), 1982, c. 11

Canadian Human Rights Act, R.S.C. 1985, c. H-6

Civil Marriage Act, S.C. 2005, c. 33

Criminal Code of Canada, R.S.C. 1985, c. C-46

Criminal Law Amendment Act, 1968-69, S.C. 1968-69, c. 38

Criminal Law Amendment Act, 1975, S.C. 1974-75-76, c. 93

Customs Act, R.S.C. 1985, c. 1 (2nd Supp.)

Processing and Distribution of Semen for Assisted Conception Regulations, S.O.R./96-254

Tackling Violent Crimes Act, S.C. 2008, c. 6

Jurisprudence

A.A. v. B.B., [2007] O.J. No. 2

Bedford v. Canada, [2010] O.J. No. 4057

Bowers v. Hardwick, 478 U.S. 186 (1986)

Brooks v. Safeway Ltd., [1989] 1 S.C.R. 1219

Chamberlain v. Surrey School District No. 36, [2002] 4 S.C.R. 710

D.P.P. v. Boardman, [1975] A.C. 421 (C.A.)

Egan v. Canada, [1995] 2 S.C.R. 513

Frame v. Smith, [1987] 2 S.C.R. 99

G.(J.R.I.) v. Tyhurst, [2003] 6 W.W.R. 402

Halpern v. Canada (Attorney-General), [2003] O.J. No. 2268

Hislop v. Canada (Attorney-General), [2004] O.J. No. 4815

Janzen v. Platy Enterprises Ltd., [1989] 1 S.C.R. 1252

LAC Minerals Ltd. v. International Corona Resources Ltd., [1989] 2 S.C.R. 574

Latreille c. R, [2007] J.Q. no. 11274 (Q.B. C.A.)
Little Sisters Book and Art Emporium v. Canada (Minister of Justice), [2000] 2 S.C.R. 1120
M. v. H., [1999] 2 S.C.R. 3
MacDonald v. Brighter Mechanical Ltd., [2006] B.C.H.R.T.D. No. 326
Makin v. Attorney-General for New South Wales (1893), [1894] A.C. 57
McInerney v. MacDonald, [1992] 2 S.C.R. 138
Mercier v. Dasilva, [2007] B.C.H.R.T.D. No. 72
Miron v. Trudel, [1995] 2 S.C.R. 418
M.K. v. M.H., [1992] 3 S.C.R. 6
Mossop v. Canada (Attorney-General), [1993] 1 S.C.R. 554
Non-Marine Underwriters, Lloyd's of London v. Scalera, [2000] 1 S.C.R. 551
Norberg v. Wynrib, [1992] 2 S.C.R. 226
North Vancouver School District No. 44 v. Jubran, [2005] B.C.J. No. 733 (C.A.)
Nova Scotia v. Walsh, [2002] 4 S.C.R. 325
Oncale v. Sundowner Offshore Services, 118 S. Ct. 998 (1998)
Pappajohn v. The Queen, [1980] 2 S.C.R. 120
R. c. Archontakis, [1980] J.Q. no. 196
R. v. Alderton, [1985] O.J. No. 2419
R. v. B. and S., [1957] C.C.S. No. 921
R. v. B.(C.R.), [1990] S.C.J. No. 31
R. v. B.E., [1999] O.J. 3869
R. v. Bernard, [1988] 2 S.C.R. 833
R. v. B.(F.F.), [1993] 1 S.C.R. 697
R. v. Blake (2005), 68 O.R. (3d) 75
R. v. Bolduc, [1967] S.C.R. 677
R. v. Brodie, [1962] S.C.R. 681
R. v. Butler, [1992] 1 S.C.R. 452
R. v. Chase, [1987] 2 S.C.R. 293
R. v. Clarence (1988), 22 Q.B.D. 23
R. v. C.(M.H.), [1991] 1 S.C.R. 763
R. v. Collins, [1985] O.J. No. 51
R. v. Cormier, [2009] O.J. No. 2937
R. v. C.P.K., [2002] O.J. No. 4929
R. v. Crowe, [1987] O.J. No. 1671
R. v. Cuerrier, [1998] S.C.J. No. 64
R. v. D.I., [2008] O.J. No. 1823
R. v. Dick, Penner and Finnigan, [1965] 1 C.C.C. 171
R. v. Ellison, [2006] B.C.J. No. 3241
R. v. E.S., [2006] O.J. No. 1750
R. v. Esau, [1997] 2 S.C.R. 777
R. v. Escobar, [2008] O.J. No. 264
R. v. Ewanchuk, [1999] 1 S.C.R. 330
R. v. Finelli, [2008] O.J. No. 2242
R. v. F.(J.E.), [1993] O.J. No. 2589
R. v. F.L., [2003] O.J. No. 4040
R. v. Gavrilko, [2007] B.C.J. No. 2154
R. v. G.B., [1982] N.W.T.J. No. 40
R. v. G.G., [2003] N.W.T.J. No. 88

R. v. Handy, [2002] 2 S.C.R. 908
R. v. Hay, [1959] M.J. No. 4
R. v. Horwood, [1970] 1 Q.B. 133
R. v. J.A.T., [2010] B.C.J. No. 1024
R. v. J.G.E.S., [2005] B.C.J. No. 3161
R. v. J.M.H., [2003] O.J. No. 5511
R. v. Jobidon, [1991] 2 S.C.R. 714
R. v. J.R., [2006] O.J. No. 2698
R. v. Kennedy, [2006] O.J. No. 4976
R. v. K.M., [2008] O.J. No. 198
R. v. Kouri, [2005] 3 S.C.R. 789
R. v. Labaye, [2005] 3 S.C.R. 728
R. v. Larue, [2003] 1 S.C.R. 277
R. v. Legare, [2009] 3 S.C.R. 551
R. v. Litchfield, [1993] 4 S.C.R. 333
R. v. Louie Chong (1914), 23 C.C.C. 250
R. v. Mabior, [2010] M.J. No. 308
R. v. Mara, [1997] 2 S.C.R. 630
R. v. M.B., [2008] O.J. No. 2521
R. v. M.(C.) (1995), 30 C.R.R. (2d) 112
R. v. M.(L.M.), [1994] 2 S.C.R. 3
R. v. M.(M.L.), [1994] 2 S.C.R. 3
R. v. Moore, [1955] A.J. No. 1
R. v. Morelli, [2010] 1 S.C.R. 253
R. v. Nicolaou, [2008] B.C.J. No. 1331
R. v. Osolin, [1992] 2 S.C.R. 313
R. v. Park, [1995] 2 S.C.R. 836
R. v. Pelletier, [1999] 3 S.C.R. 863
R. v. Phelps, [1983] B.C.J. No. 1387
R. v. Ponomarev, [2007] O.J. No. 2494
R. v. Provincial News Co, [1974] S.C.J. No 140
R. v. R.A., [2000] 1 S.C.R. 163
R. v. R.B., [2005] O.J. No. 3575
R. v. R.C., [2003] O.J. No. 3919
R. v. Robicheau, [2002] S.C.J. No. 50
R. v. R.W.D., [2004] O.J. No. 3091
R. v. Seaboyer, [1991] 2 S.C.R. 577
R. v. Sharpe, [2001] 1 S.C.R. 45
R. v. Shearing, [2002] 3 S.C.R. 33
R. v. Smith (1915), 84 L.J. K.B. 2153
R. v. Spence, [1994] O.J. No. 981
R. (on behalf of her son) v. Squamish School District No. 48 (c.o.b. Myrtle Philip Community School), [2003] B.C.H.R.T.D. No. 49
R. v. Stewart, [2004] B.C.J. No. 195
R. v. Swietlinski, [1980] 2 S.C.R. 956
R. v. T.B., [2009] O.J. No. 751
R. v. Tremblay (1991), 68 C.C.C. (3d) 439, rev'd S.C.C.
R. v. Tremblay, [1993] 2 S.C.R. 932

R. v. Wadel, [2001] O.J. No. 4248
R. v. Whitehead, [2004] O.J. No. 4030
R. v. Worthington (1972), 10 C.C.C. (2d) 311 (Ont. C.A.)
R. v. Yusufi, [2007] O.J. No. 2321
Reference re Prostitution, [1990] 1 S.C.R. 1123
Regina v. J., [1957] A.J. No. 78
Regina v. P., [1968] M.J. No. 12
Selinger v. McFarland, [2008] O.H.R.T.D. No. 48
Smith v. Menzies Chrysler Inc., [2008] O.H.R.T.D. No. 35
Susan Doe v. Canada (Attorney General), (2006) 79 O.R. (3d) 586, aff'd 276 D.L.R. (4th) 127 (C.A.)
Symes v. Canada, [1993] 4 S.C.R. 695
Towne Cinema Theatres v. The Queen, [1985] 1 S.C.R. 494
Trinity Western University v. British Columbia College of Teachers, [2001] 1 S.C.R. 772
Vriend v. Alberta, [1998] 1 S.C.R. 493

Secondary Materials

Adjin-Tettey, E. "Protecting the Dignity and Autonomy of Women: Rethinking the Place of Constructive Consent in the Tort of Sexual Battery" (2006) 39 U.B.C. L. Rev. 3.
Alcoff, Linda. "The Politics of Postmodern Feminism, Revisited" (1997) 36 Cultural Critique 5.
Anderson, E. *Judging Bertha Wilson: Law as Large as Life* (Toronto: University of Toronto Press, 2001).
Aggarwal, A., and M. Gupta. "Same-Sex Sexual Harassment: Is It Sex Discrimination? A Review of Canadian and American Law" (2000) 27 Man. L.J. 333.
Backhouse, C. *Carnal Crimes: Sexual Assault Law in Canada 1900-1975* (Toronto: Irwin Law, 2008).
–. "The Chilly Climate for Women Judges: Reflections on the Backlash from the Ewanchuk Case" (2003) 15 C.J.W.L. 167.
–. "Nineteenth-Century Canadian Rape Law 1800-1892" in D. Flaherty, ed., *Essays in the History of Canadian Law* (Toronto: Osgoode Society, 1983) 200.
–, and D. Flaherty, eds. *Challenging Times: The Women's Movement in Canada and the United States* (Montreal and Kingston: McGill-Queens University Press, 1992) 186.
Baines, B. "But Was She a Feminist Judge?" in K. Brooks, ed., *Justice Bertha Wilson: One Woman's Difference* (Vancouver: UBC Press, 2010).
Bala, N. "Increasing Protections for Women and Children: Bills C-126 & 128" (1993) 21:4 C.R. 365.
Ball, C. "Privacy, Property, and Public Sex" (2008-09) 18 Colum. J. Gender & L. 1.
Bauman, C.A. "The Sentencing of Sexual Offences against Children" (1998) 17:5 C.R. 352.
Benedet, J. "*Little Sisters Book and Art Emporium v. Canada (Minister of Justice)*: Sex Equality and the Attack on *R. v. Butler*" (2001) 39 Osgoode Hall L.J. 187.
Benjamin, J. *The Bonds of Love: Psychoanalysis, Feminism and the Problem of Domination* (New York: Pantheon Books, 1988).
Berlant, L., and M. Warner. "What Does Queer Theory Teach Us about X?" (1995) 110:3 P.M.L.A. 343.
Bersani, L. "Is the Rectum a Grave?" (1987) 43 October 197.
Berube, A. *Coming Out under Fire: The History of Gay Men and Women in World War Two* (New York: Free Press, 1990).

Bevacqua, M. *Rape on the Public Agenda: Feminism and the Politics of Sexual Assault* (Boston: Northeastern University Press, 2000).

Boyle, C. "The Anti-Discrimination Norm in Human Rights and *Charter* Law: *Nixon v. Vancouver Rape Relief*" (2004) 37 U.B.C. L. Rev. 31.

–. *Sexual Assault* (Toronto: Carswell, 1984).

–. "Sexual Assault as Foreplay: Does *Ewanchuk* Apply to Spouses?" (2004) 20:6 C.R. 359.

Brett, N. "Sexual Offenses and Consent" (1998) 11 Can. J. L. & Jur. 69.

Brownmiller, S. *Against Our Will: Men, Women and Rape* (New York: Bantam, 1975).

Bruhm, S., and N. Hurley, eds. *Curiouser: On the Queerness of Children* (Minneapolis, MN: University of Minnesota Press, 2004).

Buchwald, E., P. Fletcher, and M. Roth, eds. *Transforming a Rape Culture*, revised edition (Washington, DC: Milkweed Editions, 2005).

Burgess-Jackson, K. "Statutory Rape: A Philosophical Analysis (1995) 8 Can. J.L. & Jur. 139.

Butler, J. "Against Proper Objects" in E. Weed and N. Schor, eds., *Feminism Meets Queer Theory* (Bloomington, IN: Indiana University Press, 1997) 1.

–. *Bodies That Matter: On the Discursive Limits of Sex* (New York: Routledge, 1993).

–. *Gender Trouble: Feminism and the Subversion of Identity*, 2nd edition (New York: Routledge, 1999).

–. *Precarious Life: The Power of Mourning and Violence* (London: Verso, 2004).

–. "Sexual Inversions" in J. Caputo and M. Young, eds., *Foucault and the Critique of Institutions* (University Park, PA: Pennsylvania State University Press, 1986).

–, E. Laclau, and S. Žižek. *Contingency, Hegemony, Universality: Contemporary Dialogues on the Left* (London: Verso, 2000).

Califia, P. *Macho Sluts* (Boston: Alyson Publications, 1988).

–. "No Minor Issues: Age of Consent, Child Pornography, and Cross-Generational Relationships" reprinted in *Public Sex*, 2nd edition (San Francisco: Cleiss Press, 2000) 54.

Cavell, R., and P. Dickinson, eds. *Sexing the Maple: A Canadian Sourcebook* (Peterborough, ON: Broadview Press, 2006).

Clark, L., and D. Lewis. *Rape: The Price of Coercive Sexuality* (Toronto: Women's Press, 1977).

Chunn, D.E., S.B. Boyd, and H. Lessard. *Reaction and Resistance: Feminism, Law, and Social Change* (Vancouver: UBC Press, 2007).

Cossman, B. "Disciplining the Unruly: Sexual Outlaws, Little Sisters, and the Legacy of Butler" (2003) 36 U.B.C. L. Rev. 77.

–. "Lesbians, Gay Men, and the *Canadian Charter of Rights and Freedoms*" (2002) 40 Osgoode Hall L.J. 223.

–. "The New Politics of Adultery" (2006) 15 Colum. J. Gender & L. 274.

–. *Sexual Citizens: The Legal and Cultural Regulation of Sex and Belonging* (Stanford, CA: Stanford University Press, 2007).

–. "Sexuality, Queer Theory, and 'Feminism After': Reading and Rereading the Sexual Subject" (2004) 49 McGill L.J. 847.

–, S. Bell, L. Gotell, and B. Ross. *Bad Attitude/s on Trial: Pornography, Feminism, and the* Butler *Decision* (Toronto: University of Toronto Press, 1997).

Coughlan, S. "Complainants' Records after *Mills:* Same as It Ever Was" (2000) 33:5 C.R. 300.

Cowan, S. "Gender Is No Substitute for Sex: A Comparative Human Rights Analysis of the Legal Regulation of Sexual Identity" (2005) 13 Fem. Legal Stud. 67.

Cowie, J. "Difference, Dominance, Dilemma: A Critical Analysis of *Norberg v. Wynrib*" (1994) 58 Sask. L. Rev. 357.

Craig, E. "Family as Status in *Doe v. Canada:* Constituting Family under Section 15 of the Charter" (2007) 20 N.J.C.L. 197.

–. "'I DO' Kiss and Tell: The Subversive Potential of Non-Normative Social Sexual Expression from within Cultural Paradigms" (2004) 27 Dal. L.J. 403.

–. "Laws of Desire: The Political Morality of Public Sex" (2009) 54 McGill L.J. 3.

–. "Ten Years after *Ewanchuk* – The Art of Seduction Is Alive and Well: An Examination of the Mistaken Belief in Consent Defence" (2009) Can. Crim. L. Rev. 3.

–. "Trans-phobia and the Relational Production of Gender" (2007) 18:2 Hastings Women's L.J. 101.

Delisle, R. "The Direct Approach to Similar Fact Evidence" (1996) 50:4 C.R. 286.

–. "Litchfield: Does the Supreme Court Provide Sufficient Guidance to Trial Judges on Evidentiary Matters?" (1994) 25:4 C.R. 163.

Derrida, J. "Force of Law" (1989) 11 Cardoza L. Rev. 919.

–. *Rogues: Two Essays on Reason* (Stanford, CA: Stanford University Press, 2005).

Devlin, P. *The Enforcement of Morals* (Oxford: Oxford University Press, 1965).

Dripps, D. "Beyond Rape: An Essay on the Difference between the Presence of Force and the Absence of Consent" (1992) 92 Colum. L. Rev. 1780.

–. "More on Distinguishing Sex, Sexual Expropriation, and Sexual Assault: A Reply to Professor West" (1993) 93 Colum. L. Rev. 1460.

Dworkin, R. "Foundations of Liberal Equality" in S. Darwall, ed., *Equal Freedom* (Ann Arbor, MI: University of Michigan Press, 1995) 190.

–. *Freedom's Law: The Moral Reading of the American Constitution* (Cambridge: Harvard University Press, 1996).

–. *Is Democracy Possible Here?* (Princeton, NJ: Princeton University Press, 2006).

–. "Liberalism" in S. Hampshire, ed., *Public and Private Morality* (Cambridge: Cambridge University Press, 1978) 113.

–. "Lord Devlin and the Enforcement of Morals" (1965) 75 Yale L.J. 986.

–. *Sovereign Virtue* (Cambridge, MA: Harvard University Press, 2000).

Ebert, T. "The 'Difference' of Postmodern Feminism" (1991) 53:8 College English 886.

Ellis, H. *Little Essays of Love and Virtue* (London: A. and C. Black, 1922).

Eskridge, W. *Equality Practice: Civil Unions and the Future of Gay Rights* (New York: Routledge, 2002).

–. "No Promo Homo: The Sedimentation of Antigay Discourse and the Channeling Effect of Judicial Review" (2000) 75 N.Y.U. L. Rev. 1327.

–. *Sexuality, Gender and the Law* (New York: Foundation Press, 2004).

Estlund, D., and M. Nussbaum. *Sex, Preference and Family: Essays on Law and Nature* (New York: Oxford University Press, 1997).

Estrich, S. "Rape" (1986) 95 Yale L.J. 1087.

–. *Real Rape: How the Legal System Victimizes Women Who Say No* (Cambridge, MA: Harvard University Press, 1987).

–. "Sex at Work" (1991) 43 Stan. L. Rev. 813.

Fausto-Sterling, A. *Sexing the Body: Gender Politics and the Construction of Sexuality* (New York: Basic Books, 2000).

Fineman, M., J. Jackson, and A. Romero, eds. *Feminist and Queer Legal Theory: Intimate Encounters, Uncomfortable Conversations* (Burlington, VT: Ashgate Publishing Company, 2009).

Finnis, J. "Law, Morality, and Sexual Orientation" (1994) 69 Notre Dame L. Rev. 1049.

Flood, D.R. "'They Didn't Treat Me Good': African American Rape Victims and Chicago Courtroom Strategies during the 1950s" (2005) 17:1 J. Women's History 38.

Fone, B. *Homophobia: A History* (New York: Henry Holt, 2000).

Foucault, M. *The History of Sexuality, Volume I: An Introduction*, translated by R. Hurley (New York: Vintage Books, 1978).

–. *The History of Sexuality, Volume II: The Use of Pleasure*, translated by R. Hurley (New York: Random House, 1985).

–. "Two Lectures" in C. Gordon, ed., *Power/Knowledge* (New York: Pantheon Books, 1980) 78.

Fout, J.C., ed. *Forbidden History: The State, Society and the Regulation of Sexuality in Modern Europe* (Chicago: University of Chicago Press, 1992).

Franke, Katherine. "Theorizing Yes: An Essay on Feminism, Law and Desire" (2001) 101 Colum. L. Rev. 181.

Fraser, N. "From Redistribution to Recognition? Dilemmas of Justice in a Postsocialist Age" in *Justice Interruptus* (New York: Routledge, 1996) 11.

Fritsch, M. "Derrida's Democracy to Come" (2002) 9:4 Constellations 574.

Frug, M.J. *Postmodern Legal Feminism* (New York: Routledge, 1992).

Goffman, E. *Stigma: Notes on the Management of Spoiled Identity* (New York: Simon and Schuster, 1963).

Gotell, L. "The Discursive Disappearance of Sexualized Violence" in D.E. Chunn, S.B. Boyd, and H. Lessard, eds., *Reaction and Resistance: Feminism, Law, and Social Change* (Vancouver: UBC Press, 2007) 127.

–. "The Ideal Victim, the Hysterical Complainant, and the Disclosure of Confidential Records: The Implications of the *Charter* for Sexual Assault Law" (2002) 40 Osgoode Hall L.J. 251.

–. "When Privacy Is Not Enough: Sexual Assault Complainants, Sexual History Evidence and the Disclosure of Personal Records" (2006) 43 Alta. L. Rev. 73.

Green, L. "Men in the Place of Women, from *Butler* to *Little Sisters*," reviewing *Gay Male Pornography: An Issue of Sex Discrimination* by Christopher Kendall, (2005) 43 Osgoode Hall L.J. 473.

–. "Three Themes from Raz" (2005) 25 Oxford J. Legal Stud. 503.

Greenberg, J.A. "Deconstructing Binary Race and Sex Categories: A Comparison of the Multiracial and Transgendered Experience" (2002) 39 San Diego L. Rev. 917.

–. "Defining Male and Female: Intersexuality and the Collision between Law and Biology" (1999) 41 Ariz. L. Rev. 265.

Halberstam, J. *Female Masculinity* (Durham, SC: Duke University Press, 1998).

Halley, J. "The Construction of Heterosexuality" in M. Warner, ed., *Fear of a Queer Planet: Queer Politics and Social Theory* (Minneapolis, MN: University of Minnesota Press, 1993) 82.

–. "The Politics of Injury: A Review of Robin West's *Caring for Justice*" (2005) 1 Unbound 65.

–. "Sexual Orientation and the Politics of Biology: A Critique of the Argument from Immutability" (1994) 46 Stan. L. Rev. 503.

–. *Split Decisions: Taking a Break from Feminism* (Princeton, NJ: Princeton University Press, 2006).

Halperin, D. *Saint Foucault* (New York: Oxford University Press, 1995).

Hampshire, S. *Public and Private Morality* (Cambridge: Cambridge University Press, 1978).

Hanson, L. "Sexual Assault and the Similar Fact Rule" (1993) 27 U.B.C. L. Rev. 51.
Hart, H. *Law, Liberty and Morality* (Stanford, CA: Stanford University Press, 1963).
–. *The Morality of the Criminal Law: Two Lectures* (Jerusalem: Magnes Press, 1965).
Herman, D. *Rights of Passage: Struggles for Lesbian and Gay Legal Equality* (Toronto: University of Toronto Press, 1994).
Holland, J., and L. Adkins, eds. *Sex, Sensibility and the Gendered Body* (London: Macmillan Press, 1996).
Hoyano, L., and C. Keenan. *Child Abuse: Law and Policy across Boundaries* (Oxford: Oxford University Press, 2007).
Hutchinson, A. "In Other Words: Putting Sex and Pornography in Context" (1995) 8 Can. J.L. & Jur. 107.
Irvine, J. "The Sociologist as Voyeur: Social Theory and Sexuality Research, 1910-1978" (2003) 26:4 Qualitative Sociology 429.
Janus, E. "'Don't Think of a Predator': Changing Frames for Better Sexual Violence Prevention" (2007) 8:6 Sex Offender Law Report 81.
Jolin, A. "On the Backs of Working Prostitutes: Feminist Theory and Prostitution Policy" (1994) 40:1 Crime & Delinquency 69.
Kropp, D. "Categorical Failure: Canada's Equality Jurisprudence – Changing Notions of Identity and the Legal Subject" (1997) 23 Queen's L.J. 201.
Kymlicka, W. *Multicultural Citizenship* (Oxford: Clarendon Press, 1995).
–. *The Rights of Minority Cultures* (Oxford: Oxford University Press, 1995).
Lacey, L. "Unspeakable Subjects, Impossible Rights: Sexuality, Integrity, and Criminal Law" (1998) 11 Can. J.L. & Jur. 47.
Lacey, N., C. Wells, and O. Quick. *Reconstructing Criminal Law*, 3rd edition (London: LexisNexis UK, 2003).
Laclau, E. *Emancipation(s)* (London: Verso, 1996).
Lakoff, G., and M. Johnson. *Metaphors We Live By* (Chicago: University of Chicago Press, 1980).
Langer, R. "Five Years of Canadian Feminist Advocacy: Is It Still Possible to Make a Difference?" (2005) 23 Windsor Y.B. Access to Just. 115.
LeMoncheck, L. *Loose Women, Lecherous Men: A Feminist Philosophy of Sex* (Oxford: Oxford University Press, 1997).
Lowman, J. "Prostitution Laws: Health Risks and Hypocrisy" (2004) 171 Can. Med. Assoc. J. 109.
–. "Reconvening the Federal Committee of Prostitution Law Reform" (2004) 171 Can. Med. Assoc. J. 113.
Lust, G. "Advances Less Criminal Than Hormonal: Rape and Consent in *R. v. Ewanchuk*" (1999) 5 Appeal 18.
MacDougall, B. "The Legally Queer Child" (2004) 49 McGill L.J. 1057.
–. *Queer Judgments: Homosexuality, Expression, and the Courts in Canada* (Toronto: University of Toronto Press, 2000).
MacKinnon, C. "Feminism, Marxism, Method, and the State: An Agenda for Theory" (1982) 7 Signs 515.
–. "Feminism, Marxism, Method and the State: Towards a Feminist Jurisprudence" (1983) 8 Signs 635.
–. *Feminism Unmodified: Discourses on Life and Law* (Cambridge, MA: Harvard University Press, 1987).

–. "Feminist Approaches to Sexual Assault in Canada and the United States: A Brief Retrospective" in C. Backhouse and D. Flaherty, eds., *Challenging Times: The Women's Movement in Canada and the United States* (Montreal and Kingston: McGill-Queens University Press, 1992) 186.

–. *Only Words* (Cambridge, MA: Harvard University Press, 1993).

–. "The Road Not Taken: Sex Equality in *Lawrence v. Texas*" (2004) 65 Ohio St. L.J. 1081.

–. *Sexual Harassment of Working Women: A Case of Sex Discrimination* (London: Yale University Press, 1979).

–. *Toward a Feminist Theory of the State* (Cambridge, MA: Harvard University Press, 1989).

Manfredi, C. *Feminist Activism in the Supreme Court: Legal Mobilization and the Women's Legal Education and Action Fund* (Vancouver: UBC Press, 2004).

–. "Judicial Discretion and Fundamental Justice: Sexual Assault in the Supreme Court of Canada" (1990) 47 Am. J. Comp. L. 489.

Mayeda, G. "Re-imagining Feminist Theory: Transgender Identity, Feminism, and the Law" (2005) 17 C.J.W.L. 423.

McLaren, A. *Twentieth Century Sexuality: A History* (Malden, MA: Blackwell, 1999).

Messner, M. "The Triad of Violence in Men's Sports" in E. Buchwald, P. Fletcher, and M. Roth, eds., *Transforming a Rape Culture*, revised edition (Washington, DC: Milkweed Editions, 2005) 23.

Minow, M., M. Ryan, and A. Sarat, eds. *Narrative, Violence and the Law: The Essays of Robert Cover* (Ann Arbor, MI: University of Michigan Press, 1992).

Morgan, R. *Going Too Far: The Personal Chronicle of a Feminist* (New York: Random House, 1978).

Naffine, N., and R. Owens, eds. *Sexing the Subject of Law* (North Ryde: Law Book Company, 1997).

Nedelsky, J. "Embodied Diversity and the Challenges to Law" (1997) 42 McGill L.J. 91.

–. "Reconceiving Autonomy: Sources, Thoughts, and Possibilities" (1989) 1 Yale J.L. & Fem. 7.

Nestle, J., C. Howell, and R. Wilchins, eds. *GenderQueer: Voices from beyond the Sexual Binary* (Los Angeles: Alyson Books, 2002).

Plummer, K. "Intimate Citizenship and the Culture of Sexual Storytelling" in J. Weeks and J. Holland, eds., *Sexual Cultures* (New York: St. Martin's Press, 1996) 34.

Plummer, P. *Sexual Stigma: An Interactionist Account* (New York: Routledge, 1975).

–. *Telling Sexual Stories: Power, Change and Social Worlds* (London: Routledge, 1995).

Posner, R. *Sex and Reason* (Cambridge, MA: Harvard University Press, 1992).

Raitt, F.E. "The Children's Rights Movement: Infusions of Feminism" (2005) 22 Can. J. Fam. L. 11.

Rawls, J. *A Theory of Justice* (Cambridge, MA: Harvard University Press, 1971).

Raz, J. "About Morality and the Nature of Law" (2003) 48 Am. J. Jur. 1.

–. *Ethics in the Public Domain* (Oxford: Clarendon Press, 1994).

–. *The Morality of Freedom* (Oxford: Clarendon Press, 1986).

–. "Philosophy and the Practice of Freedom: An Interview with Joseph Raz" (2006) 9:1 Critical Rev. Int'l Soc. & Pol. Phil. 71.

–. *The Practice of Values* (Oxford: Oxford University Press, 2003).

–. "Rights and Politics" (1995) 71 Ind. L.J. 27.

Reagan, R. "Authority and Value: Reflections on Raz's Morality of Freedom" (1989) 62 S. Cal. L. Rev. 995.

Reiter, R., ed. *Toward an Anthropology of Women* (New York: Monthly Review Press, 1975).

Robson, R. "Assimilation, Marriage and Lesbian Liberation" (2002) 75 Temp. L. Rev. 709.

–. "Beginning from My Experience: The Paradoxes of Lesbian/Queer Narratives" (1997) Hastings L.J. 1387.

–. "Judicial Review and Sexual Freedom" (2008) 29 Univ. Hawaii L. Rev. 1.

Romero, A. "Methodological Descriptions: 'Feminist' and 'Queer' Legal Theories: Book Review of Janet Halley's *Split Decisions: How and Why to Take a Break from Feminism*" (2007) 19 Yale J.L. & Fem. 227.

Rorty, R. *Contingency, Irony and Solidarity* (Cambridge: Cambridge University Press, 1989).

Rosenberg, M. "Similar Fact Evidence" in *Special Lectures 2003: The Law of Evidence* (Toronto: Irwin, 2003) 391.

Rotello, G. *Sexual Ecology: AIDS and the Destiny of Gay Men* (New York: Plume, 1998).

Rubin, G. "Thinking Sex: Notes for a Radical Theory of the Politics of Sexuality" in H. Abelove and M.A. Barale, eds., *The Lesbian and Gay Studies Reader* (Routledge: New York, 1993) 3.

–. "The Traffic in Women: Notes on the 'Political Economy' of Sex" in R. Reiter, ed., *Toward an Anthropology of Women* (New York: Monthly Review Press, 1975) 157.

Sanday, P. *Fraternity Gang Rape: Sex, Brotherhood, and Privilege on Campus* (New York: New York University Press, 1990).

Sandel, M. *Liberalism and the Limits of Justice*, 2nd edition (Cambridge: Cambridge University Press, 1998).

Schultz, V. "The Sanitized Workplace" (2003) 112 Yale L.J. 2061.

Sedgwick, E.K. *Epistemology of the Closet* (Berkeley and Los Angeles: University of California Press, 1990).

–. "How to Bring Your Kids Up Gay: The War on Effeminate Boys" in S. Bruhm and N. Hurley, eds., *Curiouser: On the Queerness of Children* (Minneapolis, MN: University of Minnesota Press, 2004) 139.

Seidman, S. "Identity and Politics in a 'Postmodern' Gay Culture: Some Historical and Conceptual Notes" in M. Warner, ed., *Fear of a Queer Planet: Queer Politics and Social Theory* (Minneapolis, MN: University of Minnesota Press, 1993) 105.

Shachar, A. *Multicultural Jurisdictions: Cultural Differences and Women's Rights* (Cambridge: Cambridge University Press, 2001).

Shaver, F.M. "The Regulation of Prostitution: Avoiding the Morality Traps" (1994) 9 C.J.L.S. 123.

Sheehy, E. "Causation, Common Sense and the Common Law: Replacing Unexamined Assumptions with What We Know about Male Violence against Women or from *Jane Doe* to *Bonnie Mooney*" (2005) 17 C.J.W.L. 87.

Sheppard, A. "The Supreme Court of Canada and Criminal Evidence Reform: Recent Cases on Sexual Abuse of Children and Spousal Murder" (1991) 9 Can. J. Fam. L. 11.

Smart, C. "Desperately Seeking Post-Heterosexual Woman" in J. Holland and L. Adkins, eds., *Sex, Sensibility and the Gendered Body* (London: Macmillan Press, 1996) 222.

–. *Feminism and the Power of Law* (London: Routledge, 1989).

–. "A History of Ambivalence and Conflict in the Discursive Construction of the 'Child Victim' of 'Sexual Abuse'" (1999) 8:3 Soc. & Leg. Stud. 391.

–. "Law, Feminism and Sexuality: From Essence to Ethics?" (1994) 9 C.J.L.S. 15.

Sopinka, J., S. Lederman, and A. Bryant. *The Law of Evidence in Canada*, 2nd edition (Toronto: Butterworths, 1999).

Stewart, H. "Rationalizing Similar Facts: A Comment on *R. v. Handy*" (2003) 8 Can. Crim. L. Rev. 113.

Stuart, D. "*Ewanchuk:* Asserting 'No Means No' at the Expense of Fault and Proportionality Principles" (1999) 22:5 C.R. 39.

–. "*Mills:* Dialogue with Parliament and Equality by Assertion at What Cost?" (2000) 28:5 C.R. 275.

–. "*Shearing:* Admitting Similar Fact Evidence and Re-Asserting the Priority of Rights of Accused in Sexual Assault Trials" (2002) 2:6 C.R. 628.

Stychin, C. "Essential Rights and Contested Identities: Sexual Orientation and Equality Rights Jurisprudence in Canada" (1995) 8 Can. J.L. & Jur. 49.

–. *Governing Sexuality* (Oxford: Hart Publishing, 2003).

Sunder, M. "Cultural Dissent" (2001) 54 Stan. L. Rev. 495.

–. "Piercing the Veil" (2003) 112 Yale L.J. 1399.

Sutherland, K. "Legal Rites: Abjection and the Criminal Regulation of Consensual Sex" (2000) 63 Sask. L. Rev. 119.

Taylor, C. "The Politics of Recognition" in A. Gutman, ed., *Multiculturalism: Examining the Politics of Recognition* (Princeton, NJ: Princeton University Press, 1994) 25.

–. *Sources of the Self: The Making of the Modern Identity* (Cambridge, MA: Harvard University Press, 1989).

Temkin, J., and B. Krahe. *Sexual Assault and the Justice Gap: A Question of Attitude* (Oxford: Hart Publishing, 2008).

Valdes, F. "Queers, Sissies, Dykes and Tomboys: Deconstructing the Conflation of Sex, Gender and Sexual Orientation in Euro-American Law and Society" (1995) 83 Cal. L. Rev. 3.

Vance, C.S., ed. *Pleasure and Danger: Exploring Female Sexuality* (London: Pandora Press, 1989).

Vandervort, L. "Honest Beliefs, Credible Lies, and Culpable Awareness: Rhetoric, Inequality, and *Mens Rea* in Sexual Assault" (2004) 42 Osgoode Hall L.J. 625.

–. "Mistake of Law and Sexual Assault: Consent and *Mens Rea*" (1987-88) 2 C.J.W.L. 233.

Van Kralingen, A. "The Dialogic Saga of Same-Sex Marriage: *EGALE*, *Halpern*, and the Relationship between Suspended Declarations and Productive Political Discourse about Rights" (2004) 62 U.T. Fac. L. Rev. 149.

Waldron, J. "Autonomy and Perfectionism in Raz's Morality of Freedom" (1989) 62 S. Cal. L. Rev. 1097.

Warner, M., ed. *Fear of a Queer Planet: Queer Politics and Social Theory* (Minneapolis, MN: University of Minnesota Press, 1993).

–. *The Trouble with Normal: Sex, Politics and the Ethics of Queer Life* (New York: Free Press, 1999).

Weed, E., and N. Schor, eds. *Feminism Meets Queer Theory* (Bloomington, IN: Indiana University Press, 1997).

Weeks, J. *Against Nature* (London: Rivers Oram Press, 1991).

–. *Invented Moralities: Sexual Values in an Age of Uncertainty* (Cambridge: Polity Press, 1995).

–. *Sexuality*, 2nd edition (London: Routledge, 2003).

–. *Sexuality and Its Discontents* (London: Routledge, 1985).

–. *The World We Have Won* (London: Routledge, 2007).

–, and J. Holland, eds. *Sexual Cultures* (New York: St. Martin's Press, 1996).

West, R. "Legitimating the Illegitimate" (1993) 93 Colum. L. Rev. 1442.
Wilson, B. "Will Women Judges Really Make a Difference?" (1990) Osgoode Hall L.J. 507.
West, R. *Caring for Justice* (New York: New York University Press, 1997).
Wintemute, R. "Sexual Orientation and the Charter: The Achievement of Formal Legal Equality (1985-2005) and Its Limits" (2003-04) 49 McGill L.J. 1143.
–, and M. Andenaes. *Legal Regulation of Same Sex Partnerships: A Study of National, European and International Law* (Oxford: Hart Publishing, 2001).
Wright, J. "Consent and Sexual Violence in Canadian Public Discourse: Reflections on *Ewanchuk*" (2001) 16:2 C.J.L.S. 173.
Yoshino, K. "Covering" (2002) 111 Yale L.J. 769.

Index

Note: All legal cases are indexed in shortened form under "jurisprudence"; cases are indexed only on their first note citation in each chapter.

Lesley Erickson
Westward Bound: Sex, Violence, the Law, and the Making of a Settler Society (2011)

David R. Boyd
The Environmental Rights Revolution: A Global Study of Constitutions, Human Rights, and the Environment (2011)

Laura DeVries
Conflict in Caledonia: Aboriginal Land Rights and the Rule of Law (2011)

Jocelyn Downie and Jennifer J. Llewellyn (eds.)
Being Relational: Reflections on Relational Theory and Health Law (2011)

Grace Li Xiu Woo
Ghost Dancing with Colonialism: Decolonization and Indigenous Rights at the Supreme Court of Canada (2011)

Fiona Kelly
Transforming Law's Family: The Legal Recognition of Planned Lesbian Motherhood (2011)

Colleen Bell
The Freedom of Security: Governing Canada in the Age of Counter-Terrorism (2011)

Andrew S. Thompson
In Defence of Principles: NGOs and Human Rights in Canada (2010)

Aaron Doyle and Dawn Moore (eds.)
Critical Criminology in Canada: New Voices, New Directions (2010)

Joanna R. Quinn
The Politics of Acknowledgement: Truth Commissions in Uganda and Haiti (2010)

Patrick James
Constitutional Politics in Canada after the Charter: Liberalism, Communitarianism, and Systemism (2010)

Louis A. Knafla and Haijo Westra (eds.)
Aboriginal Title and Indigenous Peoples: Canada, Australia, and New Zealand (2010)

Janet Mosher and Joan Brockman (eds.)
Constructing Crime: Contemporary Processes of Criminalization (2010)

Stephen Clarkson and Stepan Wood
A Perilous Imbalance: The Globalization of Canadian Law and Governance (2009)

Amanda Glasbeek
Feminized Justice: The Toronto Women's Court, 1913-34 (2009)

Kim Brooks (ed.)
Justice Bertha Wilson: One Woman's Difference (2009)

Wayne V. McIntosh and Cynthia L. Cates
Multi-Party Litigation: The Strategic Context (2009)

Renisa Mawani
Colonial Proximities: Crossracial Encounters and Juridical Truths in British Columbia, 1871-1921 (2009)

James B. Kelly and Christopher P. Manfredi (eds.)
Contested Constitutionalism: Reflections on the Canadian Charter of Rights and Freedoms (2009)

Catherine Bell and Robert K. Paterson (eds.)
Protection of First Nations Cultural Heritage: Laws, Policy, and Reform (2008)

Hamar Foster, Benjamin L. Berger, and A.R. Buck (eds.)
The Grand Experiment: Law and Legal Culture in British Settler Societies (2008)

Richard J. Moon (ed.)
Law and Religious Pluralism in Canada (2008)

Catherine Bell and Val Napoleon (eds.)
First Nations Cultural Heritage and Law: Case Studies, Voices, and Perspectives (2008)

Douglas C. Harris
Landing Native Fisheries: Indian Reserves and Fishing Rights in British Columbia, 1849-1925 (2008)

Peggy J. Blair
Lament for a First Nation: The Williams Treaties of Southern Ontario (2008)

Lori G. Beaman
Defining Harm: Religious Freedom and the Limits of the Law (2007)

Stephen Tierney (ed.)
Multiculturalism and the Canadian Constitution (2007)

Julie Macfarlane
The New Lawyer: How Settlement Is Transforming the Practice of Law (2007)

Kimberley White
Negotiating Responsibility: Law, Murder, and States of Mind (2007)

Dawn Moore
Criminal Artefacts: Governing Drugs and Users (2007)

Hamar Foster, Heather Raven, and Jeremy Webber (eds.)
Let Right Be Done: Aboriginal Title, the Calder *Case, and the Future of Indigenous Rights* (2007)

Dorothy E. Chunn, Susan B. Boyd, and Hester Lessard (eds.)
Reaction and Resistance: Feminism, Law, and Social Change (2007)

Margot Young, Susan B. Boyd, Gwen Brodsky, and Shelagh Day (eds.)
Poverty: Rights, Social Citizenship, and Legal Activism (2007)

Rosanna L. Langer
Defining Rights and Wrongs: Bureaucracy, Human Rights, and Public Accountability (2007)

C.L. Ostberg and Matthew E. Wetstein
Attitudinal Decision Making in the Supreme Court of Canada (2007)

Chris Clarkson
Domestic Reforms: Political Visions and Family Regulation in British Columbia, 1862-1940 (2007)

Jean McKenzie Leiper
Bar Codes: Women in the Legal Profession (2006)

Gerald Baier
Courts and Federalism: Judicial Doctrine in the United States, Australia, and Canada (2006)

Avigail Eisenberg (ed.)
Diversity and Equality: The Changing Framework of Freedom in Canada (2006)

Randy K. Lippert
Sanctuary, Sovereignty, Sacrifice: Canadian Sanctuary Incidents, Power, and Law (2005)

James B. Kelly
Governing with the Charter: Legislative and Judicial Activism and Framers' Intent (2005)

Dianne Pothier and Richard Devlin (eds.)
Critical Disability Theory: Essays in Philosophy, Politics, Policy, and Law (2005)

Susan G. Drummond
Mapping Marriage Law in Spanish Gitano Communities (2005)

Louis A. Knafla and Jonathan Swainger (eds.)
Laws and Societies in the Canadian Prairie West, 1670-1940 (2005)

Ikechi Mgbeoji
Global Biopiracy: Patents, Plants, and Indigenous Knowledge (2005)

Florian Sauvageau, David Schneiderman, and David Taras, with Ruth Klinkhammer and Pierre Trudel
The Last Word: Media Coverage of the Supreme Court of Canada (2005)

Gerald Kernerman
Multicultural Nationalism: Civilizing Difference, Constituting Community (2005)

Pamela A. Jordan
Defending Rights in Russia: Lawyers, the State, and Legal Reform in the Post-Soviet Era (2005)

Anna Pratt
Securing Borders: Detention and Deportation in Canada (2005)

Kirsten Johnson Kramar
Unwilling Mothers, Unwanted Babies: Infanticide in Canada (2005)

W.A. Bogart
Good Government? Good Citizens? Courts, Politics, and Markets in a Changing Canada (2005)

Catherine Dauvergne
Humanitarianism, Identity, and Nation: Migration Laws in Canada and Australia (2005)

Michael Lee Ross
First Nations Sacred Sites in Canada's Courts (2005)

Andrew Woolford
Between Justice and Certainty: Treaty Making in British Columbia (2005)

John McLaren, Andrew Buck, and Nancy Wright (eds.)
Despotic Dominion: Property Rights in British Settler Societies (2004)

Georges Campeau
From UI to EI: Waging War on the Welfare State (2004)

Alvin J. Esau
The Courts and the Colonies: The Litigation of Hutterite Church Disputes (2004)

Christopher N. Kendall
Gay Male Pornography: An Issue of Sex Discrimination (2004)

Roy B. Flemming
Tournament of Appeals: Granting Judicial Review in Canada (2004)

Constance Backhouse and Nancy L. Backhouse
The Heiress vs the Establishment: Mrs. Campbell's Campaign for Legal Justice (2004)

Christopher P. Manfredi
Feminist Activism in the Supreme Court: Legal Mobilization and the Women's Legal Education and Action Fund (2004)

Annalise Acorn
Compulsory Compassion: A Critique of Restorative Justice (2004)

Jonathan Swainger and Constance Backhouse (eds.)
People and Place: Historical Influences on Legal Culture (2003)

Jim Phillips and Rosemary Gartner
Murdering Holiness: The Trials of Franz Creffield and George Mitchell (2003)

David R. Boyd
Unnatural Law: Rethinking Canadian Environmental Law and Policy (2003)

Ikechi Mgbeoji
Collective Insecurity: The Liberian Crisis, Unilateralism, and Global Order (2003)

Rebecca Johnson
Taxing Choices: The Intersection of Class, Gender, Parenthood, and the Law (2002)

John McLaren, Robert Menzies, and Dorothy E. Chunn (eds.)
Regulating Lives: Historical Essays on the State, Society, the Individual, and the Law (2002)

Joan Brockman
Gender in the Legal Profession: Fitting or Breaking the Mould (2001)